A RELIGION
OF ONE'S OWN

A RELIGION
OF ONE'S OWN

A Guide to Creating a Personal
Spirituality in a Secular World

THOMAS MOORE

GOTHAM BOOKS

GOTHAM BOOKS

Published by the Penguin Group
Penguin Group (USA) LLC
375 Hudson Street
New York, New York 10014

USA | Canada | UK | Ireland | Australia | New Zealand | India | South Africa | China
penguin.com
A Penguin Random House Company

LIBRARY OF CONGRESS CATALOGING-IN-PUBLICATION DATA
has been applied for.

ISBN 978-1-592-40829-0

Printed in the United States of America
1   3   5   7   9   10   8   6   4   2

Set in Bembo
Designed by Elke Sigal

Dedicated to:
James Hillman (1926–2011)
and Ben Moore (1912–2012)

CONTENTS

CONTENTS

PART FOUR
A Poetic Life

PART FIVE
Beyond the Self: Inner Guidance

PART SIX
Soul and Spirit

PREFACE

I was born with the themes of this book buried like seeds in my heart. I hold the religious traditions in the highest regard, have always given art a central place in my life, believe in a spiritual existence in a secular world, and find joy in the erotic life—these ideas are so etched in my being that it feels natural to write about them.

I tell many stories from my own experience and from the lives of people past and present. The people of the past I mention feel very much alive to me. They're not ghosts, not just names but real people who tried as hard as you and I to make sense of life and to live it as well as possible. They are on my own list, my community of the past who speak loudly to me. Perhaps you've read about them in my books before. I have to keep quoting the ones who mean so much to me.

The living people I mention are also my teachers. In most cases I try to be as accurate as possible in representing them. As for people who come to me for counsel and consultation, I'm always careful with privacy issues. In this book I may disguise them by using different names and changing certain details so they can't be traced. In a few rare cases I blend two or three people who share the same life issues to make a richer story. You should be able to tell when I'm citing people directly and when I'm disguising them.

If James Hillman is more prominent than usual in these pages, it is because he died as I began writing. We had been close friends for thirty-eight years, and the intimate conversations we had, especially toward the end of his life, made a big impression. As the book took shape, my father also died, and his spirit was strong in me as I navigated my way through a challenging topic. I owe more than I can say to these remarkable men.

Introduction

THE PLANET
IN THE WINDOW

The world is changing so fast that some days I feel dizzy from it. I'm a youthful spirit living in an aging body, trying to keep up with the changes around me. In one way or another, religion has always been a big part of my life, and that, too, is changing in ways I couldn't have predicted ten years ago. The question is: Should I try to live without it? Should I resist change and keep my religion traditional? Or should I rethink what religion is all about?

I've always believed in a strong, exciting secular life, given a soul through a deep, spiritual outlook and an active religious practice. I've thought of myself as a religious humanist. But religion is not only changing; in many areas it is disappearing, going the way of bookstores, print newspapers, and landlines. I resist the advancing secularism and want to put up a fight for religion, but a religion essentially and radically reimagined for our time. That reimagining is the gist of this book.

We don't seem to appreciate how deeply we are affected by changes in science, technology, and culture. Today there is little room left over for religion. Science wants to answer all your questions, and technology wants to make life livable. But you still get depressed and anxious. You feel the absence of purpose and meaning. Whether you like it or not, you have a soul that complains when you neglect it. And that soul needs religion. It's not an option.

Nothing is more important than bringing soul to everything we do. But there can be no soul without a vivid sense of the sacred, without religion. Since both "soul" and "religion" are difficult words to get hold of, maybe this is the place to offer some definitions: In my in-depth understanding of the word, religion is our creative and concrete response to the mysteries that permeate our lives. When I refer to religion as an institution or organization, I'll be explicit, calling it formal religion. My intention is to deepen our understanding of the religious traditions, but I'm aware, of course, that they can get in the way of the deep religion I'm seeking.

I use the word "soul," another mysterious word that eludes definition, the way it comes up in everyday speech. We talk about people, places, and houses that have soul. Soul is the unreachable depth, felt vitality, and full presence of a person or even a thing. A person with soul gives you the feeling that he has really lived and has a strong personality. For millennia theologians and philosophers have said that the world has soul, too.

Soul is the invisible, mysterious, and softly radiant element that infuses your being and makes you human. Like plasma in your veins, it gives you a sense of meaning, feeling, connection, and depth. If you have soul, you have a visible glow and are alive and present. When people encounter you, they see a real person.

Without soul, we and our world are dead. Without soul there is no real substance and value, no possibility for love and care, no heart and no real power or tenderness. Without soul we live shallow and metallic lives, not really touching each other and not engaged with the world. Without soul we feel a hollow emptiness and a vague sense of being lost. Without soul many act out their unconscious passions in antisocial behavior. When you encounter them on the street, they look past you, because there is a vacancy where the soul should be. Without soul we become preoccupied with ourselves, because it's the soul that gives us a real life.

When I think of a place having soul, I remember the old homestead near Auburn, New York, where my family settled after emigrating from Ireland in the nineteenth century. The weathered barns and sheds, the rusty rakes and plows, the cozy, musty house without running water and the antique smells of the kerosene stove and closed-up rooms—in my memory the place reeks of soul.

People often focus on the spiritual side of religion: beliefs, morals, eternity, and the infinite. But religion also has a soul. Like the old farmhouse, religion has its rich history of evocative teachings, paintings, architecture, music, and stories. It can feed the soul as well as inspire the spirit. What I remember most about my Catholic childhood is the smell of beeswax candles and smoky incense and mysterious chanting in Latin. To my soul, sensing was more important than understanding. Sensations remain in my memory, inspiring affection for the religion, while the teachings and admonitions fade.

As I was in the thick of writing this book, my father died—two months after celebrating his one hundredth birthday. I loved and appreciated him every day of my life. He was a devout Catholic, and at his death my brother and I had to confront an unexpected problem: We couldn't find a local priest whose schedule allowed him to conduct the funeral.

If you had told me when I was a young man that the churches would be closing their doors and the seminaries and convents emptying, I wouldn't have believed it. The emptying and graying of the churches feel much like climate change—something big and ominous is happening to us.

I see the effects of this in my work as a psychotherapist.

People come to me with deep-seated problems: They're not sure what it means to be married, they're having trouble with their children, they're depressed, they drink too much or depend on drugs, or they despair of finding work that's rewarding. They live in a world where a psychiatrist gives them pills to blunt their emotions and where anything but a literal, scientific explanation for life's mysteries faces ridicule. It's a world where formal religion, even at its best, has been squeezed out.

The disappearance of religious feeling goes hand in hand with a loss of soul, because at its best, religion speaks to the soul and feeds it. Traditional religion may well need an overhaul from top to bottom, but personal religion is a requirement. It is the indispensable foundation of an intelligent, openhearted approach to life.

Religion with a Soul

When you're religious in a deep way, you sense the sacred in things—a faint and mysterious pulse. Both in the world and in yourself you catch sight of the numinous, a hint of something more than human. In developing a religion of one's own, it's important to cultivate an eye for the numinous, a sacred light within things or an aura around them, the feeling that there is more to the world than what meets the eye. You don't have to be naïve or literal about this; it's simply a capacity in human beings to catch a glimpse of the infinite in the finite world, or deep vitality and meaning in what would otherwise be hollow and only material.

Spirituality may be abstract and largely internal, but traditionally the word "religion" implies some kind of action, often one that is symbolic or ethical—one reason I prefer the word "religion" over "spirituality." Personal religion is both an awareness of the sacred and concrete action arising out of that awareness. When you realize that something is sacred, say a special stream or lake or even old farm buildings, you may want to protect them from destruction. Deep religious realizations lead to specific responses.

Take the tragic mass shootings that shock people into spontaneous religious action. They place candles, bouquets, and sometimes handmade angels at the place where the violence occurred. You also see crosses and flowers on the highway where there has been a fatal accident. These are personal religious responses to a mysterious and tragic act that can't be dealt with rationally. These rituals come from the direct inspiration of people trying to deal with something they can't fathom. They help restore the original spirit of the place and render it sacred, and often bring soul back to a community.

A New Secularism

I have been involved with formal religion all my life. I grew up in a devout Catholic family and then left home to study for the priesthood. For thirteen years I enjoyed life in a religious community, as a solemn-professed brother with the Servites, an Italian order founded in the thirteenth century. Servites live together in priories and convents but also have work outside, such as serving a parish or teaching at a school. The men are not strictly monks but friars. As a student for the priesthood I didn't do outside work, and so my life with the Servites was almost identical with that of a monk. At twenty-six I left the order and eventually abandoned formal religion. Yet, almost every day I miss my former life in a monastery. I don't regret my decision to leave it or to end my preparation for the priesthood, because in retrospect it's clear that I was destined for a different form of religious life that is equally intense.

I went on to pursue doctoral studies in the field of religious studies. Although I no longer wore a black habit with a rosary dangling off my belt and no longer meditated every morning and evening in a highly polished wood choir stall with sleepy confreres around me, my interior life became more deeply religious.

At this point, forty years later, I feel more religious and even more Catholic than ever before, although you would see few external signs of it.

As I describe my personal religion during the course of this book, I draw on several sources: my years in a monastery, my studies of religion, my practice of psychotherapy, my ongoing study and writing. They are all part of my personal religion. I've moved further away from organized religion and much deeper into my own personal mode of spirituality. It may be more accurate to say that I have changed significantly in my relationship with the spiritual traditions. Today they are an essential part of my personal practice, though I am not an active member of any. The more traditions I study and borrow from, the deeper my spiritual life becomes.

Strangely, my personal religion becomes more individual as I study the various traditions. In the past, when I restricted my vision to Catholicism, I had almost no spiritual individuality. But now that I'm open to many traditions, paradoxically I have an intense personal experience of religion.

In the past twenty-five years my personal religion has been enriched by my wife's own religion, largely a mixture of her native Catholicism and her chosen Sikhism. I don't want to become a Sikh, but I've been affected by her devotion. Most mornings we take a walk with our dog and she talks to me about her theological ideas, her Sikh understanding. I don't want to join her in this, but I'm affected. Her views influence my religion, which is always changing and developing.

I can recommend this practice to you. If you have a spouse or friend pursuing a spiritual life different from yours, and this person is willing to talk with you without trying to convert you, listen. You need all the information and help you can get to make a religion of your own.

This book comes from my own experience, the emergence of my own spiritual life over many years. I have lived it and now want to show others how it can enrich life, give it meaning, and make ordinary days worth living. I want to proclaim that nothing is not sacred. I want to promote a religion that is felt and not just thought out, meaningful and not just emotional, my own and not just an ancient tradition. I'm convinced that this kind of personal religion, as real as the Vatican and as holy as the Dalai Lama, could offer a solution to the problem of faith in the modern world.

Every day I add another piece to the religion that is my own. It's built on years of meditation, chanting, theological study, and the practice of therapy—to me, a sacred activity. But I use my own inspirations, knowledge, taste, and understanding to give shape to this religion that suits the person I am today. I'm a more mature person, I hope, than that boy of thirteen who became a monk, and I need a religion for a grown man in the maturity of his years.

I don't want to convert anybody to my way, and I don't want followers. Yes, if you want to learn more about what I've discovered you can study with me, but my hope is that you will create a religion of your own. I'd reverse the missionary urge: Instead of converting others, I'd like to help them find their own path.

Many people, like me, have a background in formal religion or are attached to a particular tradition. You can shape a religion of your own by going deep into your tradition, understanding its more subtle teachings, not being too literal in your interpretations of it, and feeling free to take it in directions that have meaning for you. The main thing is not to be passive with it but actively engaged. It can be a rich resource and a good starting point.

When you decide to create your own religion, you will want to study the traditions of the formal religions with a fervor you've never known before. You'll discover how valuable they are and how much beauty and wisdom lie in their art and texts and stories and rituals and holy images. You'll want to learn from Buddhist sutras and the Gospel teachings and the Sufi poets and the sayings of Lao Tzu and Chuang Tzu. You will be amazed at the beautiful precision of the Kabbalah and the acute spiritual sensitivity of the Qur'ān—all because you know what it's like to search for spiritual insight and express your spiritual feelings.

You may also discover, as I did, that so-called secular literature and art complete your spiritual education. You won't know what religion is until you read Emerson and Thoreau, Emily Dickinson, Samuel Beckett and Anne Sexton, D. H. Lawrence, Wordsworth, and W. B. Yeats. You won't know how to be spiritual until you finally know how to listen to J. S. Bach and Arvo Pärt. You will be astonished at what the painters Lucas Cranach and Rene Magritte can offer your religion. These, of course, are some of my favorites.

Spiritual Creativity

This new kind of religion asks that you move away from being a follower to being a creator. I foresee a new kind of spiritual creativity, in which we no longer decide whether to believe in a given creed and follow a certain tradition blindly. Now we allow ourselves a healthy and even pious skepticism. Most important, we no longer feel pressure to choose one tradition over another but rather are able to appreciate many routes to spiritual richness. This new religion is a blend of individual inspiration and inspiring tradition.

The idea for this book began with a visit to Walden Pond, which is only an hour's drive from my house, where, on the Fourth of July, 1845, Henry David Thoreau began his experiment in living alone to discover himself and jump-start a meaningful life. I was homeschooling my daughter and we went to Walden to give her a taste of the transcendentalists of New

England. It was on a quiet early spring day that we stood silently inside the replica of Henry David Thoreau's cabin and then walked the perimeter of the small lake.

Thoreau belonged to no formal religion and yet his simple act of moving out of town, not unlike the Christian fathers going off to the desert, and building his cabin on the lake became an iconic deed. He started a movement: shifting from the mammoth religious institutions to an inspired and educated personal religion.

On this visit I had a little daydream of Thoreau making the short journey from the town of Concord to the outpost of Walden and building his ten-by-fifteen-foot cabin in the spirit of the old cathedral builders. They were building a house for God, as was Thoreau in his more modest way. In the end, he wrote a small bible, *Walden*, a verbal companion to his tiny cathedral that contains a myriad of mundane details as a perfect background for profound insights into the spiritual life. You could do no better than to read his words again and again, placing them next to *Tao Te Ching* and the Gospel stories and some poems from Rumi and Hafiz. But the main task would be to emulate Thoreau and follow your own inspiration and build your own "cathedral," however personal and freely adapted, and create your own Bible and *Walden*.

Thoreau walked two miles to find a spiritual center, while astronaut Edgar Mitchell traveled more than 280,000 miles. He found personal religion in a spacecraft heading home to Earth from a visit to the moon. Sitting in his small space vehicle on his way back during the 1971 *Apollo 14* mission, Mitchell suddenly had an awe-inspiring view of his "blue jewel-like home planet." Looking at it, he said he had a "glimpse of divinity."

There he was, a highly skilled, intricately wired, and suited-up astronaut sitting in a cramped, computer-controlled space vehicle, surrounded by the high-tech paraphernalia of his day, having a near-mystical experience. Later he would write: "The sensation was altogether foreign. Somehow I felt tuned in to something much larger than myself, something much larger than the planet in the window. Something incomprehensibly big."[1]

Mitchell's comment was not a simple metaphor tossed off in the excitement of the moment. The vision he had in space changed his life. He developed a whole new way of looking at the world and became a leader in a new kind of knowledge, noetics, that he himself described as being on the cusp of religion and science. His story, a parable for our time, hints at how we might discover a new and more effective way of being religious in an era of science.

Mitchell is uncertain whether to name his experience religious and mystical. I would have no hesitation. The point is not whether we are confronting the fact of divinity or a truth, but whether we have broken through our usual materialistic worldview. Religion is about transcending, going beyond. It's more a verb than a noun. The point is not to find something but to break through. Mitchell's words about being in tune with something incomprehensibly larger than himself describes a genuine religious experience of wonder, and wonder tears open an otherwise closed cosmos.

Secular Religion

Like a sleep-inducing spray in the air, the secularism of our culture numbs us. We breathe it every day and come to take it as only natural. It's so attractive that we don't notice as it slowly removes all sense of mystery, deep wonder, and awareness of a great Something Else or Somewhere Else that could sustain religion. Gradually and silently we become hyperactive secularists or slump into being religious people with a thick wall between our secular lifestyle and our religious beliefs. Bereft of a deep religious imagination, we don't know how to deal with the challenges of life. As I said, I see the impact in therapy.

---

1 Dr. Edgar Mitchell, *The Way of the Explorer* (New York: G. P. Putnam's Sons, 1996), p. 58.

A few years ago a woman e-mailed me saying that she'd like a private consultation. Sarah breezed into my room smiling, talking nonstop, gushing over her opportunity to tell her story. She had no complaints, nothing of importance to talk about. But then her mood changed. She was silent for a while. Tears came to her eyes, and she told me about the times she overdosed on pharmacy drugs and slit her wrists. I encouraged her to talk.

She had a high-paying job, a beautiful condo in a desirable city location, and opportunities to travel. But she couldn't maintain a close relationship. In telling me her story, she'd approach some crucial reflection and then laugh and say it was probably a mistake coming to see me. I wondered if she was relating to me in the same way she attempted an intimate relationship.

After the first session—there were many afterward—I had mixed feelings. I liked her as a person and was aware of her pain. I felt that her chief problem was a spiritual one. She was lost in the breeziness of her secular existence and couldn't land anywhere. Nothing was sacred. Nothing could stop her long enough to reflect sufficiently on her life. Even our sessions were a challenge, because her self-protection took the form of avoidance in intense, unconvincing happiness—a syndrome of our time.

Sarah had no religion in her, nothing to give weight and meaning to her actions. She didn't know whether to cry or laugh because she was so cut off from the foundations of her life. I was reminded of Paul Tillich's sermon "The Shaking of the Foundations": "When man has rested complacently on his cultural creativity or on his technical progress, on his political institutions or on his religious systems, he has been thrown into disintegration and chaos; all the foundations of his personal, natural and cultural life have been shaken."[2] Later, Tillich would recommend basing religious awareness on our "ultimate concern,"

---

2 Paul Tillich, *The Shaking of the Foundations* (New York: Charles Scribner's Sons, 1948), p. 6.

thus creating a religion of our own. So far, I hadn't heard anything like an ultimate concern from Sarah.

My revered religion professor Stanley Romaine Hopper used to say in his seminars that until we discover a new deep myth to live by, we will be at the mercy of pseudomyths. I would just substitute the word "religion" there. We are assailed by people ordained by the society to convince us of its beliefs and values, leaving us with a pseudoreligion. They wear white coats, the way spiritual priests and leaders through the centuries have done; they speak a canonical language; and they consider those who don't agree with them infidels. Doctors I've spoken to don't agree with me, but I suspect that the stethoscopes they wear around their necks are vestiges of the former religious nature of their position. Spiritual leaders of many traditions wear chains and crosses and beads in the same way.

So, what are our choices? One option is to stay with the shallow religion of the materialistic sciences and another to go back to the formal religions that so many have abandoned. We could also make do with some vague and bland notion of spirituality. I opt for religion rather than secularism, but I think we need a religion that comes out of our hearts and minds and is tailor-made to our own values and sensitivities. This new approach looks to formal religions for insight, but it takes root and flourishes in an individual life.

When I speak of a religion of one's own, I'm not talking about a selfish, ego-centered, loosely patched together spiritual concoction. I'm recommending a courageous, deep-seated, fate-driven, informed, and intelligent life that has sublime and transcendent dimension. It can be shared in a community. It can be accomplished inside or outside a traditional religious organization. It is suitable for pious members of a religious group and for agnostics and atheists. To be religious even in a personal way, you have to wake up and find your own portals to wonder and transcendence.

My client Sarah didn't have any of these portals. She was caught within the narrow confines of a religion-free life. She had no idea that to live in a domain that is only secular is to lose touch with your soul, that "vast background of our being," as Emerson called it.[3] If you become cut off from that background, life doesn't go along as usual: You go crazy.

A Sacred Milieu

Until my mid-twenties I followed the current thinking of the Catholic Church. My individuality would only appear superficially and at rare moments. Interestingly, three highly individual theologians inspired me to deep spiritual change. I didn't really wake up spiritually until I began reading the blacklisted Jesuit paleontologist and spiritual visionary Pierre Teilhard de Chardin and the Lutheran theologian Paul Tillich and was studying the New Testament with the now-respected and controversial John Dominic Crossan. Later, when I left the religious order and seminary that had been my life for thirteen years, I abandoned the faith of my fathers and mothers and was a seeker for a long while.

Chardin pictures physical evolution eventually entering a spiritual phase. Spirituality is not something added on to physical life but is the natural world spinning out its fate. For Chardin, we are naturally spiritual, and the physical world has beautiful and powerful spiritual potential. Today people like to quote Chardin: "We are not human beings having a spiritual experience. We are spiritual beings having a human experience."

Chardin spoke of the "divine radiating from the depths of matter." When I was studying him, I was still in a priory, where I was taught to see the most ordinary aspects of that life, from reading to pruning fruit trees, as spiritual work. I was getting the

---

3 Gay Wilson Allen, *Waldo Emerson* (New York: Penguin Books, 1982), p. 329.

message from many quarters and it inspired me and set the direction of my life. I still live by that standard.

Now I see the sacredness of the ordinary world as an important part of making a religion of one's own. The key figures I call upon are men and women who treated the natural world and everyday activities as sacred. Georgia O'Keeffe didn't paint Madonnas; she painted flowers and skulls, but she portrayed them with such vibrancy and symbolic innuendo that their sacredness is inescapable. Glenn Gould, a Canadian pianist and interpreter of Bach, didn't promote a particular religion, but he spoke of "the presence of divinity" in certain music that he played with reverence and stunning vitality.

Ordinarily we might hear these statements as casual metaphors, but I take them seriously. They suggest a new kind of theology, one that is not limited to any tradition or organization, that appreciates the sacredness of the secular, and that rises out of personal experience.

And so we arrive at another key principle of the book: *You can discover the sacred and the divine inside or outside a church or other spiritual organization.* You may be inspired by spiritual pioneers to discover your own sacred elements in life and the world and thus shape your own religion.

Where Is God in All of This?

"Where is God in all of this? Isn't religion based on belief in God?"

God is everywhere in it, but not in the usual ways. I understand that human beings need tangible, sometimes personal images for their more ethereal ideas and beliefs. Most people would deny that their God is an old man with a beard sitting in the clouds. But the theologians and mystics make every effort to describe God in the purest terms possible. They don't want the object of their devotion to be an idol, a too-limited notion of the infinite. Toward the opening of *Tao Te Ching* you'll find this stark and challenging line: "The Tao that can be expressed is not the everlasting Tao." Jewish writings, for their part, intentionally avoid the word "G-d," using instead "Yahweh" or "I am who am."

Personally, I'm cautious to the extreme in my use of the word. I sometimes just use the letter G. I often feel as though I need a long footnote to disclaim any naïve or too human and concrete an idea. To me, G is a mysterious reality that I discover only in my deepest reflections and meditations.

I can speak of God under unusual circumstances and "glimpse" God in nature and in certain events in human life. I can pray to God and can address God directly in times of urgent need or fear. But in every case I try not to restrict the idea of God by the limitations of my intellect and my small life.

I don't like to fill in what I don't know with poor substitutes for knowledge. I'll use traditional language when it offers a greater, deeper, and more beautiful expression. I'll speak to God out of extreme need. But I don't want to make little of God by pretending God is a "he" pulling strings in the sky. I'd rather not use the word if it's going to be so small and inadequate.

And so my religion has the word "God" in it, but it is used so sparingly, you'll have trouble finding it. I feel comfortable talking to atheists, because my idea of God is full of atheism. Like an atheist, I recoil from common appeals to God that are unrefined and lack the proper mystery and awe. Most atheists attack a naïve, too-concrete idea of God and assume that religious people are at the opposite end of their continuum. For the most part, I agree with them. We need to grow up out of that kind of religion. But the mystics around the world are not so naïve. Generally, they have a more sophisticated notion of God, and I prefer theirs over the atheists'.

I am influenced by many pious mystics from the far and recent past. Medieval theologian Meister Eckhart said, "I pray to God to get rid of God." Twentieth-century martyr Dietrich Bonhoeffer observed, also paradoxically, "God would have us know that we must live as people who manage our lives without him."[4]

I'd rather live with glimpses of God than sightings. A sense of the divine oozes out of an extraordinary presentation of beautiful nature or art. We might even sense God in a special manifestation of ugly violence: Oppenheimer's famous quotation on the occasion of the atomic-bomb explosion in the New Mexico desert: "I am become Death, the destroyer of worlds."

Since this entire book is about making a concrete response to the mysterious and to honor the most profound, most important aspects of life, it is, in my view, all about God, even if I don't use his name much. In fact, the name of God might well take away from the sense of divinity I want to evoke. God is in the space between sentences. God is the unspoken and unwritten. God is who is summoned but not seen.

If you say too much, you chase away precisely what you're trying to evoke. I'm reminded of the ancient formula: God is a sphere whose center is everywhere and circumference is nowhere. You need both insights into the nature of God: God is everywhere and God is nowhere. Theologians have referred to this as the apophatic approach or the *via negativa*—the way of negating. You look until you see nothing tangible, and that is God.

The religion I am putting forward is not the domesticated, tame, rehearsed, and constantly repeated variety. It is ever revealing and renewing itself. When I say that it is your own, that's what I mean. It is not someone else's summary of what you should do and be. It is the constant new revelation of the deep truths that can shape your life.

---

4 Dietrich Bonhoeffer, *Letters and Papers from Prison*, ed. Eberhard Bethge (New York: Collier Books, 1971), p. 360.

Religion Is Concrete

As I write, I sit in a room in my home designed as a writing studio. It looks out on a small circular pond with a fountain in the middle, every part suggesting the squaring of a circle, a traditional theme in religions and in alchemy, where symbolically it evokes the incarnation of the invisible, the square of the body intersecting the circle of spirit. One of the main themes of this book, finding the sacred in ordinary life, lies hidden in the symbol of that foundation. In this room, which looks quite monastic, I'm surrounded by books and figures from many different spiritual traditions. I had the room built according to ancient musical proportions. We discovered after it was completed that it works beautifully as a sounding box for a small music system—the speakers are up high near the ceiling. All of these details reflect my religion—not my Christianity or Buddhism or Sufism, but my personal, concrete religion, my own way of engaging the mysteries that hide behind the ordinary, my own inspired way of incarnating the spirit.

From my desk I can see out the window into the garden and watch butterflies and bees doing their quiet work all day long. I wonder why the Greeks used the same word for "butterfly" and "soul." Two alarmingly fast-growing, colorful fish swim constantly in the pond beneath the lily pads and in apparent harmony with the frogs that like to perch on the base of the fountain. Fish have long represented the thoughts and fantasies and emotions that swim within us. The garden is a large, beautiful outdoor terrarium, a universe in miniature in which, like the rivers of Paradise, the water flows and splashes. It is an emblem of life at its purest.

PART ONE

❧

A New Natural, Secular Spirituality

"Reality" overwhelms one walking home beneath the stars and makes the silent world more real than the world of speech—and then there it is again in an omnibus in the uproar of Piccadilly. Sometimes, too, it seems to dwell in shapes too far away for us to discern what their nature is. But whatever it touches, it fixes and makes permanent. That is what remains over when the skin of the day has been cast into the hedge; that is what is left of past time and of our loves and hates. . . . So that when I ask you to earn money and have a room of your own, I am asking you to live in the presence of reality, an invigorating life, it would appear, whether one can impart it or not.

—VIRGINIA WOOLF, *A Room of One's Own*

Chapter 1

❧

THE SPIRITUAL
TRADITIONS TODAY

Every manifestation of the sacred is important: every
rite, every myth, every belief or divine figure.

—MIRCEA ELIADE[5]

T he Lord is my shepherd" is a beautiful psalm, but people
are tired of being sheep. Fewer are willing to do whatever the priest, rabbi, or minister tells them. Fewer want to pack
into a crowded church and go through the motions of a meaningless rite. Fewer want to curtail their sexual interests because
a celibate or a sexually repressed or obsessed cleric tells them
to. Fewer women want to remain second-class observers to a
male hierarchy. And so many of the churches are emptying and
graying.

For some, the answer is to resist changes in culture and insist
on old-time religion. Others see no need to keep any kind of
religious or spiritual practice, whatever form it takes. Both

---

5 Mircea Eliade, *A History of Religious Ideas*, Volume 1, trans. Willard R.
Trask (Chicago: University of Chicago Press, 1978), p. xiii.

approaches have their dangers: You can be brainwashed in one and too shallow in the other. A third group is looking for a new alternative. I recommend a new and deeper way of being religious, not just spiritual, that can satisfy both believers and seekers.

Roughly four out of five people in the world are affiliated with an organized religion, and they, too, need a fresh approach that is more personal and engaging. Even they feel an urgent need to shape themselves into spiritual beings and not just follow a creed or go through the motions.

If you are among the twenty percent who are atheists and agnostics, you, too, can create a concrete spiritual way of life—you probably don't want to use the word "religion"—and you, too, can benefit from the spiritual traditions and religions without believing in them. They are there for you as much as for their followers. You can be proud that you are among the 20 percent of enlightened humanists and yet humbled at the beauty of the ancient traditions.

Skeptics call this freer approach to the religions of the world "the cafeteria approach," "salad-bar religion," or "spirituality sprawl," sampling a little of this and a little of that. I happen to enjoy cafeterias and salad bars and don't mind the comparison. There's no reason why you can't go deep into the teachings and even the practices of a formal tradition without surrendering to the whole religion. In my case, key ideas from Taoism, Greek polytheism, and Zen Buddhism, added to my substantial Catholic experience, make for a rich treasury from which to draw images, stories, teachings, and wisdom. The sheer beauty of architecture, music, the visual arts, and other artistic representations in the traditions makes them even more valuable.

My father was a devout Catholic, in many ways liberal in his thinking and yet traditional in his practice. One year for Christmas I gave him a book on Asian religions. He read it right away and told me it was one of the best and most important books he had read. Over the years he read it several times and

never tired telling me how much he appreciated it. His own
Catholic piety increased as he moved closer to his one hundredth
birthday, and yet his affection for that book never diminished. I
figure that if my hundred-year-old father, to whom I affection-
ately refer as the "philosophical plumber," could be a good
Catholic and study Taoism seriously, anyone can.

Many Traditions, Many Wisdoms

Spiritual traditions around the world, large and small, have two
major gifts to offer: wisdom and beauty. Those who understand
religion as truth etched in granite probably wouldn't make much
of these soft benefits. For them, religion is about hard conviction
and absolute correctness. But you can build a life on wisdom and
beauty, cherishing insight into human experience and the glorious expression of that insight in art and craft. The first approach
may make you crusty and inflexible, but the second may make
your life beautiful.

This is one of the main differences in the new personal religion: going deep rather than being right. This means studying
your tradition or others that attract you and following them in
your own way sincerely and wholeheartedly. The point is not to
join the right group, but to find resources that will take you deep
into your search and give you penetrating insights.

My own guides include the *Tao Te Ching*, the Gospels, stories
of the Greek gods and goddesses, teachings of the Zen masters,
Sufi poems, Native American epic songs and tales, and the
writings of the New England transcendentalists. These solid
sources collectively give me the insights I need to be on sure
footing in my spiritual life.

To these I also add secular writings that go so deep in their
reflections on human experience that I place them alongside the
sacred texts. For me, the plays of Samuel Beckett and the poems
of Rainer Maria Rilke and Emily Dickinson stand out for their
stark portrayal of the ultimate concerns that confront each of us.

The sensuous and penetrating poetry of our contemporary Jane Hirshfield is rich both in traditional and natural spirituality. The list of poets and playwrights who verge on the holy is a long one.

The writings of C. G. Jung, especially his deep autobiographical memoir, *Memories, Dreams, Reflections*, along with his work on alchemy and the spiritual traditions, serve as a basic theology and psychology. Just as theologians like Paul Tillich help me expand my Christian background, Jung helps me ground my personal religion. I can also continue to find support in the many Jewish sources available today, for me in particular Rabbis Lawrence Kushner and Harold Kushner, and, of course, always Abraham Joshua Heschel.

The spiritual traditions offer the basics of a religious life. They tell you how to live and how to envision a meaningful world. You can search them out, study them, and adapt them for your own purposes. If you study them, not necessarily like a scholar but like an earnest searcher, you will not be a dilettante. You will be a serious student of the religion you are creating for yourself.

Reading Is a Spiritual Practice

I recommend reading the classic spiritual texts from around the world, especially those that particularly appeal to you. Read them slowly and carefully—meditatively. In many formal religions reading is a spiritual practice. Portions of the New Testament were read aloud as early as the first century AD. In Christianity, too, we find *lectio divina*, reading as a kind of meditation. In Islam reading the Qur'ān[6] is a devout spiritual practice, surrounded by a precise spiritual etiquette. You shouldn't even handle a copy of the Qur'ān unless you purify yourself first. I remember, as a

---

6 S. Sayyid, "Rituals, Ideals, and Reading the Qur'an," *American Journal of Islamic Social Sciences, i-epistemology.net/ . . . /893_ajiss-23-1-stripped%20-%20Sayyid*. This excellent article is not about the actual reading of the book but about how to go about understanding the Qur'ān.

Catholic altar boy of eleven, holding a leather-bound copy of the Missal against my forehead while the priest read from it during a solemn high Mass. In Judaism the great honor given to the scrolls of the Torah also demonstrates the sacred importance of books and reading. Sikhs give great honor to the Guru Granth Sahib, a collection of traditional writings teaching the Sikh way of life.

You can practice your own *lectio divina*, reading for spiritual insight rather than information or entertainment. Select a short text from a classic source and slowly read one phrase after another. Read it more than once, perhaps aloud, so that you can let the word enter you sensually. Let the meaning and the beauty of the language impress itself on you. You may have to try different translations until you find one that works for you. Or, as I do, you may use several translations at once, trying one after another. Let the nuances of the texts give you a layered notion of what is being said.

You could create a special shelf of books, sources for your spiritual reading, books that you hold sacred. Mine includes the Bible, the Qur'ān, a special translation of the Psalms, Jane Hirshfield's inspiring collection *Women in Praise of the Sacred*, Jung's autobiography, and Homer's *Odyssey*. You can do the same on your electronic reader, giving these books a special place. You can read them regularly and reverently. The Christian *lectio divina* practice involves four acts: read, meditate, pray, and contemplate. You read thoughtfully, then you turn over the thoughts in your mind. Next, you engage in dialogue with the divine, and then you open yourself to the world around you. Really open yourself.

My *lectio divina* would be slightly different: read slowly, reflect on the words, let them take you to a deep place, take a message or lesson from that place. Go into the world with your imagination educated and primed by the images of your meditative reading. If prayer seems appropriate, let it take place after the four steps.

A Key Idea in Each Tradition

Each spiritual tradition has certain key ideas to offer to your overall spiritual understanding. I turn to the *Tao Te Ching* to be reminded of what David Hinton translates as "dark enigma." I know this phenomenon well in my life. I tire of hearing about the light from spiritual types, because it seems to me that the great mystery is darker than it is bright. You don't encounter it only in the light of pure hope and bliss. At times, you have to approach the darkness and the puzzle of your life and go through torments of self-confrontation. You may also feel the finger of the divine at work at the onset of cancer or the loss of a child.

I turn to the Gospels for other specific accents in the spiritual life. There I find a list of four special instructions: 1) Be a healer. 2) Deal with the demonic. 3) Respect your neighbor but not just those in your circle. 4) Wake up and stay awake. This last step is the deep, personal, and existential meaning of resurrection. These are real challenges, first given by Jesus to his close followers as they went on their first mission.

From the Sufi poets I learn to be inebriated with the divine that is all around me. To seek divinity, they say, is like standing in a lake and feeling thirsty. They show me how to dance like a planet circling the sun, embodying the attraction of every being to its source of life.

From Saint Francis, who may have been influenced by the Sufis, and from Native Americans I learn to relate to the natural world as to family. Brother sun and sister moon. The grandfathers and grandmothers in the sky. I feel connected rather than detached from the world, living on an enchanted planet rather than one that has been merely explained and exploited.

In the Jewish Kabbalistic tree I behold yet another series of archetypal passions framed in a beautiful tightly bound pattern of flow and tension, contraries and tandems, and the movements upward toward spirit and downward into the soul.

Most of all, in the elaborate tales of the Greek gods and goddesses, of nymphs and strange animals, I learn how deep ordinary desires and fears reach and how they relate to each other. I watch how the spiritual interplays with the depths of the soul, how the religious and the psychological work in the same spectrum. Polytheism is not only a belief in many gods, but devoted attention to many often contradictory sacred moments in ordinary life.

The spiritual traditions educate and enrich the imagination. Without them, how could we possibly see the great range of powers that push us in all directions as we try to make sense of life? Each tradition gives us a clue about how to address a particular aspect of the mysteries that challenge us, especially the big one of how to make sense out of a life that doesn't go on forever. Almost all offer some version of the paradox by which we most fulfill ourselves by caring for others. The word might be "compassion," "charity," "seva," or "selflessness": They all point toward a capacity for empathy.

The tale of the Good Samaritan in the Gospels is not a lesson about helping someone in need, being a "Good Samaritan" in the usual meaning of the phrase. It's about responding to someone in need when that person is not usually within your scope of compassion, someone who is not a relative or an immediate neighbor, someone who is not only not in your circle but is definitely on the fringe or even someone you think of as a foe. That radical kind of awareness and freedom from self-centeredness is the measure of compassion.[7]

Borrowing Ideas and Practices

The spiritual traditions don't have to sell us their precious cargo but can lend it to us. Language, ideas, techniques, methods, and rituals are all there to be borrowed. We can learn from many

---

7 I recommend the books of John Dominic Crossan on this point.

different traditions how to meditate, how to honor special days, how to venerate remarkable people, how to go on pilgrimage, how to pray, how to fast and abstain, how to gather in sacred community, how to forgive and heal and offer gratitude, how to marry and lay our loved ones to rest.

The traditions are rich with ideas and examples of how to take care of the spirit and soul throughout the arc of our lives. In these important matters we don't have to rely entirely on our originality, because we have plenty of powerful instructions and models. All we have to do is adapt them to our times and our situation. It makes a big difference whether you feel free to borrow this wisdom or feel you have to buy into it.

For a number of years when my children were younger we held a small ritual in our home occasionally on Sundays. We'd shift the furniture around in our living room, and neighbors and a few friends joined us. Generally we borrowed the simple form of the Mass but never considered that what we were doing was the Mass. We had readings from many different spiritual and meaningful secular sources and sang songs from around the world. We made every effort to be inclusive, not sexist, and nonauthoritarian. We also took time to discuss the readings and always invited the children to participate in everything we did, including the discussions. Animals were also always present, attentive, and curious.

I knew that the ritual we had in our home had ancient roots in early Christianity and even further back. I used that venerable form as the basis of our gathering, its structure. But on that skeleton we put some interesting pieces from our own imagination. For instance, we included "sacred" readings from secular novelists and poets and spent a half hour discussing the readings. We also baked bread and used a bottle of good wine for the "communion." We had friends from many different traditions present, and they all seemed to respond positively to the form, even though it wasn't native to them.

We often ended with a song or poem from Native American literature or from Ireland. You can't beat the Celtic prayers for a sense of community with all beings. I also have a penchant for Sufi poems that evoke a sense of ultimacy and absolute divinity not anthropomorphized.

I've been at rituals that seem like a long string of prayers and rites from one tradition after another. But our gathering didn't feel that way to me. We did sample many different sources, but the overall effect was a new, unified ritual that was ours and not just a string of pieces taken from the world's religions. Above all, it was a religion of our own and it felt like ours, even as we connected to ancient rites and prayers.

The Spirituality of Daily Life

I encounter many people in therapy who need more spirit in their makeup. Spirit is the element that wants to perfect, purify, and transcend. It directs our attention to the future, the cosmos, and the infinite. It is abundant in education, progress, and vision. It allows us to advance and move upward in all our pursuits. It directs our attention away from ordinary life, the body, and sensual existence. Soul is the opposite: It lies embedded in our struggles and pleasures, in our ordinary circumstances and relationships, and in the emotions and fantasies that lie deep. We feel our soul stir at family gatherings and visits home, in deep friendships and romantic relationships. Comforting dinners and friendly lunches—food in general—makes the soul come alive. People often bring their soul issues to therapy and yet may need better ideas and a vision for their lives.

Christina, for example, is a bright and intelligent woman who owns a shop where she sells handmade goods produced by artisans in her region. People love her store, and they are grateful for all that she has contributed to her community.

But Christina is unhappy. She's in love with a local lawyer, who is not too happily married and has three children. Christina pines for him. They've had an on-off affair that is thrilling for a short while and then falls apart. As in many situations like this, the lawyer is ambivalent. Christina reaches deep places of depression and feels like giving up her shop and moving away. She doesn't know what to do.

Christina is one of those people swamped by her emotions, clouded by what Jung might call "anima moods." She seems immersed in the liquid of love, unable to breathe and see the greater picture of her life. She lacks a philosophy of life, a way of understanding events, and a list of priorities—her own livable value system. Such a philosophy of life would be a spiritual achievement for her. Just as a formal religion might offer a bigger picture, a personal philosophy can also help.

I didn't say to Christina, "You need a philosophy of life." Instead, I worked with her in developing such a philosophy. I asked her what was more important, her shop or her out-of-reach lover. I wasn't looking for an answer but for an examination of her values, which would lead to her philosophy of life. We explored the roots of her business enterprise and the roots of her dissatisfaction in love.

Christina's condition was complicated: She had never taken her emotions seriously and had grown up without maturing in that area. She was sophisticated about making a living and being creative in work but unsophisticated in love. In other words, while her community skills were sharp, her emotional intelligence was mush.

As we talked, not about her lover but about her vision of life, over time her attention to the lawyer waned. After a few months, she came to me wondering what that was all about. She had expanded her shop and found a man who was really available to her. They got married and worked at the business together. I thought that this last detail was significant because it represents a concrete union of love and life.

Spirit can offer some necessary dryness to a soul dampened

with desire and attraction. It puts air into a stifling romantic entanglement, whether it's a relationship or a need for adventure. A great vision puts the small frustration into context and allows the rest of life to break free and flow. The soul needs spirit, as much as the spirit needs the humanizing influence of the soul.

What I appreciate in author David Chadwick's wry stories of his strenuous efforts to learn Zen Buddhism in Japan is his understanding that soul and spirit go together.[8] David goes to Japan to find Zen as practiced in the much-revered monasteries. He's looking for guidance from the tradition. He gets it, but it comes mixed in with so much interpersonal conflict and cultural confusion that he has to extract it like gold from ore. Maybe that is the lesson for us: Don't take the traditions as they're offered. Struggle with them, work hard at extracting only what is valuable in them, and be ready to discard the dross.

He writes about relationships in the monastery, the neighbors, visitors, his romantic partner, and his very human failures. In my mind, the story of his experiences in a Japanese Zen monastery doesn't show a failure, as his title suggests, but subtle and complicated success. In Zen and in soul work, failure is often the superficial façade of deep success, or it's a way to the kind of success that matters. Of course, David knows this. He usually writes with tongue in cheek, full of irony and every other form of wordplay.

I asked David to answer a few questions about his spiritual search and the way he formulates his current ideas about formal religion. His response was brilliant but long. I can give you only a few sentences: "The modern rational atheists and skeptics to me are like guardians at the temple gate ridiculing the idiotic away while themselves unaware of what lies within."

---

8 David Chadwick, *Crooked Cucumber: The Life and Zen Teaching of Shunryu Suzuki* (New York: Broadway Books, 1999). *Thank You and OK!: An American Zen Failure in Japan* (New York: Penguin/Arkana, 1994).

This is close to my assessment, when I say later that a little atheism can keep your faith in God honest but too much can destroy your religion. David concludes his note to me with a rousing summary of his approach: "I throw out the chaff and save the wheat then throw out the wheat and save the chaff then keep them both then throw them both out, then dance and laugh and sing and shout!"

Tradition as a Resource

Although the making of a religion of one's own can be satisfying, it can progress further and faster with the aid of the spiritual traditions. Your own spiritual path risks being too personal and limited. What resources do you have compared to the traditions that have thought of things you will never consider? They have refined ideas and images and teachings and moral guidelines expressed in elegant and inspiring ways. They have produced spiritual beauty of a kind no single person could ever create. Read Emerson's journals and you find that he was reading Hafiz for months, and Thoreau's homespun spiritual insights come wrapped in references from the Western and Eastern traditions.

The formal religions are often overdone, with useless formalities, immature psychological notions, and pompous authorities. Recently I witnessed the funeral of a famous politician and noticed that the language of the church service required arcane knowledge and failed to speak to the strong emotions of the people present. There was an abundance of academic theology and little psychological awareness of people's emotional needs, as though feelings have nothing to do with spirituality.

But behind all that detritus may lie certain insights you could spend years searching for. As the religious authorities often say, the institution is human, while the substance of the religion is transcendent.

During the writing of this book I have had a desk calendar at my elbow with a saying from Lao Tzu on the cover: "The world is ruled by letting things take their course."[9] It's worth meditating on these few words for the next twelve months. All year long I will try to let things take their course, and this sliver of philosophy can be my guide, reminding me of a truth that will carry me on. For twelve months I'll base my religion on a calendar.

There's another secret here, too, that I hope to go into further. Not only do we need good ideas; we need them expressed elegantly and beautifully. If I had to do it over, I think I'd become a translator of sacred texts.

From my Catholic tradition, I always remember the teaching of one of my favorite theologians, Nicholas of Cusa (1401–1464), who felt that we should all become sophisticated enough to know what we don't know. Here's a line that guides me in my own spiritual path:

A theology of unknowing is necessary for a theology of knowing because without it God would not be worshipped as infinite but rather as a creature, and that would be idolatry.[10]

My own Catholic tradition shares the central realization of Zen Buddhism: that we should never be attached to the technical language we use in our spirituality. We should know, every time we use it, that it is inadequate, empty. When I find myself being too caught up in a particular word or teaching, I remember Zen and Nicholas. I take to heart both the Zen teachings and Nicholas's way of thinking. That love for the traditions keeps me on track and saves me from being too enamored of my own ways.

---

9 *Zen 2013*, produced by Laura Livingston (Darien, CT: Ziga Media, 2012).

10 Nicolas of Cusa, *De Docta Ignorantia*, quoted in Pauline Moffitt Watts, *Nicolaus Cusanus: A Fifteenth-Century Vision of Man* (Leiden: E. J. Brill, 1982), p. 60. Translated by Thomas Moore.

A major purpose of formal religion is to be an art of memory, keeping in mind a certain vision of life and values that flow from that vision. We forget the important things. I know the philosophy of letting things take their course. It's second nature to me. But I'm happy to be reminded of it every morning when I open my desk calendar.

We all need to be reminded again and again of the underlying truths of our existence, and that is a good reason to read the texts repeatedly. In formal religion you often go through the major writings, reading them one after another over the course of a year. You can do that with your own reading. Select a particular book for Sundays or Fridays, whatever works, and read a little each week.

A liturgical calendar is useful. If this is Christmas, it's time to recall that light appears out of darkness, joy out of gloom, and hope out of despair. If it's Passover, it's time to remember that freedom can issue out of slavery and liberation out of captivity. If it's Ramadan, remember the instruction to take care of people. These festivals celebrate archetypes, eternal patterns that underlie social movements as well as personal developments.

In my personal liturgical year, if it's March 25, I remember the birth of my mother on the Catholic feast day of the Annunciation. I remember that she was named Mary Virginia, or Virgin Mary. I also honor July 1 as the day she married my father and the day she died. My dad died last Thanksgiving Day during the writing of this book, another collective holiday that now finds its place on my sacred calendar.

These are holy days for me, times of intense piety and meditation in my own religion. The synchronicities in these days only intensify their meaning and their sacredness. If you want to see real religion, look at my liturgical calendar, a combination of civic, world religious, and personal holy days.

My intention is to intensify rather than weaken our reliance on the world's religious and spiritual traditions, to do that by letting go the habit of feeling obligated and coerced. We could instead freely and happily turn to the spiritual ways of the past for ideas and inspiration. Our personal spirituality could then mesh with tradition in a creative and joyful way.

Emerson's Way

Ralph Waldo Emerson was steeped in formal religion and yet willing to go his own way spiritually. Educated at Harvard, he became a Unitarian minister in Boston. But soon he got involved in a controversy about holy communion and left the ministry, becoming a spiritual teacher and lecturer. In his midthirties he gave the lecture at Harvard known now as the "Divinity School Address." Only a small number of people were present, but the impact of the speech was significant. The religious establishment criticized him and didn't invite him back to Harvard for almost thirty years. This one talk set his life off in a new direction, becoming what could be the very model for creating a religion of one's own.

In the "Divinity School Address," a forerunner of this book you hold in your hands, Emerson criticizes Christianity for emphasizing the personality of Jesus and yet making little of his humanity. He complains about the churches giving too much attention to miracles. "The very word Miracle, as pronounced by Christian churches gives a false impression; it is a monster; it is not one with the blowing clover and the falling rain."

I'd become a follower of Emerson for that one sentence: the miracle of "the blowing clover and the falling rain." Just imagine what it would do for your religion if you shifted your sense of the miraculous from some astounding feat of a master magician to a profound appreciation of the miracle of rain. You would be a different kind of person living a different kind of life. You wouldn't be sad from the weight of your religious obligations, but rather joyful at the beauty and holiness of the natural world. You'd be happy, open, and graceful, all because of your positive, world-based spiritual vision.

Emerson emphasizes the spiritual power of the individual person. "The man on whom the soul descends, through whom the soul speaks, alone can teach." He speaks of the divinity of the person. "In how many churches . . . is man made sensible that he is an infinite Soul; that the earth and heavens are passing into his mind; that he is drinking forever the soul of God?" He continues, "It does little good to try to create new myths, rites and forms. The remedy to their deformity is, first, soul, and second, soul, and evermore, soul." You see why I, an author of several books on the soul, like Emerson so much.

Emerson doesn't recommend making new religions, because you can't manufacture a religion. Nor does he advocate becoming an atheist. Atheism tends to be nothing more than yet another too-earnest religion with the added problem of being excessively rationalistic. The best way is to live a more soulful life, allowing for mystery and arranging life around that mystery. This keeps the reality of God, but emptied of our ideas of who or what God is. Faith and atheism blend into a sacred theology. You don't need the word "God." You need the reality, the sense of otherness in creation, an opening to the transcendent.

The Conviviality of the Religions

Like me, my wife was raised as a devout Catholic, but at an early age she became seriously involved with the Sikh religion. One day a yoga student of hers gave her a small gift. "I wanted to give you a statue of Saint Francis," the student said, "but I thought you might be offended since it would be Christian." My wife shrugged. She feels no conflict between her native Catholicism, which she still cherishes and practices in her own way, and her Sikhism. She'd be delighted to get an image of Saint Francis as a gift.

This simple exchange demonstrates our challenge of the moment: learning to appreciate the mutuality and conviviality of the spiritual traditions. Far beyond tolerance and ecumenism, this is a new way of being religious: positively taking in the beauty and wisdom of all the traditions, treating them as resources for your own religion, and going as deeply as you want into any tradition that inspires you. Now is not the time to *tolerate* the religions of the world; it's time to seek them out and study them and be affected by them.

To create a religion of one's own, start by never again sensing any conflict between one tradition and another. Enjoy their overlap, their mutuality, and their conviviality. Be sure one day to give a Saint Francis to a Sikh or a Buddha to a Native American.

The criticism about drawing from several traditions, that it's like eating in a cafeteria, has a point: It can be superficial. So, when you become interested in Rumi or the *Tao Te Ching* or Greek tragedy, don't just dabble in it. Take it seriously. Study it in some depth. Incorporate its deep insights into your practice and weave it into a religion of your own.

You've learned how to operate your electronic equipment and computers and you know a fair amount about how the body works and how to be healthy; now become sophisticated about religion and the spiritual life.

The one ingredient missing in much of modern spirituality is intelligence. Yet, when you examine the religious traditions of the world you find study, study, and more study. Monks amass libraries, whether in France or Tibet. Spiritual teachers amass ancient wisdom, whether in Germany or Africa. To be spiritual, you have to be on guard against flimsy ideas and practices. The whole area of religion and spirituality invites flimflam and is filled with con men and con women. Both the real teachers and the charlatans are asking you to accept their approach to insoluble mysteries. It's difficult to know where to stand. You need your intelligence and your skepticism.

But amid all the chaff lies real spiritual nourishment. Just don't be gullible. Don't be swept away by anything not worthy of you. It might be better to be more of a skeptic than a believer, less open-minded and more critical. The problem in the modern spiritual landscape is not only a plethora of genuine, useful material but also a marketplace teeming with questionable ideas, practices, and leaders.

One valuable variation on creating your own religion is to return in a different way and more seriously to your family or childhood traditions. I know several people who have returned to Judaism and Christianity after finding fresh, imaginative, and well-educated teachers. "I realize now," one woman told me, "that the translations I always used were archaic and out of date. I have a young rabbi now who is knowledgeable about new approaches, and I find it exciting. I'm back in the fold and happy to be there."

Usually today you find that teachers coming out of the good theological and divinity schools understand this idea of the conviviality of traditions. They appreciate what other formal religions have to offer and they get the point about each person appropriating traditional teachings and practices for themselves. Culturally, there couldn't be a better time for creating a religion of one's own.

Chapter 2

✣

THE NATURAL MYSTIC

In my daily life I don't analyze.
I am part of a natural rhythm
A miracle and a wonder!
Splitting wood, hauling water.

—LAYMAN P'ANG

It was the 1960s, and I was a Servite friar at Our Lady of Benburb Priory in Northern Ireland. One day we all packed up for a holiday on the Donegal coast, not far away. The sight of that rugged stretch of land and the beaches marking the edge of the vast ocean; the impressive headlands reaching into the sea; the waves smashing against the rocks and pooling in the coves; the tall, hard spray of water getting you thoroughly soaked as you tried to see across the ocean with your imagination—this sensual display has stayed with me as a mystical moment in my youth. It continues to feed the special Irish spirituality that was in my blood long before I was born.

During those memorable days in Donegal I had a close encounter with nature, so huge and powerful and beautiful that I've never gotten over it. I can still sense its impact on me. I wasn't in space circling the moon and beholding the universe up close. I was just standing at the ocean's edge, but it was enough to give me one of my awakenings and a memorable, natural mystical experience.

Many people have negative attitudes toward mysticism and often use the word "mystic" pejoratively to indicate someone who is seriously and deliriously out of touch with reality. As a student of religion I say the opposite: Mystics are the ones who have actually gotten in touch with what is real. They have powers of receptivity and sympathy that are particularly acute. They are porous and have the ability to be so open as to stretch beyond the usual small and protective ego, and they are often unusually courageous. Out of that wide and sometimes painful stretching of an ego they find ethical opportunities special to them.

Simone Weil, Unaligned Mystic

Simone Weil, an unusual twentieth-century mystic particularly relevant today, was born into a Jewish family in Paris in 1909, and even as a child she identified strongly with the oppressed and persecuted. As an adult she fought for their rights, whether by becoming a factory worker, a soldier in the Spanish Civil War, or a member of the French Resistance.

For years, she was a brilliant university professor and found inspiration in several different religious traditions, though, like her family, she was agnostic. Then, at twenty-eight, in Assisi, in the church of Saint Mary of the Angels, in a chapel important to Saint Francis, she had her first mystical experience. Later, she would have other moments of spiritual ecstasy "when Christ came down and took possession of me." The phrase makes one think of another mystic, Saint Teresa of Avila, widely known from Bernini's sculpture in which orgasmic swoon and mystical possession seem to overlap. But remember, Simone wasn't Christian.

With her penetrating mind, Weil developed her own theology,

presented in a number of unsystematic books, in which several traditions play a role. She didn't approve of blending religions and made a point that could be a rule of thumb for us as we craft our own religion: "Each religion is alone true, that is to say, that at the moment we are thinking of it we must bring as much attention to bear on it as if there were nothing else . . . A 'synthesis' of religion implies a lower quality of attention."[11]

Simone Weil went deep into several spiritual traditions without concluding that they all were saying the same thing in different language—a common sentiment today.[12] She also demonstrates that a religion of one's own is more than an intellectual piecing together of a puzzle culled from the traditions. Your religion makes real demands on you. For many people a mystical experience inspires an ethical life, but Weil began with a powerful, innate ethical passion and created her religion out of that. Whichever way you go, learn from Simone that your religion isn't complete without an ethical vision. Mysticism and ethics form a perfect tandem at the base of your religion.

Despite Weil's growing up in a Jewish family that was basically agnostic, her mystical experiences led her to Christianity, especially its ethics. She had an inborn rule to "love your neighbor," and she could see a direct connection between her spiritual ecstasies and those of Christian mystics. She was a remarkable woman: a Jewish, agnostic, almost-Christian, mystic activist. She had much to teach about creating your own religion, especially about preserving your skepticism even as you deepen your spiritual vision.

Mystical Possibilities in the Ordinary
Mysticism involves a constructive loss of self and a feeling of being connected to the whole of life. Mystics meditate intensely

---

11 Simone Weil, *The Notebooks of Simone Weil*, trans. Arthur Wills (Oxford: Routledge, 2003), vol. 1.

12 Karen Armstrong, *Visions of God* (New York: Bantam Books, 1994), p. ix.

and eventually feel at one with the very core of existence and with the totality of all that is not them. You can see how a loss of self can lead to ethical passions. The "other" may sometimes be simply another person in need. Because they are so different, mystics sometimes appear to be special or even disturbed people. One wonders if their unusual psychological makeup is just part of their calling to a rare way of life in which boundaries are thin and porous.

Anyone can be an ordinary mystic. You may not experience a regular loss of ego and absorption in the divine, but now and then you may feel lifted out of your body and become lost in a beautiful piece of art or a scene in nature. As a parent, you may have a moment of bliss as you step back and look at your children. As a creative person, you may finish a project and suddenly feel light-headed with the joy of having created something worthy. You may enjoy occasional bursts of wonder and know what it means to extend the boundaries of a self.

In a religion of one's own, occasional, simple mystical moments are sufficient. Brief experiences of sublime absorption, as ordinary as being struck by the brilliant blue of a cloudless sky, may contribute to your sense of being religious. The mystical moments multiply and over time you extend the borders of your self, you are less prone to protecting yourself, and you have more empathy with the people and the world around you. If you define religion as a strong sense of the divine, your daily mysticism contributes to that sense by drawing you out of yourself into nature and then beyond.

It helps if you take these experiences seriously and make something of them. Adapt your life to them and find ways to cultivate them. Just having one sublime experience after another isn't enough. You have to weave them into your thinking, feeling, and relating. They become part of your life and identity. People look at you and see a mystic in there somewhere.

You could make a little ritual of visiting a special place in nature. I know an office worker who goes every day to a spot by the river in her city and just sits for a half hour. I used to do that when I was a summer professor at the University of Windsor in Canada. I'd sit by the Detroit river and watch the water and the river activity, especially the passing freighters. That's mysticism? In my religion it is. I was absorbed momentarily in nature and culture. I was lost, mesmerized by that special view of life and was meditating not on it but with it.

Many people find their mystical side spending hours in a garden. I have my piano. My wife paints and does yoga.

In one of his insightful talks Zen master Shunryu Suzuki said that in your practice you should walk like an elephant. "If you can walk slowly, without any idea of gain, then you are already a good Zen student."[13] There's a mantra for your religion: Walk like an elephant. It means to move at a comfortable pace. No rushing toward a goal. No push to make it all meaningful.

The sometimes inscrutable texts of Taoism and Zen teach that it's important to do what you do without trying to accomplish anything. One of the benefits of a religion of one's own is its ordinariness and simplicity. You don't need a magnificent ceremony, a specially ordained minister, or a revered revelation to give you authority. You don't have to get anywhere. There are no goals and objectives: nothing to succeed in, and nothing in which to fail. You can sit in your house, as Thoreau did, and be attentive—his suggestion. "We are surrounded by a rich and fertile mystery. May we not probe it, pry into it, employ ourselves about it—a little? . . . If by watching all day and all night I may detect some trace of the Ineffable, then will it not be worth the while to watch?"[14]

---

13 Shunryu Suzuki, *Not Always So*, ed. Edward Epse Brown (New York: HarperCollins, 2002), p. 30.

14 Henry David Thoreau, *I to Myself* (New Haven: Yale University Press, 2007), pp. 98–99.

Thoreau's advice echoes the ancient *Tao Te Ching*:

See simplicity in the complicated.
Achieve greatness in little things.[15]

My wife and daughter have spiritual names given them through a mysterious process in the Sikh tradition. They asked me if I'd like a spiritual name. "If I could choose," I said, "I'd like to be called Wu Wei—accomplishing something by doing nothing." The name hasn't stuck, but I'm doing my best to merit it.

Walk like an elephant is good advice, but Suzuki says that you should also sit like a frog. Zen practice comes down to sitting. Not sitting and doing something, but sitting. Speaking about frogs, Suzuki said:

When something to eat comes by, they go like this: Gulp! They never miss anything, they are always calm and still. I wish I could be a frog.[16]

The mystic is empty and lost in a positive way, and yet she is alert, ready for the next revelation and opportunity.

Thoreau describes in *Walden* how in his cabin he had three chairs: one for solitude, two for friendship, and three for society. He was prepared for sitting. As was Glenn Gould, who in his concerts and recordings usually used a low, merely functional chair that his father had made for him. Stories about Gould often include the famous handmade chair, as though it were a totem, an object of special significance, betraying some mystery about who Gould was.

---

15 Lao Tzu, *Tao Te Ching*, trans. Gia-Fu Feng and Jane English (New York: Vintage Books, 1972), no. 63.

16 Suzuki, *Not Always So*, p. 151.

Look at your chairs. Is there one that has special meaning? I often ask therapists about the chairs they use in their practice. The chair says something about the work, because soul work, the opus, asks you to either walk like an elephant or sit in a chair. A certain kind of inactivity linked to simplicity can make your religious practice sing. Zen students sit on cushions, but most humans sit in chairs. In our home we have two low, colorful chairs made by artisans in Afghanistan. There are little mirrors in the backs of the chairs. Maybe they're for ornament, but I suspect there's something mysterious going on. Maybe when you sit another world appears, the inner space of the mirror.

If the ordinary mystic isn't sitting in a chair, he's doing something ordinary and simple that he has somehow raised to a theological level.

I asked an old friend, Kevin Kelly, if there is any mysticism in his work of arranging and selling flowers and giving workshops on them. He told me about one tiring day when he felt he had to drag himself to the wholesale house for a job and then go home and create a design. "The moment I put the first piece of green in, my whole energy shifted. My body began to move and I knew I was dancing the arrangement. I was enthralled and filled with a sense of life. The act of creation is beyond feelings and thoughts. It unites us with the fundamental creative energy of the universe and enlivens us."

Kevin thinks of his flower shop as a chapel. He is a "priest of beauty." "Flowers do nothing, practically speaking, in daily life," he told me. "And yet they give people that moment that is a most valuable and precious aspect of spirituality: a moment of beauty."

Kevin's teaching and artistic practice has a parallel in formal religion, in the Zen art of flower arranging, or Ikebana. Here again we come to one of our basic lessons in creating a religion of our own: the formal religions can teach us how to generate our own language and practices. Ikebana not only shows how beauty can arise out of care for empty space and the display of flowers, but the flower forms can embody spiritual truths, such as impermanence, silence, and meditation.

You don't have to take a course in Ikebana or go to Japan to study flower arranging as a spiritual practice. You can simply grow or buy some flowers and carefully place them in appropriate vases and then arrange them in your home or workplace. Do it thoughtfully, with care and imagination. Remember, as you do it, that you are doing something important: making your world beautiful—a soulful way to be spiritual.

A key insight from Zen is to see the vast implications of something as ordinary as placing cut flowers in a vase or writing out a poem in calligraphy, without resorting to a grand philosophy and an intricate explanation. For some, it would be useful to start a practice of this kind by learning a traditional skill like flower arranging or calligraphy, and then perhaps finding your own home art that opens you to the great mysteries.

I can imagine a certain approach to cooking, woodworking, sewing, photography, gardening, or writing poems that could be the foundation of your own spiritual practice. For cooking, I'd recommend the cookbooks of the Zen-inspired Ed Brown, and for poetry the Jungian analyst David Rosen's books on haiku practice. In one of his cookbooks Ed Brown says about preparing food, "[Y]ou find the world appears vivid with spinach, lettuces, and black beans; with cutting boards, baking pans, and sponges. You let go of the imagined and hypothetical so that awareness can function in the world of things."[17]

The ability to lose yourself regularly in the sublime or the beautiful, even in the most ordinary settings, can make you a mystic. I use the word "portal" frequently in this book, and it applies here. It isn't just the beautiful that gives you a mystical experience, but the beautiful as a portal to the unknown and

---

17 Edward Espe Brown, *Tomato Blessings and Radish Teachings* (New York: Riverhead Books, 1997), p. 5.

unknowable. In a mystical experience you may not be able to define or describe exactly what you saw and felt. You've broken through the limits of the known and connected with the world in a way that is more like union, participation, or intimacy. Sexual union is often used as a metaphor for mystical "knowing."

Some people are professional mystics, like Thomas Merton, who lived the life of a strict monk. Some are supermystics who have truly exceptional degrees of union, like Julian of Norwich or John of the Cross. Others are ordinary mystics, like you and me, who may have momentary sensations of creative lostness, a lapse in consciousness, and attention that feels vivifying.

Astronaut Edgar Mitchell said of his experience in space: "What I experienced during that three-day trip home was nothing short of an overwhelming sense of universal connectedness. . . . I perceived the universe as in some way conscious."[18] His experience was understandably intense, but you and I can have this kind of mystical sensation in our own way and to a lesser degree and find it feeding our own religion.

Karen Armstrong, who has done much to bring intelligent understanding of religion to the world, says of mystics that "they encounter a reality in the depths of the self that is, paradoxically, Other and irrevocably separate." The experience is ineffable and can't be explained in rational terms. Mystics "encounter a presence that transfigures their lives, transcending the confines of their limited and isolated egos. They feel . . . at one with the world."[19]

These words are close to those used by Edgar Mitchell as he tried to find language to express his experience in space. They also could apply to ordinary people at special moments in their lives when they seem to get lost in an absorbing activity and feel

---

18 Edgar Mitchell, *The Way of the Explorer*, pp. 3–4.

19 Armstrong, *Visions of God*, p. ix.

the boundaries of their individuality weaken in a positive way. Ordinary absorption, being seized by an activity or a sight or sound, qualifies as a small mystical moment when it takes us beyond, to a place carved out by wonder and amazement.

Ordinary Mystics

A religion of one's own may arise out of an experience that shakes you up. Sickness, divorce, economic trouble, or the mere sight of suffering can be the beginning of a deep journey of questioning and wonder. A parallel in formal religion is the Buddha's conscience stirring to life as he leaves the protection of his home and beholds illness and suffering. The Gospels describe in strong language how Jesus, too, often feels shaken by the suffering he witnesses and is stirred into action. For the average person the transforming moment may be sensing nature's awe and beauty or feeling a strong desire to offer service to the world.

In creating a religion of one's own, you could be open to moments when your sense of self expands and the boundaries melt. The result is not really a loss of self, but an increase. The edges become softer, and, although to a rigid ego the experience may be frightening, if you're prepared, the mystical moment may allow you to enter life more fully. You feel more yourself and less lost in a negative sense.

Religion begins in the sensation that your life makes sense within a larger one, that you and the animals have a bond, that the trees and rocks and rivers are to the body of the world as your bones and hair and bloodstream are to your body. You understand, at least in some primal way, that your happiness depends on the happiness of the beings around you. You may even realize ultimately that your soul participates in the world's soul.

One etymology of the word "religion," *re-ligare*, to bind together, describes the bond between you and your world and ultimately with the hidden, invisible, yet pulsing, breathing, singing source of it all.

Religion binds us to the faint, transparent, and untouchable bloodstream of the divine, the mystic ichor that flows through all things, not making them divine but making them receptacles of divinity. You are part of that scene and have divinity flowing through you as well. You are what Nicholas of Cusa called *deus humanus*—a human-god or god-human. Paradoxically, without that divinity you have no humanity.

Many mystics are like Nicholas in saying that you have divinity inside you; it is not only outside. If you go deep enough into yourself, you will come up against mysterious creative forces. You can't know yourself completely, and you may realize, again as mystics have pointed out, that some of your problems stem from your resistance against that deep, unknown source of vitality. If you could get out of the way, who knows what you could become? The divine creator not only makes a world but also creates a self.

Károly Kerényi, an especially imaginative and probing religion scholar, a friend of Jung, describes the Roman word "*religio*" as "an attitude of respect, or beyond that, of worship, or more still, a feeling of giddiness on the edge of the abyss . . ."[20] "Abyss" may not be the best word for Kerényi's meaning, since it may imply darkness and even Hell. I imagine instead standing at the edge of the ocean or under the sky, aware of the mysterious context in which our lives play out. I would say that I feel dizzy at the edge of the infinite expanse of life I see in the sky.

Kerényi's vision brings to mind my uncle Thomas I. Nugent. I often write about him as an example of the naturally religious person. In 1878 his father, William, who came from Waterford, Ireland, purchased a 125-acre farm, set between two tall hills, in the beautiful rolling land outside Auburn, New York. Eventually my uncle Tom farmed the homestead, and I spent many summers

---

20 Károly Kerényi and C. Kerényi, *The Religion of the Greeks and Romans*, trans. Christopher Holme (New York: E. P. Dutton, 1962), p. 14.

in his company, walking the land, milking the cows, feeding the chickens, and repairing equipment.

The farmhouse had no running water. We drank cool water from a spring twenty yards up the hill from the house and washed with rainwater that collected in the cistern outside the kitchen. At first, my uncle plowed and sowed and harvested with two strong horses, a gray mare and a sorrel workhorse. Later, he modernized with a John Deere tractor. I plowed with both, under his tutelage, and was his companion all day, every day, as he took care of the animals and watched the weather.

We were quiet much of time, whenever he wasn't telling outrageous stories. We watched the clouds and felt the breeze, determining when to take in the hay or harvest the oats. On those long wonder-filled days I learned to be sensitive to the signs of nature and to feel at home in the fields and among animals. My uncle was thoughtful, intelligent, witty, and honest. But he was not religious in a conventional sense, the only one of the family not to go to church. Yet everyone loved and respected him. I adored him, and obviously still do.

The man was something of a mystic, a very ordinary mystic, who lived his life in tune with the seasons and the changing sky and landscape. He could communicate with the animals with just a nod or look, sometimes a hardly perceptible sound. He had a habit of checking the movements of the wind and the clouds and feeling for moisture in the grasses. He often mystified me because he had powers that I never witnessed in my life in the city.

You can imagine how a solitary farmer's life could have some mysticism in it. He was a hermit of sorts, living with two quiet and hardly engaging brothers who worked long and hard at their day jobs. Anyone who knew him well thought of him as being religious in his own way. He had thoughtfully rejected formal religion and just as thoughtfully followed his own deep inspirations.

He wasn't perfect. He would go on drinking binges every now and then that I hated, because during them he was in the thrall of some daimon. But later I understood that a bodhisattva, with one foot in the heavens and one on earth, will often wrestle with one of the demons as part of his or her vocation as mediator. Many spiritual leaders fall to the daimon of sex; some money. My uncle dealt with Dionysos, the god of the vine, who offers an abundance of vitality in exchange for a particular kind of madness.

A daimon, by the way, is a generic urge or impulse, while, psychologically speaking, a demon is a negative form of that urge. I discuss these terms in more detail later.

The spiritual traditions provide a background for a farmer mystic. The great medieval Christian monasteries were usually surrounded by the farmlands that provided their food and labor. Thomas Merton, himself living in a Kentucky monastery that had its own farm, said of Shakers, a religious community that centered its spiritual life on farm labor, "There is, in the work of the Shakers, a beauty that is unrivaled because of its genuine spiritual purity . . ."[21] Writing about the Shakers, Suzanne Skees notes that *Harper's Bazaar* of 1910 said of Shaker chickens: "Their white feathers are always a degree more snowy than other fowls, and their yellow feet almost appear to have been polished."[22]

My uncle Tom worked his farm with some of the Shaker spirit, though I never thought that his chickens' feet were polished, and with genuine spiritual purity, not because of any formal belief but because he was so devoted to nature. I don't think that to be a mystic he had to speak of the divinity within nature. It was enough to sense it and honor it, leaving it unnamed and unremarked.

---

21 Thomas Merton, *Mystics and Zen Masters* (New York: Farrar, Straus and Giroux, 1967), p. 196.

22 Suzanne Skees, *God Among the Shakers* (New York: Hyperion, 1998), p. 182.

Let me pause here for a general observation. Many people, like my uncle Tom Nugent, who create a religion of their own, would never use that terminology for what they do. They simply live and act in a certain way, and I come along, with my background in religious studies and my concern about the secularization of culture, and describe their lives as religious in an informal way. I call them mystics because they have found a portal to transcendence, though they use no formal spiritual or theological language. This may be the direction we are going in the future: toward a religiousness that is not separate from ordinary, secular life and that dispenses with much of the proper language.

I'm painfully aware that the experts in fields like religion and spirituality sometimes feel that bringing mysticism down so far into ordinary life is an insult to the great mystics and makes it all too light and breezy. I feel just the opposite. I believe that one day we'll understand that we've lost out on religion because we made it too lofty and distant. I see it as a simple quality of everyday life, and in that simplicity lie its beauty and importance.

Nature's Divinity

Not long before he died, James Hillman, my old friend and mentor, told me that, if the truth be told, he was a pantheist. Knowing his work and being personally close to him for many years, I think he meant that he perceived the divine in everything. James sighed when he spoke these words, as though they were a confession, as though he were finally admitting to having some sort of nameable religion but also indicating that he truly found life and the world sacred.

In some ways James was like my uncle Tom. He was allergic to religion. He refused to participate in formal religion, for the most part, but in his own way he was a deeply religious man.

Look closely at his work and I think you'll see the style of a theologian. He pushed everything to its ultimate. He discussed the gods with a level of appreciation that touched on reverence. At the same time he was always critical of formal religion. Although he expressed wonder at how I escaped being a monk without severe emotional problems, I saw his lifestyle as monastic: focused on study, books, ideas, religious themes, animals, community. He'd deny it, but I think he would have made a good monk—without the vows.

One of the many images in Christianity that disturbed him was that of Michael, the archangel, battling a dragon with a long, sharp spear, as presented, for instance, in Albrecht Dürer's complex etching or the beautiful mosaic of James Powell.

James thought of the dragon as representing the imagination, and he felt that Christianity failed to foster imagination. He favored the religion of the Greeks, who, he thought, made use of the gods to bring imagination to every aspect of life. A few years before he died I made a translation of the Gospels from Greek and applied over five hundred notes—comments of my own and of a variety of writers on various passages. I discussed the project with James, because I was fascinated by the new insights I had found by reading the Greek version closely and in light of my studies in Greek polytheism. James was skeptical.

One day I received a one-line postcard from him. "What about Mark 1:25?" it said. I looked it up. In that passage, when an "unclean spirit" asks Jesus what he wants, Jesus replies: "Shut your mouth." The Greek text is strong, more like: "Muzzle it." It was important to James that we listen to what a daimon has to say, and the last thing we should do is keep it from speaking. We shouldn't "muzzle it," but listen to it for insight and guidance.

The next time we met we discussed this passage further. I agreed it was a troublesome line but that in general Jesus was able to speak to the unclean spirits and the daimons, so much so that people thought he must be in league with them. Listening closely to me, James thought for a moment and let it go, obviously un-convinced.

I often felt that James saw the many ways in which Christi-anity had been a foe to the imagination, but he didn't know much about the other side of that religion—the mystics and theologians who appreciated the rich stories and personalities of the tradition. I also felt that many Christian practices, like the veneration of images of the saints, would fit well with James's ideas of relating directly to images and appreciating their reality.

What can we learn about creating one's own religion from James Hillman? That spirituality has its own deep shadow. That the soul's mysticism is as important as the spirit's. That is, that the focus of contemplation can be ordinary life, the natural world, deep feelings, and important relationships. That both moralism and literalism weaken the religious attitude. That religion and spirituality can take many different forms. That what looks like the opposite of religion may be its best manifestation.

A few months before he died James phoned and asked if I would preside at his graveside funeral. I found it difficult to speak. "Don't go sentimental on me," he said.

"There's a difference between emotion and sentimentality," I replied. "This is difficult."

But we went on talking. James didn't want a rabbi or cantor, but he wanted some music. He didn't want lectures or talks. He'd leave it to me to work something out.

This deeply emotional conversation again reminded me that James had his own religion. Remember our principle of the con-viviality of the traditions. James, born into a Jewish family and a passionate agnostic or pantheist, asked me, a Catholic in some sense of the word, to conduct his funeral. That was extraordinary. I can only think that, knowing me well, he understood that I had a religion of my own and he could trust me to honor his.

The Blue Sky

As I began thinking of the theme of a personal religion, Georgia O'Keeffe came to mind, especially for her vision and the inventive arc of her life. I've always believed that many people are attracted to her paintings for the sacred that shines through them: flowers, skulls, landscape, and sky. She spoke for no formal religion, and yet to me she was a religious painter.

In a letter of 1952, written when she was sixty-four, O'Keeffe said: "I realize how un-Catholic my soul is . . . I am startled to realize my lack for the need of the comfort of the Church—When I stand alone with the earth and sky a feeling of something in me going off in every direction into the unknown of infinity means more to me than any thing any organized religion gives me."[23]

The bright blue sky of New Mexico became an essential part of O'Keeffe's vocabulary and evokes the mystical in her art. In this letter we also get a clear picture of her spiritual situation. She says that she is not afraid of death, and formal religion seems to be based on that fear. She was attracted to life and vitality, as millions see in her paintings. She didn't paint angels and divinities but rather captured the divinity in things.

She owned a copy of *The Cloud of Unknowing*, a well-known mystical text of the Middle Ages, and she met and corresponded with Thomas Merton. Brenda Mitchell's dissertation on O'Keeffe's "visionary mysticism," "Music that Makes Holes in the Sky," portrays O'Keeffe as an intellectual artist influenced by writers she knew. She had ideas and was thoughtful in her simple life and art.

Mitchell also remarks that O'Keeffe's fascination with the sky led her to paint birds in flight. "In these paintings appear the opposition of black and white winged raven and snow-covered

---

23 Jack Cowart, Juan Hamilton, and Sarah Greenough, *Georgia O'Keeffe: Art and Letters* (Boston: Little, Brown, 1987), p. 263.

earth, soaring spirit and earthbound corporeality."[24] O'Keeffe was exploring familiar images for spirit and body: sky and landscape, birds and skulls, clouds and desert sand, life and death—the vocabulary of a mystic.

Where body and spirit have a solid place the soul gets into the picture through sexuality. When you look at an O'Keeffe painting, the first thing to hit you is its sensuality. Then your eye will move toward the unmistakable shapes of sex—the flower that looks like a vulva and the pistils and stamens that are unmistakably phallic.

If you find the sexuality of her images stronger than the mysticism, remember her insistence that sexuality was not her concern. Yet sexuality is there in the natural manifestation of a flower. Sex and death are also plain to see in the unique shapes and colors of the desert. I believe O'Keeffe when she says she's not interested in sexual themes. Still, in her intensity she couldn't help but present nature in all its glory, including its sexuality. You could also say that the sexual is always close to the sacred. She was interested in revealing the holy and in the process unintentionally accented the erotic.

Her mysticism was so deep that she didn't want to reduce her vision to sex, which is only a piece of a greater whole. Sex is a portal to life, a way of peeking outside the realm of the human ego into the realm of mystery and wonder. Announcing an exhibition of O'Keeffe's work, the Irish Museum of Modern Art put it this way: "O'Keeffe manages to imbue her work with an eroticism and mysticism while maintaining a careful restraint."

Yes, her restraint applies to both sex and mysticism, and there is a lesson there for us, as well. Both sex and mysticism have a way of getting out of hand and overwhelming us. In making our

---

24 Brenda Marie Mitchell, "Music That Makes Holes in the Sky: Georgia O'Keeffe's Visionary Romanticism," thesis (Urbana, IL: University of Illinois at Urbana-Champaign, 1996), p. 196.

own religion, we might remember O'Keeffe's way: Give everything to the work but maintain your modesty, your reserve, and your privacy.

It's impossible to live in New Mexico and not be reminded daily of the thick mixture of spiritual resources there: the Pueblo sacred culture, the holiness of the land and sky, and the charming churches and shrines. O'Keeffe said, "I saw the crosses so often . . . like a thin dark veil of the Catholic Church spread over the New Mexico landscape. . . . For me, painting the cross was a way of painting the country."[25]

I include Georgia O'Keeffe in this book partly because of a statement like this. She could reject formal religion as not being suitable to her own spiritual life, but she could also appreciate the power of the churches, crosses, and rituals and take an interest in and befriend priests. There was a line between her and the formal church, but it was a thin line, easy to cross. It didn't prevent her from being inspired and educated by formal religion.

In her letters O'Keeffe makes it clear that she had no need to convert other people to her viewpoint. In a letter from 1929 O'Keeffe writes: "I see my little world as something that I am in— something that I play in. It is inevitable to me. But I never get over being surprised that it means something to anyone else."[26] Whether this is humility or rugged individualism is difficult to say.

O'Keeffe, then, has many lessons to teach about being an ordinary mystic and creating your own religion. She had that inventive and curious connection with the traditions and yet she found divinity in nature. Her personal religion also allowed her to follow a track along the map of her life, recognizing a real home in New Mexico after sojourns in other places. You see in her paintings how that region could seep into her body and come

---

25 Brenda Mitchell, "Music That Makes Holes in the Sky," p. 179.

26 Cowart, Hamilton, and Greenough, *Georgia O'Keeffe*, p. 187.

out in her paintbrushes. By being obedient to her muse, she became an artist.

Part of your religion may be the search for a place to live. Marsilio Ficino, the fifteenth-century philosopher, says this: Your first task is to find the place where your soul is at home. O'Keeffe tried several. They were not completely unsuccessful, but it was only New Mexico that brought her soul to life and resulted in her art. She was like Suzuki's frog: She kept looking until one day, "Gulp!" She found her home and ate it.

I don't want to be misunderstood. Hillman and O'Keeffe chose a church-free way of being religious, and I believe both were successful in establishing a rich spiritual existence. But I also cherish the lives, decisions, and creative work of Thomas Merton and Pierre Teilhard de Chardin, who creatively, critically, and courageously brought their inherited formal religion to a new level, remaining loyal to it in spite of heavy authoritarian pressures and the temptation to go their own way. Simone Weil traced a way between the formal and informal.

One of the things I would like to do in my retirement years is to visit the graves of Merton, Chardin, and Weil, who, among others, struggled to insist on their own religion in the face of criticism and resistance. I honor Merton and Chardin for wanting to remain in the formal church as they followed their respective daimons in new directions. I respect leaders and followers today who are working hard to make formal religion a source of deep and satisfying spirituality. I also appreciate those who, like O'Keeffe, learn from the traditions but carve out their own religious lives following their own genius.

There are countless ways of blending formal religion with one's own genius for spirituality. Emily Dickinson, for example, who called herself a pagan and wondered about her family's Christian devotion, also went to church and wrote piously about

Christian ideas. Like Simone Weil, she chose to live in a crossover place. For myself, I still find it difficult to describe my relationship with the Catholic tradition: It's difficult, painful, distant, and yet appreciative, loyal, and deep. You will no doubt have your own complicated connection or disconnection with your formal religious tradition, but no matter how serious the obstacles or attachments, you can still work out a religion of your own.

Natural Mystics

A good way to satisfy the spirit's need for certain basic ingredients that were once the stuff of religion is to be a natural mystic. You don't need to meditate formally for hours or swoon from absorption in the infinite. All you have to do is pull over when you're driving on a highway, get out, and watch the sun set. All you have to do is feel the rain pouring over you on a wet spring day. All you have to do is take a walk in the woods to the point where you forget your daily routine and the busyness of life.

Of course, you can go much further and learn how to meditate. You can take up a craft or art as a spiritual practice, like Kevin Kelly's flower arranging. You can study the Zen tea ceremony, the Zen art of archery or calligraphy. You can make music, paintings, gardens, or furniture. If you really want to, you can join a strict monastery in any part of the world, but you can also be a mystic in your kitchen.

One effective way some people blend tradition and their personal spirituality is to become involved with an established monastery or spiritual community. When I visit Ireland, I try to spend time at Glenstal Abbey, a benedictine community just outside the city of Limerick. I meet people there who are formally attached to the monastery and are called oblates. They maintain their lives at home and at work and enjoy their formal connection to the monastery—another good way to shape a personal religious style.

I like to spend time with the monks because they connect me

to my past. As I keep saying, I've never let go of my status as a friar in a Catholic religious community. I may not be in good standing with the official church, but I'm in good standing with my internal, private Catholicism. It only gets better and deeper.

You can be a monk more metaphorically like Hillman, having a daily routine, digging into your work as though it were the meaning of your life, and making mealtime a special moment for concentrated cooking and celebration. Kerényi said that the essence of religion is sometimes festival, and Hillman's ability to make festival of everyday moments was certainly part of his religion.

Call this a mysticism of the soul in contrast to the spirit. It is connected to everyday life and to the things of the world. It is physical, sensual, and bodily. It may require craft and getting your hands dirty. I know for myself as an occasional woodworker that I can get involved in a project, measuring, cutting wood, marking, joining, and finishing, and the time goes by like magic. I seem to slip away from the domain of the clock into a space-time situation quite different from normal life. Why couldn't this be my form of mysticism?

Woodworking always brings to my mind a line from the Gospel of Thomas. Jesus says: "Split a piece of wood. I am there." You could extend that beautiful comment and say, "Pull open a banana: I am there. Put your shovel into the earth: I am there. Listen to the song of the robin: That's me." You don't have to believe that anyone is literally behind the song or in the banana or in the earth. You don't have to speak of God. You don't have to talk like a theologian. You only have to use your spiritual imagination to establish a world alive and mysterious and home to a presence impossible to describe but also impossible to deny.

PART TWO

✌

Clearing the Emotions, Finding Depth

The child archetype does not grow but remains an inhabitant of childhood, a state of being, and the archetypal child personifies a component that is not meant to grow but to remain as it is as child, at the threshold, intact, an image of certain fundamental realities that necessarily require the child metaphor and which cannot be presented in another manner.

—JAMES HILLMAN, "ABANDONING THE CHILD"[27]

---

27 James Hillman, *Loose Ends* (Dallas: Spring Publications, 1975), p. 30.

Chapter 3

✿

DREAM PRACTICE

The years when I was pursuing my inner images were
the most important in my life—in them everything
essential was decided.

—C. G. JUNG[28]

W orking with dreams belongs in a religion of one's own
because dreams are a vehicle of transcendence, a means
of going beyond the self and yet within the soul. They are an
open window allowing fresh information to enter from else-
where. The dream realm is like a dark, narrow passageway with
curtains at each end. They connect the world of myth, another
and related language of the soul, that is the land of the soul, with
the day world. The curtains don't open wide, so we only glimpse
the two connected realms, but glimpses are always useful.

A regular dream practice can keep you in touch with the basic
narratives that you are living and that shape your life. At first,

---

28 C. G. Jung, *Memories, Dreams, Reflections*, trans. Richard and Clara
Winston, ed. Aniela Jaffé (New York: Pantheon Books, rev. ed. 1973), p. 199.

dreams seem to be full of nonsense images, but when you look at them closely, they begin to make sense, often fascinating and challenging sense. Most important, dreams provide our lives with a backdrop of images that point to both our personal experience and the wide realm of art. Dreams help us imagine our lives as dramas that once again present the eternal journeys, longings, and struggles that define every human life.

Alex, a young man in his twenties, consulted me about his situation. He appreciated the way I have used Greek mythology in my work and wanted to go deep into those images he knew well. When he arrived at my door, I looked at him and registered my first impressions: He was a handsome man, dark and sensual, lively and a bit nervous. Like many people, he showed that he had two personalities: One was serious and concerned, but the other, which just broke through from hiding now and then, was fun-loving and even mischievous. He had a habit of wrinkling his brow seriously and then just momentarily allowing an inchoate smile to flash on his face. Ever the analyst, I wondered what this split emotional pattern was all about, but I liked him very much and wanted to build our therapeutic relationship on the eros.

He told me that he'd been in therapy before because of a tendency toward obsessive-compulsive behaviors. "It can get pretty bad," he told me. I felt a pang when I heard this—people don't often talk about the therapist's painful concern for his client. I wondered what it was in this beautiful person's life that had generated this symptom. I listened to his life story and his interpretations, and then I asked for a dream. I knew that a dream would reveal much more accurately, if a bit obscurely, what was really going on.

He had read some in-depth psychology, including my own work, and was ready to study his dreams. The first dream he presented set our agenda: "I'm walking toward a river and I'm on the bank when I see sharks in the water. I'd like to get closer and maybe go into the water, but I walk away."

It was a short dream but it felt significant. We talked about it. A dozen literary and religious references to rivers popped into my head: the rivers of Paradise; the river of life; Hesse's Siddhartha, who ends years of searching at the river; James Dickey's *Deliverance*, in which a battered man, asked what happened to him, says, "The river happened." I felt I knew the river in general, though of course I didn't know the river of this dream. Getting to know this young man from his dream was like visiting a town you've never been to before and standing at the bank of its river. You've seen plenty of rivers, but not this one.

Of course, I wasn't a friend of James Hillman for years without learning to be cautious with all my associations with a dream image. It was this man's river, not a symbol and not a universal, that we were dealing with now.

We talked about the sharks. Dreams of fish are common, and big fish in special waters are common in mythology as well, like Jonah's whale. Of course, a whale is not a shark, but we were moving into the territory of water and its creatures. I also know of the Irish salmon of wisdom and the dolphins of Dionysus. There's a charming African story about the hippo praying to God to be allowed to cool off in the water.

At first it seemed that my young man wanted to approach the river of life and maybe go into it, but the sharks were fearsome and kept him away. Was he avoiding life out of fear? Had he seen the sharks that live in the waters of life? Had he felt the teeth that threaten when you dare go right into the stream? He wanted to be wet with vitality but was kept from that pleasure by the sharks. He was afraid of his own river.

Jonah's whale teaches us that a sea creature doesn't have to be dangerous. The whale holds Jonah safe and then, on God's word, spits him out of his mouth onto the land, where Jonah then fulfills his orders. So I wonder about my young man's sharks. Yes, they are frightening creatures, with their sharp teeth and reputation for aggression. But maybe the dreamer has to learn to be in life along with its dangers. Maybe the sharks want him to join them and discover a connection, a creative relationship. His own sharkiness? But in the dream he is being self-protective and doesn't enter the stream at all.

Alex's underwater creatures are sharks, not a whale. He's not afraid of being swallowed whole, like Jonah, but of being cut up by sharp teeth and strong muscle. After that first session I wondered if Alex was simply afraid to live and venture close to life, only to back away. Was he afraid of the dangers he had seen there, especially the aggression and maybe sharp teeth? Were the threats hidden beneath the surface? Did he like to approach life but then back away out of fear? I reminded myself to be prepared for signs of this pattern in the days to come.

At the same time, I didn't want to be lured into a rigid point of view. Maybe this wasn't the moment to get too close to the river. There's a time to back away, a time to keep your innocence, a time to deny the sharks.

Another client told me how in life she's having trouble with her five children as they argue over how to split a choice property the family owns. The mother told me, "I have to help them work this out." She said this with frustration, as though it put a great burden on her. I wondered why she was making it all so difficult for herself. Her children were grown and were parents, too.

"How will they ever sort this out unless I take a stronger role?" she said. She thought she was only being altruistic. She assumed that she wasn't doing enough. But what I heard was overbearing parental control. To me she was suffering from a maternal complex: Something in her *wanted* all the responsibility. She told me a dream in which she was in charge of a great many programs at a hospital and just couldn't get the work done. It was all unraveling and she woke up exhausted. I noticed that as she told me this dream, physically she looked different. I could see the weight pressing on her. I noticed that her shoulders had dropped and her brows were knotted.

I reminded her of a recent dream in which she was a stand-up comic at a school party. It was a role she wasn't familiar with but that felt good. We discussed the difference in emotional tone between the comic and the family arbiter. Just talking about the comedy relaxed her face and body. She mentioned how much she admired certain Zen and Sufi stories in which spiritual masters resolve problems through humor and wit. "I wish I could do that," she said. "Why not?" I asked. She left the session that day with plans to take the family situation more lightly and look for ways to be more subtle and clever in dealing with her children.

Notice that in both of these cases the dreams offered themes that applied directly to life and were timely in relation to what was going on in the day world. The dreams don't have to be long and elaborate and contain obvious references to mythology and art. They may seem mundane and meaningless, until you look at them more closely. With their own kind of poetry, they show what is going on at a level invisible to the nondream world.

Dreams offer an alternative perspective on the affairs of daily life and even on grander themes that play a grander part in human existence. The mother as comedian is a role she would never have considered for herself, unless the dream had provoked her. Alex would never have told me that he was afraid to enter life. In fact, on the surface it appeared that he had done well by getting a good job and making friends in many parts of the world. The dream usually presents a point of view that accurately reflects the dreamer's position and emotions but is also foreign to him.

Often a dream surprises the dreamer. A person may believe for many years that she is generous and altruistic. Then one day a dream hints at a selfish streak. The dream affronts her, and she tries to dismiss it. "Dreams aren't important anyway," she says.

You don't have to be a trained analyst to hear the defensiveness in that statement.

After thirty years of doing therapy of depth, aiming at the mythic levels of experience, I rely almost entirely on dreams. The work doesn't get moving until a dream enters the picture. Dreams offer pieces of narrative that reveal the major themes that shape and color an entire life.

"Pieces of narrative," I say, because dreams are not usually complete stories. A story is like a complete thought or a full sentence, while dreams usually present a string of images. They may suggest a problem without offering a solution. The dreamer may tell the dream in the form of a story and imply a solution, but the one listening to the dream has to be careful not to be taken in by the dreamer's purposes. I usually make a point to look for a different angle on the dream, a contrary point of view. I consider the dream from a fresh perspective with a different set of values and expectations.

Dream Personalities

We often make tight connections between a dream and its dreamer, but the themes of dreams usually apply to people in general. Many people can identify with the dream of the sharks and some with being a stand-up comic. The effect of a dream to provide a useful set of imagery as backdrop to experience is similar to the way mythology and art provide patterns. Your dreams are not just parts of a personal myth; just as mythology and art address the human condition, dreams go beyond personal matters.

As you become familiar with your dreams, you will notice recurring themes, even specific images that appear regularly. A series of dreams may be connected to a particular issue in life, and sometimes several of these groups overlap. You may see a series of dreams in Bundle A, then a new Bundle B, then A again, and then C. Certain dreams seem related in theme, if not with specific images, and these themes may disappear for a while, perhaps years, and then return. This aspect of dreaming gives you a dynamic and layered sense of who you are.

I've often written about my flying dreams. They started out with me soaring inside a room, near the ceiling, on my own power, my arms flapping. In these dreams I usually had a euphoric sensation that I wish I could experience in real life. After a dream like this, upon waking up I might move my arms and expect to float toward the ceiling. They felt so real that they bled over into my waking state.

In later years I had a series of dreams, recurring occasionally over a long period, in which a commercial jet plane was trying to take off while navigating streets and tall buildings in a large city. Sometimes the plane would never get off the ground but just taxi successfully on a high-traffic road. Thinking about this dream at the time, I wondered if I was having trouble flying freely and openly. I seemed to be grounded by the restrictions of a complicated life. On the other hand, this take on the dream may represent my ungrounded nature, my near-neurotic need to be free and unencumbered. Maybe I need all that complicated life—the streets and traffic—to ground my soaring, *puer* nature.[29]

When I meet people and talk turns to dreams, I sometimes ask if they are flyers, like me, the type of person, perhaps the idealistic, ambitious, and spiritual men and women Jungians call *puer*, who have the spirit of youth in them and like to be high off the ground, away from the burdens of making a living and getting along in life. One of my recurring dreams seems to suggest this issue: I'm in a small plane, flying not too high. I see my family standing on the ground below me and I wave to them.

---

29 Here, I'm referring to the *puer aeternus* discussed by Jung and Hillman. It is a positive, indeed valuable and attractive spirit of adventure based on the image of the young man—in Latin, *puer*. *Puer* men and women often have dreams of flying, signifying their wish not to be held down by the demands of life and their excursions into the realms of inspiration and imagination.

One more take on my downtown airplane dream: I still have my vehicle for flight, but now I'm in the midst of life, especially cultural life. The many books I've published and my years as a psychotherapist have placed me in the heart of life more than I ever thought would be possible. Yet, down here, in the thick of lives and marriages and the world's attempt to get itself in order, I still have my ideals and ambitions.

Because of my dream practice—writing my dreams and keeping my notebooks—I can go back years and see the direction of my dreams at different points. From a later perspective the dreams look different. I can now see how they foreshadowed developments. For instance, I look in the red-leather-bound blank book I made for recording my dreams in the mid-1980s and find one from exactly twenty-five years ago:

I'm in a car with several people, going through a strange place where a building is collapsing and debris is held back above our heads with netting. A young woman is in the car. She looks like Chris's daughter, only older. She stands and begins to pull at the debris. I warn her that it may collapse if she continues doing that. But she persists.

A policeman appears and tells me to go with him. I'm surprised, because I've been trying to stop her, and besides, I'm dressed nicely. At the station a team of social workers and other staff interview me. They want to know what I know about this girl. I tell them that she's young and does things like this. They huddle and decide to keep her for three hours. It's dawn now. My parents are in the car, and I wonder why they're involved. I have the keys. I'm shocked then to learn that the police staff has assumed all along that the girl is my daughter. They never asked about our relationship.

At the time, which happened to be two years before I began writing *Care of the Soul* I made a note saying that the girl of my psyche is in trouble. In those days, I had a degree of innocence that wasn't useful to me—like being dressed nicely, thinking that should satisfy the "police." My "girl" was tearing apart the ceiling, the world above, which may have been my theology and ideas about religion. I felt that I was perhaps too innocent about my efforts to deconstruct religion and psychology and replace them with care of the soul. It's odd that this dream would show up at this moment, today, when I'm writing this book in an effort to rearrange the sky, an image for my thinking about spirituality. I see this book as a second *Care of the Soul*, suggesting a new turn in culture, shifting away from religion as we've known it, only to become more religious and spiritual in a fresh manner. I shouldn't be innocent about this, because many people might be disturbed and angered by my implied criticisms of established religion. Others will be unhappy about my not accepting a fully secular world.

Jungian reading of the girl would no doubt see her as an anima or soul figure. You could call her a *puella*, Latin for "girl," in line with the *puer*. I have this inspiration to redo religion, but it's a dangerous project. The sky could fall. So police appear. In my own psychological imagery police play a big role. Probably because of my Catholic background, I'm sensitive to any judgment about doing wrong and committing a sin.

The girl is my daughter, it turns out. This is fascinating to me, twenty-five years later, because now I have a daughter who is twenty-one and in her own way is carrying on my work. She, too, occasionally runs into "police" who just don't understand her. In this way, as I picture the arc of my life, the dream has a prophetic quality, an aspect of dreams noted for centuries but today not taken seriously by scholars and professionals.

Dreams get to our very essence; they are mythic, sacred texts that tell the deep story of our destiny and progress. Altogether they constitute a personal Bible, many stories in many different genres strung together in one book of life. Therefore, a dream practice fits well as part of a larger spiritual way of life, as a piece of your own religion.

If you have a practice of meditation, yoga, and prayer, you could easily add a little more time to record and reflect on your dreams. All of these approaches would fit together snugly. Alternatively, a dream practice could stand alone as a valuable spiritual activity that would keep you in touch with the deepest and the most sacred aspects of your being.

One significant advantage would be to link your psychological development with your spiritual progress, two areas that are often separated. Dreams address both soul and spirit, the life of emotions and relationships and the search for meaning and purpose. They are both profound and transcendent.

Dream Therapy

Often, people who are intent on a spiritual journey overlook the psychological dimension. Their emotions get in the way. Their relationships suffer. They live out their psychological complexes in their spiritual activities. They need a therapeutic cleansing before their spiritual advance can be clean. Dream work can be an effective part of this catharsis, helping to clear up psychological tangles and confusion.

As our dream work continued, Alex told me more about his obsessive behavior. He mentioned that when he went home to his apartment in the city, he had to walk up a long, steep stairway, and he couldn't do it without counting each step. He was aware of internal instructions that he could not disobey. Freud's perceptive colleague Sandor Ferenczi said that an obsessional neurosis like counting is a way of deflecting painful thoughts and avoiding sensual life. Counting also puts an intellectual, controlling, and defining barrier around life.

Alex's problem is one for our times: We avoid life by counting everything we do. We get depressed because we are not entering life and then may deal with our cultural depression by taking drugs.

Some turn to spiritual teachings, leaders, and rituals, looking for a way out of a quantified existence. In their desperation, often they either get swayed by the wrong teacher or take on a spiritual system in a way that doesn't give them what they crave.

My young man Alex may be intelligent enough to find his way successfully. But the dream offers a caution. If he is avoiding the sharks, natural aggressors or images for the aggression in ordinary life, he will be susceptible to a sentimental psychology or spirituality. He may not have the toughness or the cutting critical mind, represented by the sharks, that he needs. His compulsive rituals, like the need to count his steps, betray his masochism, a failure of personal power. He is at the mercy of rules that come from an unknown source and doesn't have the strength needed to resist them.

Dream Practice

We are a mechanistic people living in technological times. When confronted with something puzzling or dazzling like a dream, automatically we ask, *How does it work?* We want tools for figuring it out. We'd like to get control of it.

But inquiring into the mechanics of things may be to ask the wrong question. Many studies are being done on dreams, and the scientific ones tend to be reductionistic. They want to tell us that dreams are only products of the biological brain. Since dreams are presented as images, it might be more productive to deal with them as images, similar to the way we respond to images in art and religion. Even there, of course, the modern mind usually overlooks the imagery to focus on biography, history, and technique—the mechanics rather than the substance.

As your work with dreams eventually reveals much about the psyche and the deeper layers of ordinary life, you may realize the importance of these night images. Again and again in therapy I've watched as skeptics discover the value of a dream practice and become devoted to it.

Dreams are narratives or short dramatic pieces in which I the dreamer may play an active role. The images come partly from personal experience and partly from some mysterious realm we know nothing about. They may derive from the far distant past and from the events of the day before the dream. We remember only parts of the dream and even then our memory may be faulty. Because of all of this fragmentation of images we may conclude that dreams are meaningless and unimportant, but we might also learn to appreciate this special genre of images, one that is fragmentary and layered.

Considering dreams as dramatic pieces, I turn to the theater, myth, fiction, poetry, and film to get insight into dreams. These various forms seem related and perhaps are facets of a single image-making process that defines the soul. Jung's comment quoted as a caption to this chapter makes this point dramatically. Work with our images can be the catalyst for an entire life.

Dreams fade quickly from consciousness, so it's important to catch them as soon as possible. It helps to have a notepad or book and pen near your bed. When you wake up, write down any images from the dream that you can recall, even if they make no sense. A dream is not a story, so it's better to write the images as you remember them, resisting what Freud called "the primary revision," an immediate effort to make sense of confusing images.

At first, you may not have much to write. However, a one-sentence dream can be surprisingly fruitful. So write down what you remember and don't worry if it doesn't make sense or seems incomplete. Develop an appreciation for incomplete sentences and odd juxtapositions.

Some people recommend writing your dreams in the form of a poem. Those methods are fine and work well for some people, but I prefer to see the dream as remembered. Just the images. I worry that further revising takes us away from the original experience of the dream, giving us more a picture of the ego than of the deep world of images.

After writing the dream as faithfully as I can, I draw a line under it and write any thoughts I might have about it: personal associations, memories, interpretations, and related images from art, literature, and religion. These help "amplify" the dream, to use Jung's word for this phase. We are not aiming at a final interpretation of the dream, but we do want rich reflection on it.

I follow Hillman closely in not wanting to transform a dream image into a strictly defined meaning. No dictionaries of dream images and no final solutions. But it's still useful to come up with a number of provisional interpretations that help open the image to understanding. After that, you can continue to relate to the pure image.

I find that now, after years of dealing with dreams, the sense of another person's dream comes through quickly. Right after hearing it, I feel intuitively what it's about, though it still may not be completely clear. I sense the meaning more in my body than in my mind. But my reaction is similar when a client gives me his interpretation of an experience. If there's something odd in his point of view, I sense it physically. Then I have to read my body's reaction.

I make a point of empathizing with characters in the dream that seem at first to be the antagonists. It's tempting to side with the dreamer, either in the dream or outside of it. But often, once we shift from the bias of the dreamer to the point of view of another character, a fresh and surprising idea appears. I try not to be taken in by the dreamer's honest judgments. The main thing I can offer is a different slant on the dream, an angle that I get from being open to the negative characters and events. Like Alex's sharks. I don't have to be persuaded by Alex's fear. Maybe the sharks are nothing more than life's ordinary dangers and threats. You can't live without them.

Some people want to control their dreams, come up with happier endings or resolve longstanding problems. They want to go back into a dream and change it. To me, that's like painting a mustache on the Mona Lisa. This is another lesson I got from James Hillman: Treat a dream with respect and don't try to make it into something that you want or prefer. Don't try to outsmart the dream; rather, always be its servant. We have enough ego in the world and not enough deep, autonomous imagination.

It's helpful to tell your dream to someone you trust and even better if that person can give you some insight. Your friend doesn't have to interpret the dream but only say what comes to mind. He may notice something familiar in the dream that you missed or know something about you that is reflected in the dream. My wife does this for me frequently, and she almost always has something worth saying about my dream without interpreting it.

When the dream comes to mind during the day, I continue to reflect on it. Sometimes an event or something someone says will bring a recent dream to mind. But often the dream drifts into awareness quietly and quickly on its own. You have to be alert to make connections and take some insight when dream intersects with life. According to Veronica Goodchild, professsor of Jungian and mythological studies at Pacifica Graduate Institute, the sudden appearance of a dream in the midst of an ordinary occasion is a form of synchronicity.[30] Something happens in life, and you suddenly remember a dream, maybe from the night before. The dream and the life event may feel mysteriously connected. The surprise of their conjunction startles you into a realization or opens your mind to a fresh insight.

Dreams, then, may have an effect on you not directly connected to their content. Dreaming takes your awareness down into the deeper regions of the psyche, where you wonder who you are and what you're doing in the world. Whatever your dream is about, the dream itself is like a fantastic submarine, a vehicle for exploring your depths.

---

30 Veronica Goodchild, *Songlines of the Soul: Pathways to a New Vision for a New Century* (Lake Worth, Florida: Nicolas-Hayes, 2012), p. 106.

A dream may startle you into a realization that you can't figure out from the content. A dream may be an action, a punch in the face, a feather caressing your back. You don't always have to ask, "What does this dream mean?" Instead, you can ask, "What did your dream do to you?"

What You Can Discover in Dreams

The images of a dream, of course, are important. They can give you insight into the narrative fragments, the themes that ultimately make up the stories of your life. I say "stories" in the plural, because the canonical story we tell about our lives is only one possible version out of many. Dreams may not themselves be full-rounded stories, but they hint at the narratives we are living out in daily life. We all seem to have major themes and defining stories, as well as minor themes and stories that are not necessarily at the heart of our existence.

I've been using Alex's dream of the river full of sharks as a primary image for his essential attitude at this moment. If he were to narrate the events of his life, you would see episodes that remind you of the sharks. For example, in his first years of college he ran into professors who gave him a hard time, so much so that he switched his major and took a tangent away from his life plan. Alex isn't the first person to think of his professors as sharks.

But there is also a matter of timing with dreams. The shark motif may be strong now, but in the coming months and years he may notice a shift taking place away from sharks toward some new theme. Life doesn't stand still, and even the undercurrents of a life shift.

To appreciate the psyche in its full and beautiful complexity, it might help to have a three- or multidimensional model. A dream might cut across all levels. I can imagine a layer of recent experiences, one of more distant events, and yet another for childhood. But we could go deeper. There might be a level of fairy tale–like events and then myth and finally some deep, quiet primal level of the deepest psyche.

I had a client, Caroline, who was going through a life passage I think of as "finding your depth." Many people go along unconsciously, living fairly superficial values and following the crowd. Then one day something happens, internally or externally, and suddenly they become engaged in a life-and-death search for depth. Several myths offer insight into this process, such as the Greek story of Demeter and Persephone, a young girl at the peak of her innocence being seized by the lord of the underworld. Many people can identify with this myth because they feel seized, against their will and contrary to their plans to discover their own underworld.

Caroline had a dream early in our conversations in which she was happily riding along a narrow road on her bicycle when she unexpectedly veered off the path and was trying to keep her bike going on rough terrain. This dream announced a new development that only became more challenging as time went on. At first, riding her bicycle happily in idyllic surroundings reminded me of Persephone happily picking flowers just before Hades appeared. In fact, Caroline's superficial happiness disappeared right around the time of the bicycle dream, an early development that I thought foretold a painful road ahead. In fact, she entered a long period of disorienting transition in her career and in her marriage.

Whenever I come across a bicycle in dreams, I pause to consider its many dimensions. The word means "two cycles." In Caroline's dream we are witnessing two different cycles in her existence: her old way of life and new possibilities. You might remember that Buddhists use the image of a cart with wheels to describe two rounds of existence: the cycle of samsara and the cycle of nirvana, the everyday struggle and release.

The dream indicated that Caroline's vehicle of the moment was like a bicycle. Since she was in her midforties, maybe it was too childlike, or, as our discussions implied, maybe it involved issues that had roots in her childhood. That bicycle wasn't dependable. On it she drifted away from her path and found herself on a rough road. Or, in another but not incompatible way of seeing it, she was destined to go off the easy path in order to find a new way.

I can't describe adequately the intensity of Caroline's descent and the range of emotion she went through once she had this dream of veering off the road more traveled. Other dreams kept us apprised of her situation all along the way. As her guide, I depended on the dreams to know how to react and what to say. I can't imagine the process without them.

I felt that Caroline was being asked to make stark changes in her way of perceiving the world and finding her way in it. I didn't know if she would have the tenacity to remain loyal to her process, but I had faith in her. I had seen others back away or ultimately refuse the challenge. My guess is that half of my clients decline to take the risk. They all have their reasons, but it always comes down to preferring the comfort of the messy status quo over the promise of a challenging new way of life.

What is at stake is not really psychological but psycho-spiritual. Deep relationships, the past, current connections, and a way of life come up against the spiritual possibilities of meaning, hope fulfilled, transformation, and the fulfillment of vision. These latter seem like lofty goals, but they are also frightening, and many people decline them.

A person like Caroline is offered the opportunity to transcend, to go beyond the life she has known, to go much further in her profession and to find happiness in marriage she didn't know was possible. Her dreams and her passage in life offer her a new personal religion: a new vision and a new ethic, a new aesthetic and a new spirituality. I've known people to refuse an opportunity to leave a rutted, well-worn path because it can be so disorienting at times and also lengthy. In the Gospels Jesus uses this very imagery when he says, "Go through the narrow gate, because the wide gate and the broad road lead to disaster. Many go that way, of course, and yet a narrow gate and a little lane lead to life. Unfortunately, few choose them" (Matthew 7). Thoreau adds to that advice: "I might pursue some path, however solitary and narrow and crooked, in which I could walk with love and reverence."

Jung called the process I'm describing individuation, becoming an individual, a real person not continually swept away by his passions or influenced by his culture. Each person has a unique opus, a soul work, because each has a particular makeup and history. For Jung the opus was a process of getting to know yourself deeply, not only a psychological process of painful advance in self-knowledge; but a religious initiation involving spiritual ideals and the search for meaning.

Jung could have called this process the discovery of one's own religion, a process that engages both the spirit and the deep soul, the yearning for transcendence and the depths of personal history. Dreams are important to the process because they reveal the depths and heights of our struggles. They address the concerns of both soul and spirit and reach far beyond our rational capacity for self-knowledge.

Just as the earth has visible memories of geologic times, we, too, are structured in a deep way by events either far in the past or deep in our nature. It's sometimes difficult to distinguish between what is essential and what is remembered. You may dream about a crucial moment in your childhood when you got lost in a woods. The dream is about that memory, of course, but it may also call to mind other, more recent times when you have felt lost in a metaphorical forest of business deals or worries about raising a family. Dreams seem to unite these different strata, placing you in situations so familiar that they seem innate to your being. So when you look at your dream, you may be discovering psycho-spiritual fault lines and drifting plates, ancient aspects of your soul, that account for some of your achievements and difficulties, your joys and pains.

At this deep level of personal myth and innate constitution, spirituality and psychology overlap and conjoin. For that reason, paying close attention to dreams aids any spiritual activity, keeping it grounded and in contact with the elements that have shaped you. Dream work becomes as important as meditation, quiet reading, and prayer, and fits tightly into a developed spiritual way of life.

Another important benefit: Giving dreams careful attention allows you to see the dream aspect of everyday life, the dramas you're in as you go about your affairs. It allows you to glimpse the deeper narratives and key images that lie beneath everyday experiences. In general, it brings your attention and focus down into an underworld of special emotion and meaning where the foundations of your existence stand invisible and yet influential. In dreams you behold your Genesis and your Exodus, your revelations and reformations.

Caring for your dreams also helps you understand other dramatic and imagistic activities such as art and sport and religious ritual. They are all closer to the plane of dream than of rational thought. As you seek insight in your dreams, you may be drawn to the arts for more information about the imaginal realm that holds so many important secrets for individuals and for society. In turn, your dreams may help you see the deeper meaning in play, games, and sports.

Dreams in Religion

Many have seen dreams as portals connecting this world with another world, and in that way dreams have played a role in religious stories. In the Old Testament, Joseph, son of Jacob, dreams that his brothers are showing him honor. This makes them angry and eventually leads to his position in Egypt. Daniel interprets the dream of King Nebuchadnezzar and is rewarded with power over Babylon. Joseph, Mary's husband, has dreams in which an angel gives him warnings and advice, and he obeys.

One of the most beautiful dreams in religious history concerns the birth of the Buddha:

One night, Queen Mayadevi dreamed that a white elephant came down from heaven and entered her womb, and on that night she conceived a pure and powerful being. Later, in giving birth to the child, instead of experiencing pain, she had a vision in which she stood holding the branch of a tree with her right hand, while the gods Brahma and Indra took the child painlessly from her side. When the king saw the baby, he knew that his wishes had been fulfilled and he named the young prince "Siddhartha." Later, the mother died, and her sister raised the child.

This dream tells of the conception and birth of the Buddha and our own Buddha nature, our best self. It is not just a story about the biological birth of a rational animal but the birth of a soul. That's why a white elephant, an image for the greatness of the spirit, is the inseminator, just as in the paintings of Jesus's conception it's a holy spirit in the form of a white dove that provides the seed. We're talking about the conception and birth of a thinking, feeling, visionary, sensitive, sensual, moral person. In the land of story it takes a huge, white animated source to create a being of such magnitude.

You are born with your spirituality; you don't have to go looking for it. It is a huge presence that wants to live through you and be embodied in your life. Your spiritual self was born in a dream, and when you dream you are returning home. Your natural self is at home in the land where everything is both a physical fact and a poetic metaphor. When you dream, you are returning to the home, the very womb of your spirit and a world that speaks the language of your soul.

Imagine that your spirituality is pure white, while physically you are one of many colors, that it is huge while your self is relatively small.[31] You have a spiritual animality that is instinctive and at home in nature. You have a Buddha in you and a Jesus and a liberating Moses. In you is the spirit of Thoreau and Dickinson, Socrates and Lao Tzu. Your own spirituality has so much vast potential that it is indeed like a big white elephant that crawled into your mother's body at the moment of your conception.

These are just a few thoughts engendered by meditation on the story of the Buddha's birth. Now make it your own. Reflect on it. Let your imagination float and soar. Let the story be a vehicle for developing your own theology. Don't think of it as a Buddhist story but as a story for all Buddhas, of which you are one.

Let the story teach you more about dreams and how they support a spiritual existence, a great dream of birth. Birth is one of the major themes that need not be taken only physically. You are born again and again. You are born into your spirituality as well as into your ongoing natural life. You are born into many personalities and new dimensions of experience. Birth, eternal, and never-ending.

At a deep level the story of the Buddha's birth to Mahadevi has even more in common with the story of Jesus's birth. Mary conceived in a special way, without the loss of her virginity. In the Buddha's story there are two mothers; in Jesus's, two fathers: the spirit, often portrayed as a bird, and Joseph the carpenter.

Jung emphasizes this point in his reflections on this story: that we need a mother for the body and another mother for the spirit. It isn't enough to be born physically. "Man is not merely born in the commonplace sense, but is born again in a mysterious manner, and

---

31 This statement is not intended to glorify the color white. Beautiful and mysterious black plays an equally important role in the opus of the soul.

so partakes of divinity. Anyone who is reborn in this way becomes a hero, a semi-divine being."[32]

In this context, to be a hero means to be engaged fully in the work of becoming a human being in body, soul, and spirit. It is more than automatic, unconscious living, more than physical survival and success. Being the hero is to be on the path of soul-making, dealing with your natural materials, and making something of yourself as you deal with life's challenges. It is perhaps what Keats has in mind when he says, "Do you not see how necessary a World of Pains and troubles is to school an Intelligence and make it a soul?" It's what Joseph Campbell means when he speaks of "the hero's journey." He writes: "Everywhere, no matter what the sphere of interest (whether religious, political, or personal), the really creative acts are represented as those deriving from some sort of dying to the world; and what happens in the interval of the hero's nonentity, so that he comes back as one reborn, made great and filled with creative power."[33]

We are on the hero's journey when we submit to the deep processes of life and allow them to affect us and bore their necessities into us. We are the hero when we take on the challenges and go through our initiations and transformations, enduring loss and gain, feeling happy and sad, making progress and falling back. The hero is engaged in life. The hero is not the one who displays force and muscle without deep insight or the courage to be. The hero may not look heroic from the outside but may go through powerful developments in a quiet way. The difference is that the real hero engages life and reflects on it. She becomes more and more what he or she is destined to be.

---

32 C. G. Jung, *Symbols of Transformation*, trans. R. F. C. Hull, CW vol. 5, 2nd ed. (Princeton: Princeton University Press, 1967), p. 494.

33 Joseph Campbell, *The Hero with a Thousand Faces* (New York: MJF Books, 1949), p. 37.

All of this is implied in the classic story of the dream birth of Siddhartha Gautama, who became "the awakened one," the Buddha. Perhaps this is the ultimate dream, the deep journey of life that ultimately makes sense of your existence. It's your ur-myth, your primal and most profound identity, the deepest self that you only glimpse in moments of epiphany. Dreams are the windows and doorways to that essential identity, without which we feel lost and wandering. Dreams reveal the odyssey of the soul and the path of spirit.

Chapter 4

❧

THERAPY AT HOME

[M]y most important patient was myself . . .
—SIGMUND FREUD

I was thirteen and getting ready for bed in the attic room my father had set up for me after giving up his stamp-collecting space. Nervously I was telling my mother of my wish to go away to a seminary to study for the priesthood. "Why don't you wait until you get a little older?" she said wisely. But the passion was strong in me. Years later she would remark at how upset I was not to get her immediate support. Eventually, of course, she gave in.

I reach back for this memory to demonstrate how powerful spiritual emotions can be and how they can shape a life. Not all feelings are psychological. The spiritual ones can be just as disturbing and require attention, reflection, and even therapy.

The spiritual emotions include a longing for meaning, the need to be creative and make life worth living, wondering about death and afterlife, having the pleasure of feeling in tune with your destiny, and worrying about ethical behavior. These are just feelings, but they can turn into anxieties and depressions and cause serious problems. Many people I have seen in therapy over the years say that some of their adult problems go back to religious teachings and personalities that affected them when they were children.

Psychological issues may also lie behind spiritual experiences. I'm sure there were deep psychological reasons for my willingness to leave a warm, loving home and spend many years in an emotionally cool school environment run by men who lacked maternal qualities. I was always close to my mother. But maybe I needed to begin my separation from her. And maybe I needed to prove myself. There are many "maybes" in my thoughts about this crucial time in my life that was especially difficult since I had to choose between a home for my soul and one for my spirit.

Without knowing anything about it, I certainly needed to stretch my experience and vision. Looking back now, I can see how that wrenching from my family started a process that made my life what it is. You might look back, too, on early events that revealed their meaning only years later. You might see current developments with the bigger picture in mind. This is a kind of spiritual assessment of meaning and destiny, important elements in becoming a person.

People get so caught up in the content of their spiritual enthusiasms that they may give little thought to the emotions involved. Some adults tell me that they still follow the values taught in the church where they grew up simply because their family believed in it so firmly. It's the family that accounts for the strong faith, not the spiritual ideas.

It's important, then, not only to create a religion of your own but also, in the process, to be aware of psychological matters that are linked to the spiritual ones. Once you understand how religion can be personal and embedded in daily life, you can narrow the space between the spiritual and the psychological. Then, too, you can get involved in a self-therapy that is psycho-spiritual. You could begin to clear up any emotional blindness that could have a negative impact on your spirituality.

Most spiritual guidebooks recommend that a spiritual practice begin with attention to the basics of everyday life. The Catholic Ignatian Exercises, used by millions to foster personal spirituality, begin with a life assessment. *The Kama Sutra* opens by recommending a close study and caretaking of your everyday existence before going on to the advanced states of erotic ritual.[34] The Jewish Kabbalah Tree of Life embraces many aspects of ordinary living and connects them to high spiritual awareness. The Qur'ān, too, links ordinary responsibility to the community with the highest goals of the spirit.

Many people begin a spiritual project—meditation, yoga, a new religion—while they have complicated emotional problems entangled in their spiritual longings. A priest once told me that the only reason he became a priest was that his father had tried to be one and failed. He wanted to make his father happy. The emotional element doesn't have to be negative, as in the case of a man who told me he took up yoga to meet a woman with an interest in spirituality.

From a different angle, we talk about being emotionally healthy and often overlook the spiritual emotions. People feel lost and depressed when their source of meaning dries up, as when they lose a job that has given them purpose or when they no longer believe in a formal religion they've known for years. Divorce can create guilt and a deep sense of failure. Some people feel distress over the loss of their once supportive religious community and tradition. These problems are psychological from one point of view, but they have strong spiritual implications, as well.

---

34 *The Kama Sutra* is easily misunderstood as a sex manual. But it is a rare spiritual text that offers an erotic way of life, essential for any deep-seated and visionary spirituality.

As you develop a religion of your own, you might address your spiritual emotions in two ways: First, you may need to work through events of the past in which your strong spiritual feelings wounded your deep soul. I still feel bad about leaving my family at a young age, and yet I know that the meaningful life I now enjoy required the sacrifice. Second, in the future you can find ways to address both soul and spirit, because both need your attention and need to be connected.

My wife links soul to spirit by bringing tea to her yoga classes and inviting her students to spend an hour after class sitting, talking, and drinking her homemade chai. She'll also ask her students to stop in the middle of their practice to paint images. In my practice of therapy, I respond when people bring up their childhood religion or their efforts to find a spiritual home or their thoughts about afterlife, belief, and wonder. We keep spirit and soul engaged and connected.

The Neoplatonic teaching on the soul, on which I base most of my ideas, sometimes sees the soul as distinct from spirit and yet at the same time spirit is part of the soul. That means that your spiritual life comes under the heading "care of the soul." People often intuitively understand that their spiritual practices enhance their souls. What they often forget is that their spirituality is affected by their emotions, family background, and current relationships—the stuff of their souls.

I recommend self-therapy, exploring your fear, desire, sexuality, anger, personal past, and relationships. I don't see therapy as fixing what is broken but rather tending to the whole of your psyche. Getting to know your deep soul may prevent you from venting raw emotions, acting out, and being depressed and addictive. It can clear the way for a spiritual life not sullied by psychological matters left untended. And it may accomplish some needed healing.

Prima Materia

We know only a small portion of who we are, for we are many. We have innate personalities, mythlike, archetypal figures that live through us in our daily lives. We also absorb pieces of the people we encounter and are shaped by events. The novelist Michael Ondaatje puts it beautifully: "There is the hidden presence of others in us, even those we have known briefly. We contain them for the rest of our lives, at every border that we cross."[35]

Therapy involves an exploration of these "hidden presences" that affect us so profoundly. The people and events of our past and the archetypal figures that shape us make up our own periodic table, the basic stuff out of which we make a life and become a person.[36]

Borrowing language from alchemy, Jung referred to the raw stuff of the soul as *prima materia*, raw material. We all have material—experiences, relationships, emotions—that hasn't been sorted out sufficiently. The main task in psychological alchemy is to take this raw material and help it change into a more refined resource for a thoughtful and effective life. When our emotions and memories are raw, they often interfere with our ideals and goals and certainly with our spiritual aspirations. All that is needed is some deep reflection and serious confrontation. The raw stuff becomes less unconscious and less autonomous when subjected to the process of reflection.

When I was just beginning as a therapist I had a key dream in which I was in a house under construction and walking on an unfinished stretch of flooring and almost fell through it. The founder of Neoplatonism, Plotinus, said that work with the soul is like making a piece of sculpture: You chisel away until a beautiful form appears. Therapy is a creative act, a making, a craft, and an art. John Keats called it soul making. I could call it soul carpentry or soul sculpting.

---

35 Michael Ondaatje, *Divisadero* (New York: Alfred A. Knopf, 2007), p. 16.

36 I'm not forgetting the purely imaginative figures that appear in our dreams and fantasies, and the archetypal, mythic themes that structure our lives.

It's far better to be under construction than to be shabby and in need of repair. The person who hasn't sorted out his life experiences acts them out in daily life, repeating negative patterns. The alchemical or therapeutic work not only liberates you from your past, it makes you a thoughtful and less impulsive person, less prone to acting on raw emotion. You also become a better leader, parent, teacher, friend. You become a person of substance, liberated from the raw, interfering patterns and emotions that are useful only when refined.

During your own therapy, you have insight into your soul and you cooperate with an alchemical process already under way. It is not an ego-centered construction job, but more a close observation and the subtle fostering of what you want to achieve. You're constructing a thoughtful life, but in a non-doing way. The *Tao Te Ching*, a basic spiritual resource for anyone, describes ancient masters on the way, and they could be your model:

> The ancient masters were like people crossing a winter stream . . . yielding, like ice about to melt.[37]

Many people want to change but also want everything to stay the same. They're not yielding, because they don't want their hard ice to melt and the water to begin flowing. When you feel a softening, when you realize that something hard in you is moving toward melting, you can let it happen. Melting is a good metaphor for exactly what is needed in many people's lives. They've been frozen, hard, rigid, cold, and fixed and now can soften.

In your self-therapy you may discover how interesting your soul is. You can glimpse its mysterious patterns and movements in your dreams and notice how your raw material lies in the

---

37 Tzu, *Tao Te Ching*, no. 15.

background of your life story. I try to approach therapy not with knitted brow as a painful process of improvement, but as a pleasurable and hopeful exploration of the soul. You can do this on your own to a point, but you will need a part of you in the background, noticing when you're protecting yourself from painful realizations.

One woman described her anxiety to me this way:

One can try and understand why and come up with a million different reasons but it doesn't change anything. One can end up with a battle between the ego wanting to remain safe and the soul wanting to live. Apathy can cling to you like a cloud around a mountain and feel like a chain around your soul until it just feels tired.

How do you do self-therapy when you feel this way—soul tired? I suggested that she stop looking for reasons and just go over the stories of her life as vividly as she can. There's a difference between looking for reasons for feelings like apathy and gaining insight through stories and dreams. The latter is less rational. You may be surprised when fresh realizations suddenly surface, and you gain a perspective you've never had before. It's easier, of course, with a therapist who can lead you deep and help you catch insights. But you can do it alone.

In going about your own therapy, it's helpful to be concrete and methodical. Write down your memories. Speak them into a recorder. Draw and paint your images. Give your life a spiritual and psychological timeline. Talk openly and substantially to family members and friends. Take your self-therapy seriously.

Let me frame these essentials of home therapy as a series of lessons. Just remember that the actual number of lessons is infinite.

Lesson 1: Tell Your Story

Therapy is sometimes called the talking cure and consists for the most part in telling the stories of your life. Essentially, it is not about interpreting your stories and explaining who you are, but telling the stories with some intensity for insight. A good therapist knows how to listen and how to encourage effective storytelling. So in your informal therapy it would be good to find someone who will listen to your special stories, the ones that are not superficial but stir your emotions and hint at the meaning of your life.

Generally, people are not good listeners. They may be thinking, all the while you speak, about what your story means and how you're put together. Just as people like to gossip, they also like to psychoanalyze. A good therapist doesn't do this. She avoids instant analysis and advice giving. If your friend is prone to either, it might be better to find another ear.

Once, a young, vulnerable woman, Joanne, was telling me about her home life with her two children and her shy husband. "He gets angry, like my father, at small things. A nurse once told me to stay away from him when he's like that, but I think it's my job to stay close to him in good times and bad." The word "nurse" came through sharply.

"What nurse?" I asked. "Does your husband beat you? Does he get violent?"

"No, of course not. Well, sometimes his anger gets the better of him. Once, just once, he hit me and we had to go to the emergency room. He was embarrassed and begged me not so say anything."

"Just once?"

"Not often."

You see how the story develops and how much soul material lies in certain potent words. You notice how several statements contradict the facts. They're not lies, just evasions, worry that the story will really reveal what is going on. Most people have a need both to tell their stories and to keep them hidden. In therapy, both needs have a place. Keep certain things private, but at the same time take risks and step over thresholds into new revelations.

In Joanne's story, look at all the rich images that have come up in a few sentences: a "shy" husband—shy can be good, but it can also mean repressed and maladjusted; angry like her father, an indication of childhood problems; the rule about protecting him because of the marriage vows; the husband begging her to keep quiet—control.

If you're the listener, you have to hear what is being said at many levels. Often, our ordinary speech is full of code words and phrases that mean much more than the mere words suggest.

I don't want to romanticize stories. They can become habitual and canonical, and you can come to believe in the stories that you always tell. And, of course, most of us at one time or another tell stories intended to mislead and avoid the facts. Stories have a dark side that people often ignore.

Sometimes your emotions may be so strong that you can't find a complete story. All you have are images and episodes, impressions and fragments of memory. These are also useful and may give up their insights in a good experience of art therapy. I don't mean using images to diagnose, but to be an artist and let images come out and be realized on paper or in sound or poetry. Good art therapy escapes the problem of using stories for self-protection and too easy explanation.

Joanne was a spiritual person interested in meditation and many diets and systems of spiritual practice. She spent years studying with several different teachers, some of them strong in their ideas about what she should do with her life. She seemed susceptible, gullible, and too innocent about men. Soon the stories of her malicious male spiritual guides melded with tales of her husband's need to control her.

Joanne's story demonstrates how spirituality has the potential for sadomasochistic pleasure in control, dominance, and ultimately violence. Spiritual leaders and practices look so well intended and positive on the surface that you may not see the shadow in them. The same is true of teachers and doctors and, unfortunately, fathers, grandfathers, and uncles. And people may be reluctant to tell dark stories that cast their leaders in a bad light.

As you tell your stories, you may glimpse patterns you haven't noticed before. You may have small epiphanies and revelations. You may get insights into your situation. But to get the full benefit of your exploration, your story has to go deep and take risks. You may censor your story as you tell it, and that holding back may obscure the lessons the story has to give. That's why you need a good friend who can listen and give you feedback or encourage you to go further.

Tell your stories, and when you sense fear and reluctance, try to relax. The more your stories pour out unimpeded, the better chance you have of glimpsing your soul. You need to see it before you can work with it.

There is more to therapy than storytelling, but this is the starting point and the most important aspect. Let the stories rise to the surface. Tell them with candor. Listen to what you're saying and glimpse the revelations in a nuance, a tone, and a gap between words. Therapy begins with words that are not fully under your control, words that not only come out of your mouth, but speak to you and tell you things you've either forgotten or never knew.

Lesson 2: Go with Your Symptoms

The next lesson baffles many people and sounds contrary to common sense. I get it from James Hillman and Patricia Berry, two Jungian analysts and archetypal psychologists with whom I worked closely for many years. I saw how they "preserved the symptoms" and honored the many twisted ways the soul presents itself.

Dr. Berry asks, "Where is the symptom headed? What would happen if it were fulfilled rather than removed?" She's skillful at seeing value to the soul where a superficial look would only see trouble. For instance, she has written about the value of feeling stuck and frozen.[38] Your symptom may be that you let people push you around, and you think you should be stronger. But maybe the symptom is pointing you toward being more effectively vulnerable. Things are often the opposite of what they appear to be.

In practice, this means being sympathetic with your troubling emotions and bad habits, always assuming, of course, that you're not being violent with someone or acting out in dangerous ways. Accepting your symptoms for what they are can be the first step in letting them loosen and transform.

Jung says that alchemists often described the *prima materia*, the raw material, as chaos or the sea.[39] The latter was bitter from the salt in it, just as our raw material is often pungent; it was chaotic, just as we might sense our lives as full of chaos. It's understandable that a person would be reluctant to dredge up the bitter raw material of the psyche for examination. Better to let it remain undisturbed and forgotten. Yet, if there is no material, the work can't even begin.

I would go further. The more bitter and distasteful the raw material, the more promise it has for clearing out the soul and making life richer and more self-aware. It may take a while, and you may have to develop some confidence and courage before you get to the rich material of your soul. This work is not for the fainthearted. The more seriously you look into yourself, the more good you can do.

If you are engaged in real soul work, becoming a deeper person, being more of an individual and thoughtful about

---

38 Patricia Berry, "Stopping: A Mode of Animation" in *Echo's Subtle Body* (Dallas: Spring Publications, 1982), pp. 147–161.

39 C. G. Jung, *Mysterium Coniunctionis*, trans. R. F. C. Hull, CW vol. 14, 2nd ed., (Princeton: Princeton University Press, 1970), p. 246.

ordinary life, then your spiritual efforts will have a strong, fertile base. Soul and spirit often interact and overlap, your maturing soul supporting your evolving spirit. Your glowing ideas about a spiritual existence need the bitter, salty, and chaotic feelings.

Keep your symptoms in mind and don't try to get rid of them. Be patient. As you hold them and explore them, they will release some of their hold on you. Often they transform from troublesome habits to useful traits. I've witnessed people go from hot, destructive jealousy to satisfying relationships in which they can be vulnerable and self-possessed. Jealousy, rooted in an urge to be deeply involved, morphs into a suitably complex way of being intimate. What was once a symptom can become a mark of character. You don't want to get rid of such a symptom but rather allow it to transform until it blossoms, revealing the good seed it had in it from the beginning.

In my practice of therapy, I am always encouraging people not to be so negative about the psychological issues that bother them. I don't actually tell them to "go with the symptom," but I model that principle myself. I look at my own motives to be sure that I'm not trying to eradicate problems. I see therapy as a method for getting *through* life's problems rather than trying to make them disappear.

Let me give you an example. A woman I know in her fifties is plagued by her elderly mother, who dominates and micromanages her life. The daughter has tried to deal with this intolerable situation by traveling, moving away, and shouting and ranting. But she keeps listening to her mother's criticisms and bad advice. It appears to me that something in the daughter wants to be her mother's child. So I encourage her to stop fighting it and, at least temporarily, admit that she wants to remain close to her mother. We keep the symptom rather than move in an opposite direction. It may take time, but I expect that eventually she will embrace her need to be close to her mother, sort out its positives and negatives, and live it out in a more graceful manner.

In my own case, I'm aware of some of my complexes, those

overwhelming urges or habits that control you just when you don't want them to. For example, I have an odd problem with a certain kind of woman. I think of it as my "auntie" complex. Certain women in their fifties or sixties cast an odd spell over me. I feel compelled to listen to them or care for them or do what they want. I was in a grocery store when "auntie" appeared in the guise of a produce worker. I was picking out some olives that I liked, and she told me to take some white beans. I would never have taken beans. I said no, but several times she repeated her advice. I ended up leaving the store with beans I didn't want.

I could try to fight this annoying complex, but instead I go into it. Here's an idea for you: If you spot your complex somewhere, don't hide, don't avoid. Go right into it. I spot "auntie" somewhere and I go up to her and start a conversation. If the issue that comes up is serious, I'll be aggressive with it, but ordinarily I don't fight it. This "auntie" complex of mine is a mild mania, of course, though it can become serious. One of the most important rules is to admit to your problems. Don't deny them. Acknowledging your emotional issues is one simple way of "going with the symptom."

You can also turn your symptoms into strengths by finding creative and effective ways to live them out. Once, I was speaking to a group of nurses and asked how many of them had a mother complex. The majority put their hands up. They had a natural tendency to mother people and found expression for it in nursing. There, the complex allows the person to do demanding work with passion, even if sometimes it also provides opportunities to go too far in mothering or doing it in inappropriate ways. You cannot "go with your symptom" perfectly.

Lesson 3. In Relationships, Respect the Mystery

In my definition a "soul mate" is a person to whom you feel so deeply connected that you wish their fulfillment more than any surface happiness and more than the apparent success of the relationship. There is a sense of the eternal and the destined in a soul-oriented connection with another person that may give rise to a special selfless love, and that sensation signals the presence of both soul and spirit in the couple.

One of the basic problems in close relationships is the tendency to expect the other person to be and act the person you want them to be. It takes considerable maturity to allow the other to live his or her own life. You may have certain needs that you hope your friend or lover or family member will fulfill. You may live by certain rules and habits that you hope everyone will adopt. You may have a worldview that works for you, and you can't understand why someone close to you doesn't share it. This clinging to self-interests has to change. You may have to learn to appreciate and ultimately enjoy the other person's ways and especially the mysteries that lead them on.

Allowing the other his or her own life and destiny is a spiritual achievement, a religious act, if you will, that raises the relationship above the level of mere human connection. In love you discover what the gospels again and again call agape, a profound respect for another's value, an outgoing effort of the heart to transcend your own self-interest and discover the enlivening space outside yourself where you can find meaning. Agape is the spiritual side of love that asks you to transcend yourself and your needs.

Taking this lesson a step further, you might also realize that another person is not only a mystery to you but also to herself. She doesn't know why she does the things she does. She has fears and hopes that may look clear to you but for her come out of a fog. She may be driven by desires and anxieties that are far beneath the surface of awareness. Therefore, you may have to respect her mysteries and expect that she will go in her own direction.

Modern views on life and relationship overlook the mysterious and in so doing dismiss both soul and spirit, rendering a relationship materialistic and ego-centered. Yet fate and destiny, essential parts of every person's experience, are largely beyond the limits of our knowing and predicting. How do you live out a human relationship under such conditions? You honor the mysterious in the whole of life.

You can positively and thoughtfully support tentative moves into new territory on the part of those close to you. You can see the importance of her mystery, which is her soul opening up and responding to its innate potential or to developments in life. You may think about living from your own soul, but you can also share the lives of others as they live from theirs and work out their destiny.

Developing this understanding about people and their connections is part of therapy. Allowing another's mystery and openness to change usually helps you allow your own. It's a two-way channel: You can't respect another's response to fate if you can't respect your own, and you can't be open to your own changes if you are not open to those in others.

Lesson 4. Depression

We are an extraverted society. We interpret our lives by external causes and influences and give almost no heed to our interior. And so, in compensation, we fall deep into ourselves, sensing and feeling our souls, by means of depression. Depression is a symptomatic way of remaining in touch with our souls.

People think of depression along the lines of the common cold. It's an aberration that comes along like an affliction carried by germs in the air. We don't imagine that our depression could have to do with the meaning, or lack of it, in our lives. We treat it as though it were an objective reality, like an organ breakdown rather than an invitation to further life. We think it comes from nowhere or descends like a parachute into our lives. We deal with it by means of pills and mechanical treatments like electric shock. We don't see the literalism and materialism in our remedies and certainly don't see that the very use of these methods is part of the problem that leads to depression.

Medieval and Renaissance medical books suggest that melancholy is a gift to the soul, something that could heal us rather than just afflict us. I am not referring to long-term clinical depression here, but rather the times in life one feels drawn inward and downward. Depression gives us valuable qualities that we need in order to be fully human. It gives us weight, when we are too light about our lives. It offers a degree of gravitas. It was associated with the metal lead and was said to be heavy. It also ages us so that we grow old appropriately and don't pretend to be younger than we are. It grows us up and gives us the range of human emotion and character that we need in order to deal with the seriousness of life. In classic Renaissance images found in old medical texts and collections of remedies, depression is an old person wearing a broad-rimmed hat, in the shadows, holding his head in his hands.

If depression is your issue, don't simply try to get rid of it. Don't run to places of entertainment to escape it or to settings of happiness to evade it. Let it be. Let it settle. Don't indulge in it or merely sink into it. As it forms a dark cloud around you, allow it to seep into your pores, giving you some of its qualities, while not overwhelming you. "Put it in a suitcase," James Hillman said, "and carry it with you." Keep it contained and yet close. Make sure it's available, but don't let it get out and take over.

Some people are depressed because they don't have spirit in their lives. They lack vision and purpose and find their relationships weak and faltering. They fear for their happiness and desperately want their spirits to lift. The tie between depression and spirituality is tight. Therefore, it makes sense to deal effectively with any depression you have as you consider bringing a new kind of religious sensibility into your life.

Depression might also settle in because you have allowed your religious background to make you feel guilty and bound, unable to enjoy life's pleasures. You may have to think hard about these influences and notice them even when they're subtle. You may have to have many heart-to-heart conversations with friends to finally see how your spirituality may be weighing on you.

Lesson 5. Anger and Aggression

Many people today go through their lives heavy with anger. It may be obvious in their touchiness and tendency to criticize. It may be more subtle in their depression or unwillingness to be positive and constructive. For many, anger is a shadow quality that they want to keep secret and hidden, and yet they feel it and it may put a scowl on their faces or an abruptness in their actions.

Some are angry about things that happened years ago, events that were never resolved and therefore continue to press and create a chronic feeling of rejection. I've known men whose language is largely coarse and negative, betraying longstanding and bitter resentment. They walk angry, talk angry, and carry themselves in an angry fashion.

Some people turn their anger against themselves and do what they can to deprive and punish themselves. It may seem odd, but for some it may be more satisfying to hurt themselves than to turn their aggression outward and punish the world. They hope that the world will suffer at seeing how they have hurt themselves. Technically speaking, anger has sadomasochistic qualities, satisfaction in hurting others or in hurting oneself.

Hillman always said that his work, so original and bold, was the result of his anger. He lectured and wrote about Mars, the spirit of aggression, with appreciation, and he always spoke publicly with force and argument. He wrote a challenging book called *A Terrible Love of War*, in which he spoke for the human need to be assertive and even aggressive. In his personal manner, Hillman often stung people with his strong, critical style. The very quality that made him worth reading turned some people away. But he had many followers and close friends, like me, who loved him. Allowing your anger to be a constructive force in you rather than a destructive indulgence can bring more love into your life, not less.

Part of our self-therapy must include coming to terms with our anger. I can't imagine a human being who doesn't have a complicated connection to Mars and the anger that has built up in him. As usual, it would help to tell stories that might account for some of the anger and frustration that have become habitual.

It might also help to make an anger timelime, listing the various occasions over time that have given rise to anger in a notable way. You could list the ways you reveal your anger in a measured and camouflaged fashion. You could note the situations that most give rise to anger and ways you either vent it or repress it.

Interestingly, anger doesn't always look like anger. I sit with a mousy person who feels that the whole world is toying with her and not giving her a break. She's a volcano waiting to erupt. I sit with a man in therapy who says little and seems to be waiting for me to do the wrong thing so he can leave. He's angry at me from the start, misplacing an anger that has spoiled his life for years. At least, as classical analysis teaches, showing it in therapy, even in passive-aggressive ways, gives us a chance to work through it.

As a therapist, I do my best to go directly into the heart of a conflict between me and my client. I stick with it until a resolution appears or at least the stage is set for some progress. Many temptations go through my mind, ways I could avoid the confrontation and language that could mitigate it. Immediately on recognizing these temptations for what they are, I refocus and stay in the heat. The appearance of anger becomes an opportunity to bring some fire to the work and become yet more seriously engaged.

If you're often angry, trace the roots in story and then apply your anger as a force and a sharp edge to whatever you do. Don't indulge in venting. Always convert and transform your anger into something worthwhile. Let people see and feel your anger, but don't explode every time you feel it. Like all strong emotions, anger requires a process of alchemy to transform it from raw feeling to a cultivated and meaningful quality of action and personality. Dip into your anger as if it were a precious resource, which it is.

Sometimes our language imprisons us. We speak too easily of anger, when the emotion might be more subtle. We may feel frustrated, betrayed, let down, unreasonably challenged, tired of criticism, or disillusioned. It's helpful to use exactly the right words for our feeling and experience. The right word helps us know how to respond.

In ancient Rome, Mars, the god of anger, was closely allied to the spirits of agriculture. It was said that he helped protect the fields from pestilence. Notice that imagery: Mars, anger, helps us weed out annoying obstacles to growth. It serves the natural process of maturation and nurture. It's in the service of the spirits and gods of basic nurturance. It's primal, instinctive, protective, and healing. Yes, Mars heals. Your anger heals.

Anger can give you the strength to make difficult decisions and deliver painful messages to people who need to hear your displeasure or your desire. If you're out of touch with your anger or can't express it effectively, you may keep it inside, where it may turn against you.

I worked with a man once whose anger would explode on rare occasions. Otherwise he was passive and eerily quiet. I knew that he had many plans for his life, but they remained internal simply because he couldn't summon up the force needed to get them into the outside world. His marriage suffered and his career stalled, until one day he started making big changes. He connected with his anger and quit the job he hated and had words with an annoying neighbor. His marriage improved almost overnight. I could see the agricultural Mars at work in him, weeding out bothersome obstacles and sowing seeds for a new life.

I know this is not the anger that has been repressed and has become dark and violent. No, this is anger at first blush. Not denied. Pure anger—the alchemist might say "eternal or essential anger" as distinct from anger twisted into indirect expression—is your ally.

Even your symptomatic anger can be purified if you return to its origins. Remember how you have been misunderstood, violated, offended, taken advantage of. That primal anger is useful to you now. Don't undervalue it. Let it influence how you behave; let it teach you. Don't be an angry person, chronically afflicted with it. Let your anger provide the fuel for everything you do.

More Lessons

MASOCHISM

One of the common, underlying problems is classic masochism: being pleased with suffering or finding an odd happiness in being the victim of an imagined oppressor. It's complicated, because sadism and masochism breathe on each other and follow each other like a moon hovering around a planet. The masochist may be trying to control with his weakness, and the sadist is only expressing his weakness with his excessive aggression.

Problems in life often stem from the failure to draw strength from one's own nature and from life. People believe in being small and weak, whereas being strong and big could help resolve their emotional blockages and actually allow them to be effective in relationships and in positions of leadership. Many fear being too forceful, but in fact excessive force usually comes out of weakness, not strength.

Find precisely where you are weak and at the mercy of others, see any hidden control in those very places, and consider having an easy strength, giving up both the need to control and the need to be passive. Mere insight into your sadomasochistic patterns can help you find an alternative style.

You might also understand the difference between force and strength, the former pressing too hard to achieve questionable ends, the latter a deep-seated power of soul. You might notice the difference between ego power and soul power, the former anxious and self-centered. Finally, you might appreciate the paradoxes involved, where being more vulnerable in a comfortable way gives you strength, and when you have some deep strength, you can finally be vulnerable.

Most people tend toward masochism. When you are feeling the weight and emotional tension in relationships and just getting on with life, you may be slipping into that "love of weakness" that is a mysterious dynamic in the human soul. It isn't easy to shake because at some level it satisfies. You may have to get some insight into that particular satisfaction to be relieved of your pain. You can also make some simple efforts to learn how to enjoy your strength: Notice it. Practice it. Enjoy it.

Sadomasochistic tendencies can lead to actual sadistic and masochistic behavior that plagues all aspects of life, including traditional religion. New spiritual groups sometimes have leaders who demand docile followers. Teachings may still be an onus on people and require various kinds of suffering. Swept away by their enthusiasm for a new spiritual movement, young people may leave their families and give up their futures. They may surrender their life decisions to a leader or adopt values that make life unnecessarily difficult. All of this in the name of religion.

WHY ISN'T THIS TURMOIL OVER?

In formal therapy people often ask: "Why isn't this dark night over and done with? How long is it going to go on? I thought I'd be through this by now." Sometimes dark nights are over and done with much sooner than you would expect. Sometimes they go on and on and one wonders if they'll ever end. It isn't up to the person going through the dark night to predict how long it will take. The task is to stay with it and make use of any encouraging signs. You need patience and hope.

Jung makes an interesting comment on timing: "Many alchemists compute the duration of the opus to be that of a pregnancy,

and they liken the entire procedure to such a period of gestation."
We've seen that the opus is the work of becoming a person of
depth, a process that asks you to confront your fears, explore your
desires, and engage in life wholeheartedly.

For many people the process of creating a soul-centered life
entails at least one period when they feel lost and maybe depressed and anxious. Using the language of mystics, I have referred to this as a psychological dark night. Jung says that after
going through a dark period of development, some people look
back and see that it has taken nine months. Dreams may also
show this in their imagery.

In my experience, it helps to have such a natural sense of
timing. The nine months may not be literally true of the experience, but the sense of gestation helps both the initiate and the
guide get through the process with a positive attitude and with
patience. In general, a good sense of timing can be useful when
you tend your spiritual and psychological unfolding: when to be
patient and when to make a move. To live a meaningful life, it
helps to take note of crucial moments in your past and watch
when that time of year or a particular date returns. In their
groundbreaking book *Why People Get Sick*, authors Darian Leader
and David Corfield give many examples of people becoming seriously ill on dates associated with painful moments in their
pasts.[40] They also point out that medical professionals usually fail
to notice these correspondences because they don't look for
meaning in illness. By focusing on the opus, Jung directs our attention to the long process by which we discover meaning and in
which illness can be a significant factor.

For your process of self-therapy, then, I recommend Jung's
image: a nine-month gestation. Give yourself time, be patient,
see your process as a natural one. Remember, nine months is a

---

40 Darian Leader and David Corfield, *Why People Get Sick* (New York:
Pegasus Books, 2008).

metaphor, not a literal time frame. Your nine months may actually last a few weeks or a few years. Just keep the image in mind and cooperate with the process.

RELAXED THERAPY

Therapy doesn't have to be intense analysis, where every word is weighed for its meaning and every gesture interpreted. I like to spend the hours of consultation in such a relaxed way that an observer would suppose we were just having a normal conversation. I don't worry if the talk is easy and distracted and unfocused. I let it go where it wants to go. I may ask a question here and there that underlines something said or some feeling that has arisen, but even then I don't want to lose the easy flow of words. I want the process to lead, as we follow.

Explore your past life, your emotions, and your relationships in your own way, using any art and craft, any form of dialogue. Relax. Stay free. There are no rules. But try to go deep into whatever fantasies and narratives are directing your life. Go somewhere with them. Get some insight. Give them some depth. Get to know your soul through them. If you go in any particular direction, make it downward and upward. Overall, it's better to think of self-therapy as a vertical process rather than a horizontal one.

AN OPEN HEART

Today when people have to get their hearts unclogged they may go through "open heart" surgery, a good metaphor for emotional surgery that most of us need. Many relationships fail because one or both of the people involved can't open their hearts enough to love in a way that will sustain the relationship over the struggles and confusion that pop up in every life.

By "open heart" I don't mean a romantic gushing of emotion.

I mean the capacity to receive another person into your life, free of your self-protective defenses. Open hearts are relatively rare in an anxious world and yet are clearly the basis of a spiritual life.

"Open heart" doesn't mean "dangerously exposed heart." We need to protect ourselves and we can't achieve perfection in this sensitive matter. I often turn to Emily Dickinson's wise words on this point: "The soul should always stand ajar." "Ajar" is a good word for the kind of openness that is ready to accept new life but is not in a position to be overwhelmed or overstimulated. I've seen this image in people's dreams many times: a door left ajar. It may be frightening, full of fantasies of intruders and robbers, or it may be convenient—a little openness to allow life in.

You may not be aware that your heart isn't open. You may imagine that you are loving and available when you are not. In this matter, your self-image as an open person may be a cover for your failure to truly open your heart to be influenced and connected.

In his book *The Thought of the Heart*, James Hillman gives three different ways the heart could be open: first, in wonder; second, in being intimate; and third, relating to an object or another person as a "thou" rather than an "it,"—living in an ensouled world rather than an inanimate one.[41] In the Gospel of Mark, Jesus is upset by the hardness of people's hearts (Mark 3:5). The word used sometimes means "marble" or "callus," the thickening of the skin. The soul's heart has to be soft and capable of wonder, intimacy, and personhood.

This special combination of Jesus and Hillman offers rich ideas that could well become central in your own religion. You could engage in practices that wake you up to wonder, like standing under the day or night sky; that show you how to do everything

---

41 James Hillman, *The Thought of the Heart and the Soul of the World* (Dallas: Spring Publications, 1981), p. 32.

in an intimate rather than distant way; and that help you soften those emotional places where you have become hard and callused. This is a psycho-spiritual challenge, where spirit and soul come together, where your emotional openness and spiritual sensitivity coincide.

Hillman pursued Jung's interest in alchemy, the ancient psycho-spiritual practice in which the elements and processes of the soul were seen symbolically in the basic materials of the physical world, similar to the way astrology finds insight into human experience in the positions of the planets in the sky. Jung viewed the heart as the seat of passion and imagination. Hillman picks up on this idea and states it more radically: only the thought of the heart reveals the soul's concerns.

Just speaking about the heart tempts us toward sentimental language that avoids the shadow side. Hillman reminds us that the physical heart is divided into two chambers, pointing to the dual nature of the soul's heart, where an appreciation of both beauty and ugliness, love and aggression, and fear and courage all have a place. How can you see the gods, he says, if you're shocked by ugliness?

In religious imagery it's notable how often the heart is shown present and available, as in the sacred heart of Jesus, the mudras of the Buddha, Aphrodite placing one hand over her genitals and another over her heart, or the important fourth heart chakra of the yoga systems of India. The widely recited and chanted Heart Sutra addresses spiritual emptiness, a teaching that might be better expressed in English as openness.

THERAPY AT HOME

Here's a checklist of activities you can do at any time as self-therapy:

1. Keep a daily record of your dreams.

2. Talk to family members about early experiences and about personalities.

3. Talk to friends about your personal issues.

4. Read some good psychology books.

5. Spend time quietly in nature.

6. Walk meditatively.

7. Resolve some troublesome relationships.

8. Study your fears and longings.

9. Write out your personal myth, the deep story you are living.

10. Paint or draw the scenes and characters of your "inner" life.

This list is just a beginning. It will get you started. Most modern people are extraverted. They interpret their lives in terms of the visible and literal outer world. Your alchemical therapy begins with a new orientation toward the deeper, often inner patterns your life takes. It thrives on memories carefully reflected upon. Good, probing conversations also help. Let your family and friends be your informal and personal therapists (only in the sense I describe therapy here, not pretending to be professionals and not analyzing).

Twenty years ago I took a radical step by suggesting that "care of the soul" could replace psychotherapy. I was only following Plato and many other Platonists over the centuries. When I recommend self-therapy, I'm thinking of therapy more as care than as repair. Consider your spiritual emotions and keep soul and spirit tightly connected as you work through your problems. You can care for your soul every day by doing things that make your world more beautiful and intimate and by tending the wounds and bad habits that have accrued to your life. Follow your dreams, find the occasion to speak from your heart, and make a life that is more soulful than practical.

PART THREE

❧

Carnal Spirit—Spirituality and Sensuality

To renounce the realm of the senses
is to punish yourself with asceticism—don't do this!
When you see an object, really look!
Hear sounds,
Inhale scents,
Taste delicious flavors,
Feel textures.
Use the objects of the five senses, and
You will soon attain supreme Buddhahood!

—THE CAKRASAMVARA TANTRA[42]

---

42 Miranda Shaw, *Passionate Enlightenment* (Princeton: Princeton University Press, 1994), pp. 143–44. The passage is slightly retranslated.

Chapter 5

᪥

PLEASURE, DESIRE, AND THE DEEPLY EROTIC

The beauty of the waist, and thence of the hips,
    and thence
downward toward the knees,
The thin red jellies within you or within me. . . .
O I say these are not the parts and poems of the
    body only,
but of the soul,
O I say now these are the soul!

—WALT WHITMAN, "I SING THE BODY ELECTRIC"

In a famous Zen story two monks are walking together and come to a river. A beautiful woman is standing there trying to figure out how to get across. The older monk offers to help and picks her up and carries her. Later, as the two monks resume their stroll, the younger says, "I thought we weren't supposed to have contact with women." The older monk replies, "I put the woman down long ago, but you're still carrying her."

The lesson usually drawn from this story is, do what you have to do and move on. From a typical spiritual point of view, the monk picks up the woman and then lets go. No attachments, no complications, no worries.

But disturbing reflection can be a good thing. Even inner conflict and worry inspire the need to sort things out. In my interpretation of the story, the young monk who can't stop thinking about the woman would become the teacher. He's more human and has the capacity to carry his experiences for a long time and worry about them. In a way, the story contrasts spirit and soul, and I favor the soulful young man.

The traditional story may also give the impression that erotic touch is no big deal. You can do it and then forget about it. But we all know how potent touch can be, how it can stir up both warm-blooded memories and feelings of guilt. A monk carrying a woman across a stream is no small thing. If I were a monk and picked up a woman and and felt an erotic charge, I'd be haunted for a long time.

Those of us gifted with a body know the zing of eros, the afterglow of touches, images, and even words. Whitman's "I Sing the Body Electric," quoted at the beginning of this chapter, is itself an electric body of words. For Whitman, writing is a sexual act showing us that words have flesh and blood.

I lived in a Catholic monastery long enough to know the many ways monks slip away from the demands of eros. "Don't think about it" is not a good solution. To repress erotic fantasies is to fan their flames. I'd rather keep carrying the woman in my mind, sorting out my confused feelings, than remain under the illusion that eros is something you can just pick up and put down.

Many spiritual people are confused about eros and sexuality. They believe in virtue and purity and end up repressing their sexuality. But repressed, it really catches fire. How many spiritual leaders have succumbed to sexual desire in inappropriate ways and lost their standing and their jobs? Imagine eroticism in the best possible light, as the foundation of your spirituality, and it will work *for* you rather than against you.

Erotic Spirituality

Eros is the spark of desire and the flame of love. It's a wind that blows in need and longing. It's the warmth of pleasure, vitality, and excitement. It's an arrow striking your heart and waking you up to want and satisfaction. These are all traditional descriptions of a spirit depicted as a young man with a bow and quiver full of arrows. The poet Charles Olson links the sound of the word "arrows" with "eros," reminding us that desire is something that can strike when we least expect it. It would be better to give up the idea that the troublesome desire is mine—why don't I stop thinking this way—and see eros as a power that arrives on its own accord.

The ancient Greeks and modern psychological thinkers like Freud and Jung thought highly of eros. Freud saw it as the principle of life and Jung as the dynamism of the psyche. For the Greeks Eros was a world-engendering god, a creative figure in the very center of things. The ancient "Orphic Hymn to Eros" begins with language we may not associate with eros today:

> *I invoke great, pure, lovely and sweet Eros*
> *an archer with wings speeding along a path of fire*
> *playing together with gods and mortals.*[43]

A materialist culture thinks of sex as physical and biological and can't seem to understand how the soul and spirit can have their own sexuality. Yet the ancient Greek image of Eros as a young man with hefty wings points to his dynamism, strength, and spirit, or, as an egg, portrays his fertility and potential. Read Whitman's words once again. Eros is not just about the body, but about the soul.

---

43 I purposely translate this ambiguously. Does Eros play together with us or does he play with us?

As part of your self-therapy you could reflect on how you were brought up to think about eros and recall experiences, good and bad, that still affect you. I remember going to confession when I was seven, reflecting on the ten commandments, and not being sure what committing adultery was all about. With the acute intuition of a child I suspected that it connected somehow to the mildly erotic games my circle of friends played, and at that early age sexual guilt set in. As I grew up, that guilt swelled, until late in my teens I realized its absurdity, but too late to expunge it from my memory. For all my efforts at a religion of my own, I still have traces of Catholic guilt, not in my head but in the cells of my body.

As you envision your own religion now, you can reverse centuries of repression by boldly blending the spiritual and the erotic. You can develop a philosophy of life that appreciates the role of desire, pleasure, attraction, and sexuality. You can meditate and pray in a sensual fashion, in tune with the material world and your own body. You can understand your erotic fantasies as poetry about your life and not always as literal invitations to sex. If you're a leader or a counselor, you can help people deal with sexual and erotic problems by affirming their sexuality. This step alone would help countless people integrate a deep sense of religion into their personal lives and relationships.

Once you stop demonizing them and embrace your erotic passions and interests, your entire sense of the spiritual may change. You may see through the antierotic condemnations of religion. You may give up any need to feel virtuous and instead embrace life passionately. Then you may be free to explore ethical possibilities that are beyond sex. You may well find more joy in life.

Some people seem to think that they're being spiritual by not being sexual. They purchase their spirituality by giving up their sexuality, or at least holding it in low regard. But this tactic makes no sense. It isn't positive. You haven't got anything for all the sacrifice. It would be better to be erotic in a soulful way at the very moment you are most spiritual.

Religion may be the cause of your depression and stand in the way of a good sex life and upset the delicate balance of your basic emotions. Many people have been convinced by formal religion that they would be better if they were free of the stain of their sexuality. But real virtue can't be bought with repression; real virtue is the rare innocence that comes from taking life on and owning your passions. Eros lifts the spirit—the purpose of his wings.

Eros Generates Life

In ordinary speech eros refers to romantic, sexual, or intimate love, and the adjective "erotic" denotes something that is arousing, pleasurable, and desirable. Today you find the word in contexts that are dark and disreputable, like pornographic movies and books. But two thousand years ago the Greeks told stories and sang hymns of the divine Eros, the creator. He was called Phanes—Light—and honored as a positive force.

Religious institutions have waged a continuing battle with eros, and they have lost the fight. The scandal of Catholic priests engaging in cruel abuse and not being stopped by the authorities and Zen masters and public preachers caught in the betrayal of their vaunted virtuousness—these examples should teach us not to deal with eros through repression and posturing. Eros is a mighty power: better to befriend him for your well-being than deal with him continually as an enemy.

Sex Is Not Always Sex

Often, sex isn't just about sex. Just as in adolescence, sexual awakening is part of a much larger awakening to a bigger life and world, so when sexual fantasy and desire stir in a marriage, the marriage may be in store for new developments. When a married person unexpectedly feels sexual attraction outside the marriage, new possibilities may be germinating. I remember one woman finding a new career in art curating and another becoming a psychoanalyst, both developments begun at a time of intense and uexpected sexual desire and marital discord. This is all confusing, because sexual desire seems to be about sex, and you can find yourself in a dilemma about what to do: be loyal to the marriage or follow your passion. The way out may be to look closely to see where the desires point, perhaps beyond plain sex.

You may understand sudden sexual desire, perhaps in an awkward or impossible situation, as a generic waking up of passion and longing. You may not have to act out the sexual desire but instead explore the awakening itself. You may be alert for new ways of making a living or a different part of the world in which to live. You may seek out fresh experiences. The point is to follow through on the sexual fantasies with a broad scope, opening your life up, finding new pleasures and satisfactions.

A clue to the greater meaning of sex may lie in the sensation you may have after a joyful sexual experience. You may not only feel good because of the sex; you may have an overall sense that life itself is good. That's why people are often in love with love: It gives the sensation that you are waking up and starting over.

In ancient art you see Aphrodite, the goddess of sex, in the company of Eros, who in myth is sometimes her son. These images depict an intimate connection between sex and eros, two closely related but different things, one about sexuality itself and the other a more general feeling of desire and pleasure, one leading toward making love and the other toward making a life. You might also detect the scent of eros in medicine, education, and psychotherapy, where passion for the work is essential. In these areas it's easy to confuse Aphrodite with Eros, sex with a more general passion. In therapy dealing with a person who is troubled by unwanted and inappropriate sexual desire—a rather common problem—I direct the conversation outward toward desire, pleasure, and longing in life. I'm not trying to diffuse the passion but rather to see whether the desire points toward a wakening in some other area of life, whether in this case sex symbolizes new life rather than embodies it.

Even in today's complicated life eros is a gigantic egg—as Greek religion pictured it—in your development: Life may be about to crack open, a new possibility ready to be born. Whether eros appears as a wish for sexual experience or for sexual images, the urge points to an increase in life. As you move toward new vitality, perhaps after being stuck or depressed, sexual dreams may become more frequent and intense, heralding the return of eros.

Biologically, sex may be about the continuance of the race, about making babies. But for the soul, sex is more about the mysteries of intimacy and vitality. The Greeks understood, as shown in their hymns to Eros, that the erotic is not just a personal passion. It's one of the main dynamics and powers of life that makes our relationships, our families, and our world. We demonize it sometimes to protect ourselves from its power.

This broader view of eros and its connection with sexuality takes us into the realm of religion. We're talking now about life and meaning. Eros is central to the spiritual life, because it is unimaginably deep and important. It keeps us moving along in life and prevents the small, provisional structures we've set up from being too rigid and fixed. Eros is the dynamic force that keeps us awake rather than asleep, alive rather than soul dead.

Another client of mine, Rose, is happy to be married and has two children, but she has a passionate interest in the man who lives next door. She wants to be faithful to her husband, but the desire is so strong she feels she can't resist it. She tries to suppress the attraction, but it preoccupies her. She becomes distraught because she doesn't want to harm her marriage. Yet the desire persists. As we discuss the situation over a few weeks, we learn that her desire is not really for further sexual experience but for a new phase in her life—fresh ways of doing things, new possibilities, even a new job. Her marriage had become too narrow for her and while she values it she needs other passions and interests to stimulate her. Some deep part of her wants to come back to life.

Once she paid attention to her broader desire and made some changes, her attraction to the neighbor diminished. She's happy now that she didn't go far in acting on it. She's free to explore her possibilities. Getting involved with another man would have been just one more obstacle to the life in her that wants to be lived.

One way to tell whether your fantasies and longings point to a person or to an expansion of your life is to look for impossible dilemmas and conflicts. If you're happily married and you still find yourself interested in other lovers, you may well consider whether the "third" party is an actual person or a screen image for life in a bigger sense. You might ask yourself whether the new person is going to be another problem or an opening to new life. Whatever the outcome, you can always take the appearance of eros as a signal to open your life to new experiences and ideas.

I'm not suggesting that sexual desire is just a metaphor but that our sexuality lies within and behind various passions and interests that are not explicitly sexual. Many people have something like an orgasm of the spirit when they find out they've been given a new job or position. Some feel about a new city the way they may feel about a new lover. Feelings about coming to life are not just *like* sex, they *are* sexual in a way. Or, let's say they are erotic, remembering that Eros is a maker of worlds closely related to sexuality.

I don't want to give the impression that working out sexual fantasy is easy. You don't just switch from sexual desire to increased vitality without confusion and effort. You may stay focused on a person as the object of your love for a long while, until it breaks open into something larger. Here is another secret of eros: It keeps going deeper. It may begin when you meet an interesting person, which soon generates a passing wish to travel. That may develop into an interest in a particular culture. You find yourself wanting to study the language of the place. Eventually you feel a need to move, and, once there, you take up photography as a new profession. With many desires, you have to be patient and keep tracking them, peeling away layer after layer.

Usually the process of sorting out the desire for a person from the need for a different life involves painful struggle and patience. The pressure to do something may become so strong that it's difficult to take the time to sort things out. But I always counsel patience—watching, waiting, making small moves. Once the process is over, it's much easier to see what was going on. In the thick of passion it's difficult to have a good perspective.

As the classical text says, eros is a path of fire. One desire leads to another, not randomly but moving closer to the heart of the matter, toward the deeper desires of the soul and spirit.

You think you want a person. You get him, and you aren't satisfied. You think you want to be in a particular place. You get there, and you aren't as happy as you thought you'd be. You think you want money. You get it and your hunger is only greater. And so it goes. Desire takes you on and on until you realize that there is nothing in this world that will calm it completely. Then you find deep religion and learn that the ultimate object of desire is God or the divine, the mysterious and unnameable.

You can find this subtle idea suggested in the biblical "Song of Songs":

> *I searched for the one I love in my bed*
> *Deep in the night*
> *But I couldn't find him. (3:1)*

Sometimes, obviously, erotic desire calls for sexual experience and an actual relationship. In fact, finding a lover with whom you can be engaged and passionate may free your erotic tension for larger game. Only then are you free to explore your desires in life. A good sex partner can and should promote the greater role of eros in your life, and ultimately a good lover will lead you to the very source of your life. Sex is not only a metaphor for spiritual eros, it is its vehicle. It can get you started on a journey toward a goal far off in the mist of your own religion.

Eros: The Fast, Full Streaming of Life

Why does religion often rail against sex? Two reasons: First, sex represents the unmitigated and fast flow of life. *Panta rhei*, says Herakleitos—"Everything flows." Life keeps coming at us with its great variety of possibilities. You get married, and yet you still might wish to have sex with or just be with someone else. Although you are faithful to your formal religion, you may come up with a new idea about how to be spiritual and how to live a moral life. Such things don't stand still as you mature. We are in a constant state of evolution. But formal religion tends to think in absolute terms, not allowing for change. Many of us were brought up with the principle "Nothing flows."

In your own new way of being religious you can be positive about eros as the longing for life. You can put the Herakleitos quote in your own personal "bible," preparing for change and even wanting it. In this way you reconcile your sexuality with your spirituality, a major component of a new, humane, liberated, and visionary way of being religious. Sex not only inspires joy in life but it also shows how unrelenting and full the flow of life can be.

Men and women complain that life never stops making demands on them. They're new on a job, and already they're thinking about the next one. They've only been married for a year, and already they're tempted to try it with someone else. There he is, Eros at work, keeping life in motion. We all want to feel alive and yet the pressures of daily life can feel like a chore or a grind, stifling us. Obviously, we have to know his ways so that we can handle the pressure of his abundance and tempo. If you acted on all his promptings, you'd go crazy. But how do you deal with his extravagance, his overreaching, without suppressing it?

You could start by not personalizing this erotic force and recognize that it is an aspect of life, not your personality or your partner's. Faced with a challenge, we are quick to blame the other person, because that's the easiest way to avoid being alive. "I want everything to be as it has always been," you might say to a spouse who is trying to work out some new project. This is an antierotic statement. Your partner probably doesn't want the challenge any more than you do. But how do you say no to life and still feel alive?

Triangles in Service of Life

Eros is often an issue in marriage, understandably, since marriage is set up to be stable and predictable. It shouldn't be a surprise that soon after people get married some new thing comes along threatening the status quo. Hillman and Pedraza talk about a triangle as a dynamic force that would be both challenging and life-giving. The triangle might be the typical pattern of a married couple challenged by a third person who may be a lover, a friend, or even a business associate. The third intruding factor might not be a person but a job, a hobby, or an intellectual interest. I've known a few married couples dealing with a new religious or spiritual fascination that captured one of the people.

Hillman's comments on marriage may sound extreme. He says that the fantasies married people have at the beginning, fantasies of togetherness symbolized by an unbroken ring, are delusional and defensive. They keep eros out. They're rooted in anxiety about the stability of the marriage being threatened. Such an arrangement can't hold, because life wants to break in on that deathly demand for absolute stability.

Hillman offers a rule of thumb: "The more we rigidly insist upon unity the more will diversity constellate."[44] He was always in favor of diversity, or psychological polytheism, making it one

---

44 James Hillman, "Schism," in *Loose Ends* (Dallas: Spring Publications, 1975), p.89.

of the foundational planks in his archetypal psychology. For myself, whenever I hear someone insisting on unity, in whatever context, I worry about the suppression of the soul, which is many-sided and full of the richness and the tension of multiple urges.

So the third factor, whatever it is—desire for another person, a new job, interest in another country, a new art—will probably disturb the status quo, the comfortable feeling that everything is settled and in place, but will allow life to go on.[45] For me this insight about the delusion of unity and the necessity of a triangle has been a breakthrough idea. I can't imagine my work in theory or therapy without it. Hillman is suggesting that our need to hold our lives together and insist on being settled and fixed is not just a mistake but an emotional protection against life's dynamism, a disturbance of mind and heart. He implies that when something new comes along, the effect might be deeply unsettling, precisely because of our strong need for stability.

You see this pattern in ordinary relationships, such as a young couple I know who have been together for only a short time but long enough to develop a sense of unity in their relationship, as they foresee a long life together and make plans for it. They have little on which to base their fantasies, and so, when the woman suddenly wakes up to what is happening to her and suggests slowing down and perhaps separating, at least for a while, the man begins to have suicide wishes or dives into other sexual relationships. The emotional response to separation may be as desperate as the former insistence on unity.

A similar pattern may arise in a person's religious life. You grow up in a family, as I did, in which a certain religious understanding and practice is taken for granted. Then you go to college

---

45 David L. Miller, *Three Faces of God* (Philadelphia: Fortress Press, 1986). This book places the ideas of the triangle and the "third" in a much more extensive context and beautifully summarizes the thoughts of Jung, Pedraza, and Hillman on it.

and discover a bigger world. You come home with your new ideas, and your family worries about you. In their anxiety, their delusion of unity or assumption that there is only one way to be religious, they find it difficult emotionally to embrace their wayward child.

This struggle over being settled and waking up to life deserves consideration in your own religion, because one of the weaknesses of formal religion, as many have known it, is a sentimental enthronement of the idea of unity and tradition, standing for the status quo. These apparently noble thoughts serve to defend against the erotic, against the very principle of life and vitality. It would be worth your effort to study Jung, Hillman, Pedraza, and David Miller on this theme, even if it is complex and challenging.

Let me try to clarify these ideas, since they go against common sense. Ask yourself why you make so much of stability, faithfulness, and even the very length of a marriage. I'm not saying that these things are not valuable, but why feel so strongly about them? Do we overstate the value of these qualities, and if so, doesn't that imply anxiety? Perhaps we are hypnotizing ourselves into believing in them so that we don't have to face the very different claims of eros. Eros and his mother, Aphrodite, are quite interested in passion and desire, but they have no regard for the sanctity and longevity of a relationship.

There is something in the nature of things that makes us want a ton of life, ceaseless and unfettered, and something else that likes moderation and the status quo. Why, when people are so committed to their marriages, does erotic desire continue to appear? In therapy I've seen it countless times, and it's the very stuff of fiction and drama. The Greek images give an answer, one that inspires Hillman to speak favorably about triangles.

The secret is not to be too literal about a new passion. Don't get into a place where you ask yourself: Should I or should I not act on my desire? A triangle is an opportunity for a new vision about life and not necessarily about a new relationship or love interest. When faced with a tempting opportunity to try another marriage or another sexual partner, the question need not be which should I choose, but what is life asking from me now?

Asking the bigger question—What does the soul want now?—allows us to stay alive and awake within a stable relationship, affirming both marital vows and erotic fantasies. The triangle should help the marriage, in the end, if it is not taken literally but seen as an invitation to be more vital. I understand why Hillman sees the insistence on stability as delusional, but at the same time I might soften his critique of marital bliss and suggest doing two things at once: aiming for intimacy in the relationship while acknowledging the important demands of erotic fantasy.

It might also help to think more seriously about eros as part of your spiritual life. Being conservative and dogmatic may mean sustaining your defensive delusional thought that resisting life is a good thing. You could instead be conservative in a loving way and still open to new ideas and new forms of vitality. It shouldn't be too difficult to sense the defensiveness in your objection to new ideas and new forms. These are signs of your delusion. Now, do you have the courage to face your delusions and be alive?

The Sacrament of Sexuality

As a Catholic, I was taught that marriage is a sacrament, a sacred institution, something immeasurably deep and valuable. I recommend this teaching to everyone, something to borrow from Catholics, because today we tend to understand marriage as a mere psychological situation or as a living arrangement, a way to create a family unit.

Church and temple weddings are full of strong symbolism expressing the mysteriousness and spiritual depth of marriage. That depth can help a couple be loyal to the marriage and not just to another person or a legal promise. In this way marriage is spiritual, or in the way I'm defining the word, religious, as well. It's interesting that when people abandon formal religion, they often go back to it for weddings and funerals, two of life's mysteries that demand religion. It's also telling that at a time when ritual is being streamlined and turned into education, weddings and funerals are still loaded with symbolism and drama.

If there is emotional depth and a spiritual vision in a marriage, it should be able to hold the erotic comings and goings bound to arise in two lives. The marriage can provide stability and depth as eros blows in yet another opportunity for more vitality. All aspects of marriage, but especially marital sex, can carry on this important soul work. For some, it may help to include experiment and exploration, qualities that are natural to eros. If you're not adventurous in marriage, you may find adventure outside of marriage.

I'm not speaking only of allowing fantasy a place in physical sex but in the erotic life of the marriage in a bigger sense. You may travel together, become engaged in each other's work, meet friends of each other, exchange ideas, look at art and film and discuss them. Pleasure, vitality, and new life keep eros alive in each partner and in the marriage. Of course, this broader erotic movement will make marital sex that much more satisfying, as well.

Today we have a tendency to be psychological rather than spiritual in our efforts to revive a marriage. We "work on" commitment and communication. But it might be better to take a spiritual approach and allow eros, which traditionally is one kind of spirit, more of a place throughout the marriage.

If you could appreciate that marriage is a sacrament, then you might see how it can deepen your sexual satisfaction. The sacrament lies far down in the soul, and as you engage in marital sex, year after year you are moving into profoundly mysterious realms. Your sex is taking you into the glorious underworld of your relationship. The process works both ways: The spirituality of marriage deepens the sex, and deepening sex brings out the spirituality of marriage.

Jung's contribution to marriage was to show how the alchemical *hieros gamos*, the sacred marriage, marriage in its broadest sense, plays out in an actual human marriage. When we marry, our family histories join together, our destinies, our deep and lost emotions, our past relationships—all eager for a happy resolution. Even more mystical elements unite: the continuation of the human race, the desire for peaceful connections between people, and the reconciliation of all opposites. A wedding ceremony is not just about two people coming together but about all differences finding a solution.

Since eros serves life and vitality, it often has a role in divorce. A partner may become interested in another party or in a different way of life. He may feel stuck in a stale and stagnant relationship, and she may feel too closed in and held back. Eros comes along, and the partners think about ending the marriage.

Some people take an ego approach and worry about being failures. Others see eros as a spirit that begins things but doesn't end them. In therapy, I often feel that ego worries stand in the way of a spiritual vision about what is going on. Maybe life does have to go forward. Maybe the marriage has exhausted its potential. Maybe the partners have changed so much that the more limited marriage can't hold it all. In these cases, too, you may have to honor eros and respect the need for an ending.

On the other hand, frequently it might be better to give up all the heroics about commitment and communication and instead focus on the mysterious, sacramental aspects of a marriage, honor movements of eros, and cooperate generously instead of blocking it out of fear. I've encouraged couples to explore each other's needs and desires, regarding them deeply and openly, and determine if the marriage can adjust to them, instead of the other way around.

The Spirituality of Sex

There are ways to make our sex lives more spiritual without piling sentimental ideals and holy language on top of them. Several years ago in *Tango Magazine* I published a list of ten steps toward spiritual sex:

Ethics: Treat your partner honestly, respectfully, and kindly.

Generosity: Give yourself emotionally and physically without undue self-protection or wariness. Push the borders of your privacy and comfort.

Ritual: Sex can have a high element of ritual, making it special and more deeply meaningful—timing, clothing, atmosphere, music, candles, setting; use of language, oils, and fragrance.

Partners: Be more than a body. Be an interesting person, bringing your intelligence, culture, ideas, values, and talents. Be a real person.

Vision: Surround sex with substantive conversation. Engage as an educated person. Go beyond concern for yourself. Connect mind and bed.

Contemplation: Sex can be meditative and calm. It can create an atmosphere that is dreamy and otherworldly.

Beauty: Beauty is part of spiritual practice. It's a means of transcending the ordinary. Appreciate the beauty of your partner and, at least sometimes, make the whole experience beautiful.

Community: Don't just draw in on yourselves. Spread your erotic joy to others. Let your sexual pleasure spill out into community as peace and joy.

Prayer: Monks have always said that work is prayer. So is play, and so is sex. Don't be overly pious, but bring some reverence to sex.

Ecstasy: Sex can be a kind of mysticism, if you allow yourself to be caught up in its spell, trusting your partner so that you can lose yourself in a positive way.

Sex and Spirit Reconciled

First, you need a philosophy of life that honors your sexuality. Think it through. Arrive at a point when you understand that your sexuality is not just biological but is your vitality and source of creative power. It is a positive resource for connecting soul to soul with your partner and in a broader sense with people. It allows you to be fully in this world, sensing it and feeling it as part of yourself. Your sexuality makes you sensitive as well as sensuous, and spiritual as well as physical.

Most of us in the course of our lives may have been in sexual entanglements and done things we're not proud of. Preparing for a religion of your own, you may want to sort through some of those past experiences and recover some innocence, not naïve and childlike, but mature and suitably complex.

Once, after a lecture and in the thick of a crowd, a fashionably dressed, middle-aged woman said to me in a low, hushed tone: "My husband died a year ago. He was a wonderful lover. I miss the sex. But I can't betray him with another man, even though he's gone. I know you can't help me in this situation, but . . ."

I always do my best in these situations, which are common, and attempt an improvised and very brief therapy. "What would he want of you now?" I asked.

She nodded. "I know. He'd want me to go on with my life. I guess I have to free myself."

"Maybe you could love your sexuality a little more. He did," I replied.

Again she nodded.

This woman's problem was a spiritual one that involved her sexuality. She felt a need to be faithful to her dead husband. That's understandable and probably needs to be affirmed. Who knows how long she should go on feeling faithful? The timing is something you have to intuit. At the same time, she wants to resume a sex life. Many times in life we are faced with such dilemmas, which are really multiple claims on us. It's the perfect time to practice psychological polytheism: You remain faithful and at the same time begin opening yourself to a new life. To the Herakleitos quote "Everything flows," I'd like to add another fundamental truth: "You can do several things at once."

Maybe the woman who asked the question is bothered by guilt. In that case, she may have to trust her sexuality and give to it what she can. In some ways hers is an ethical problem: How should I live? Not ethics as a list of dos and don'ts but as a choice about how to adjust to a significant change. Sometimes ethics demands us not to do what's right but what's best.

Trusting your sexuality means knowing that your desires, however inappropriate, have meaning. You may need to reflect on them for a while, turning them over in your mind until a satisfactory solution appears. I felt confident that this woman would find her way toward a decision. Her sexuality was speaking and she was considering it thoughtfully. It might take time, given the mass of feelings stirred up by her husband's death, but eventually she would find her way.

You may not trust your sexuality because of a tendency to denigrate it, judging it to be your lower nature. See it as your higher nature, providing the energy and push to make something extraordinary of your life.

Sex and eros are complicated and often make life complicated, and so our solutions may not be simple. My momentary client at the lecture may need more time before she can take up her sex life with a new person. She is feeling both desire and inhibition. Both need her attention.[46] She may have to mature to the point where she can do two things at once: be loyal to her husband and loyal to her new life. This is a complicated situation requiring a thoughtful, layered solution. But this complexity and dimensionality are basic signs of soul, of living deeply, with a strong sense of values, after long and challenging reflection.

---

46 On this interesting point about working out desire versus inhibition, I recommend James Hillman's essay on the "masturbation inhibition" in *Loose Ends*. I often read it not for the theme of masturbation but on how to deal with inhibitions.

Religion Versus Being Religious

You may automatically think of "religion" as a suppressive, anxious, top-heavy institution that tells you not to enjoy those very things you enjoy the most. Jung called it a "misery institute."

You may need different wording for being religious in a new way: living a life of reverence, contemplation, solid ethics; developing a sense of wonder and awe; or responding creatively to the mysteries. If you're going to use the word "religion" at all, as I do, you have to redefine it for yourself.

You want your own personal religion to be sex-friendly. You want to be thoughtful, moral, and kind. If you added these three qualities alone to your sexual behavior, free of guilt-making rules about who, when, and how many, you would start to heal the breach between your religious self and your sexuality. You can be moral without being excessively hard on yourself and others.

"Moral" doesn't mean "moralistic." Moralism is a defense against morality, its opposite. Morality means acting in ways that are sensitive to the needs of the other and of the world that is in our care. Moralism is the assumption that you know what is the right behavior for everyone and that it can be itemized in a list of right and wrong that everyone should follow. In tone, moralism is usually negative and unyielding and has little room for thoughtfulness and kindness.

The moral person appreciates the complexity of human life and emotion, and factors this into any judgment about what is the best thing to do—not moral relativism, but moral subtlety. People usually become more morally sensitive as they age, while moralistic standards are considered absolute for all times.

I have never met a person who hasn't had some moralism in him. It's convenient and always serves the self or ego. It isn't generous or understanding. In fact, it's usually sadistic and is connected to a deep desire to punish. It's more of that raw material of the psyche in need of refinement. Yet, eventually, with work, it could become morality.

Developing your own religion is an opportunity to come to peace with your sexuality. You can forgive yourself for past mistakes. You can fit your sexual desires in with your other values so they don't dangle and cause problems from the margins. Your sexual behavior can become moral instead of moralistic.

When you become aware of a sexual wish that goes against your vows and values, you can let go of the potential moralism that may have been at work in your youth and instead remember what you believe in personally and what you want in the whole of your life. You can see the wish as a wish, not a need or a demand. We have all kinds of wishes that don't need to be acted out.

You can also take the "temptation" as a cue to get more eros in your life, more pleasure and play, more connection to people and friends. You can allow yourself to be more erotic in other ways than in the direction of the literal temptation. Sex can indeed be dangerous and disrupt a life. In all of this you don't have to demand perfection but do your best. You can be intelligent and use your wits. Sometimes the best solution is to have a bigger imagination about what is going on.

You may find yourself on the edge of desire that could throw your life into turmoil. Even then you can decide not to repress but to allow the desire some play. You can avoid any acting out and yet go through it all without repression. You may feel these moments as trials and not know what the outcome would be. In the end, you may discover that by trusting eros, you don't need a heroic decision to overcome erotic desire. You may end up enjoying the eros, watching it impel life forward without acting on it.

In the face of sexual desire, you may have to allow it without necessarily acting it out. I don't mean that we never act it out, but there are other options, especially useful when acting out would contradict some other need. In the face of some erotic temptation, repression is the worst option. It will backfire and just get you into worse trouble. You can't stand still, because eros is dynamic: According to mythology, he shoots arrows and runs on a path of fire and blows in on the wind. The only alternative may be to advance slowly toward the temptation and carefully watch what develops. In my experience, this tactic often defuses the immediate pressure and allows for more thought and reflection.

A spiritual point of view helps: You sense your dedication to marriage or friendship or values and devote yourself to them, even as you feel a pull toward an enticing sensual experience. You enjoy both tugs at your loyalties and work out an interesting solution that honors both. You take the polytheistic approach. You aim for a degree of complexity that may be somewhat tense but ultimately satisfying.

You might think of eros as the urge toward pleasure and delight, not just superficial satisfactions but a deep sense of fulfillment, as well. I'd include the urge to create as one of the basic gifts of eros. In myth, eros is an originator, and so it is the special joy of creating something original that eros inspires. The obvious arena for this kind of creativity is art, but eros can inspire originality in all areas of life.

This particular kind of creativity—originating, bringing something new to light—goes deep. You may feel a need to be creative and may feel depressed and unsettled when circumstances prevent you from creating. Eros can give you the sense that you are alive and vital and that life is worth living.

As I read various sacred texts from the world's religions, I feel an erotic charge in them, even when there is no obvious sexuality. For example, both the Buddha, as the awakened one, and Jesus are celibate figures and yet I would never say they are not erotic. They seem charged with an extraordinary vitality and are intimately engaged with the world and with people. Their creativity has to do with life itself—how to understand it and how best to live it.

We could emulate this deep form of spiritual eros in our own lives by being similarly engaged and in love with life. We could be creative, as we consider our own individuality and our opportunity to embody a unique way of living out our human potential.

An Erotic Lifestyle

One way I try to honor Eros so he won't clobber me with impossible temptations is to give my life and environment an erotic tint. I enjoy thoughtful and artful erotic films, photography, painting, sculpture, and dance.

In my writing studio I have several stylized erotic paintings by my wife. In turn, I have given her some of my erotic writing, written for her and not for the public.

I speak for organizations strongly criticized for their erotic direction. Readers sometimes write me complaining about my association with these groups, but I assume they just don't understand the subtleties involved. I write endorsements for highly erotic books that I feel deserve attention, and again I am criticized for it. All I can do is shrug. A world divided between desire and repression doesn't understand the place of the erotic. It seems my critics would like me to join them in dealing with eros by avoiding it.

When I recommend creating a religion of your own and including a positive, spiritual appreciation of eros, I am only advocating what I have worked out for myself. I was born an erotic person, in the sign of the goddess of sexuality, Libra, with Venus at my midheaven. I feel that by nature I'm ordained to speak in favor of the erotic.

Let's try another list, this time ways in which you can invite eros into your life thoughtfully without either suppressing it or acting it out:

1. Say yes to new experiences.

2. Be more sensual than abstract, especially if your work involves numbers and machines.

3. Wear clothes more colorful and sensual to the touch than usual.

4. Watch some erotic movies that have some beauty and meaning.

5. Learn to cook a few gourmet meals.

6. Reveal more of your sexuality.

7. Follow the Epicurean rule: In midst of pain or hard work, find a way to have a little pleasure.

8. Touch and caress people when comfortable and appropriate.

9. Appreciate and enjoy the power of your sexuality.

10. Whenever possible, blend play and work.

I can imagine writing my own ten erotic commandments. Jesus did this, funneling the ten old ones down into the one commandment of love, agape. But Jesus's followers don't seem to trust him on this point and generally elect to go the old way, with stern, negative commandments. The Greek dictionary gives these meanings for "agape": "desire," "delight," "affection," "love of God," and "the love of husband and wife." The word is used often in the Gospels and usually translated as "love," as in "love your neighbor." Agape is certainly a close cousin of eros. Jung recommended adding Dionysian joy to any religion that has become sour, and my suggestion is to return to the Orphic Eros, the creative source of light and love. If your own religion lacks eros, it is also in need of soul.

Chapter 6

✿

SPIRITUAL SECULARITY

I find that I conciliate the gods by some sacrament as
bathing, or abstemiousness in diet, or rising early, and
directly they smile on me. These are my sacraments.

—HENRY DAVID THOREAU[47]

W hen I am walking the streets in a big city like New
York, London, or Dublin, I like to step through the
massive doors of a church and sink into the darkness and smells
of candles and incense, leaving behind the harsh light and cutting
sounds of the outside world. The sensation of moving inward
into a quiet darkness is calming and refreshing. Before I can have
a thought of what to do, my attention is already captured and
sent into a reverie that is the preamble to prayer. Already I'm
meditating as I find my way in the holy fog of altars and pews
and stained glass.

The soul needs regular excursions from reality, and a good
religious building can offer you such an excursion. For this

---

47 Thoreau, *I to Myself*, p. 40.

reason alone, it would be a danger to society to lose these important places, and the typical modern unadorned public meditation room won't do.

But as necessary and beautiful as churches and other religious buildings may be, they have a negative side: They may put up a boundary between sacred and secular. Once inside the church, you may judge the outside world as less valuable or less worthy and may feel a competition between the holy and the profane, a split that has not done religion or the spiritual life much good.

In your own religion you can heal the split between sacred and secular, your spiritual vision and your daily life. This doesn't mean that you hold back in either area. You can be as religious as you like or as secular as you like, as long as you keep the two together as a tandem. You can glimpse the sacred in the secular, or enjoy worldly life more because of your spiritual vision.

Thoreau says that taking a bath is a sacrament. I could say the same about going for a walk, teaching your child, or painting your house. These activities seem to be only secular, simply because we haven't considered how the holy and the ordinary work together. But if you study and meditate just a little, you may learn to appreciate ordinary activities for their sacredness, their sacramentality.

As a child I memorized a short and elegant definition of a sacrament: "an outward sign signifying an inward grace." That is, a sacrament is an ordinary thing or activity that, to a properly educated imagination, signifies or points to a deeper spiritual meaning and power. The priest sprinkles holy water on your head and calls it baptism. Thoreau takes a bath and says that for him it's a spiritual action. As priests and theologians of our own religion, we can take almost any aspect of ordinary life and see its sacramentality, for everything can have an inward grace.

Which is what the Greeks were getting at by seeing gods, goddesses, and spirits of all kinds in every aspect of life. The philosopher Thales said, "The world is full of gods." These figures, far from being absurd or fanciful, help us see the holiness in anything. You can find Demeter, goddess of grain, in a supermarket, and Hermes, god of crossroads, on Wall Street.

But the sacramentality in an action doesn't appear automatically. If you're unconscious and have no religion of your own, these actions will remain only secular. The religious imagination and a certain style of behavior make all the difference. Read Thoreau's *Walden*, and you will find many lessons on how to make the most ordinary actions sacred. For example, he warns against overdoing luxury, a typical spiritual admonition: "Let our houses first be lined with beauty, where they come in contact with our lives, like the tenement of the shellfish, and not overlaid with it."[48]

It's curious that we have many vast and complex religious institutions and haven't been able to sacramentalize ordinary life, while the Greeks said that the world is full of gods and yet didn't even have a word for religion. The point is that we need to see religion in everything and not removed from ordinary life. Maybe we shouldn't have a word for religion.

As I play my piano, I bring to it everything I learned about meditation from thirteen years of spiritual training. As a meditator I pull open the lid and place my fingers on the keys. Bach, Mozart, and Chopin are my gurus and my saints. An hour of playing is my *puja*, my devotion, and my practice. This gives the notion of *practicing* the piano a new level of meaning, as in "spiritual practice." But just playing the piano without the imagination of holiness or a greater context, is probably not a spiritual act. Intention and style convert the commonplace into the spiritual.

I use two different words for worldliness: "secularity" and "secularism." Secularity is the full embrace of this world with all

---

48 Jeffrey S. Cramer, ed., *Walden* (New Haven: Yale University Press, 2004), p. 39.

its allurements, pleasures, and fascinations, as well as its troubles and tragedies and imperfections. Secularism, like any "-ism," is an ideology that wants to be free of religious and even spiritual influence. Secularism tends to be the enemy of religion. It sees religion as superstitious, naïve, and fearful. Secularity, on the other hand, is friendly with a religious point of view.

Both religion and secularism have enjoyed their extreme positions for centuries. It's always pleasing to have an enemy to spar with, especially a cardboard cutout version. Religious people condemn the secular life as a vast temptation against spiritual purity, even if they enjoy secular living on weekdays. Secularists despise religion, but they tend to argue against some patently foolish expression of it.

Your challenge, then, is to create a religion of your own by being secular in a religious way, or religious in a secular way. You can learn how to see the secular from a religious angle, and vice versa.

My dog, fully in possession of the Buddha nature, has some lessons for me about the sacred in the secular.[49] He wants to go out twice a day, and I live in New Hampshire, where the winters are usually snowy and bitterly cold. I walk out on a clear, dark night. My dog shoves his snout deep into the snow, apparently catching the scent of a deer or a neighboring dog. I look up and see Orion brilliant against the dark blue-black of the sky. Coming out on a cold night I'm well aware of my earthly existence and yet I'm pulled out of myself into wonder, once again, at the brilliant stars. Who am I in this tremendous context, and what is my fate and what do I mean in the huge expanse of galaxies and multiple universes? My mind can't hold the vast openness and complexity, and I can't twist my imagination to fit myself into such a place. And yet, here I am with my dog, waiting

---

49 The classic Zen koan from *Gateless Gate:* Does a dog have the Buddha nature?

for him to do his business in the snow that mirrors the Milky Way, one of the great mysteries of my existence. Orion's two dogs, Major and Minor, are up there, too, probably taking similar advantage of the milky-white galaxy.

If you want to be fully religious, you must tap into as many of the mysteries around you as possible, and you shouldn't neglect the night sky. Religions have always taken it into account. You shouldn't overlook animals as embodiments and personifications of the mysteries. From the Lamb of God to the Egyptian Anubis, they have always been part of religion. You should know that food is a way to the divine, for many religions have communed with the divine through ritual eating. All eating can be graced with a little ritual.

The secular and the spiritual are two sides of a coin. There is no separation between them. If you want to be spiritual, you have to live fully in this world—and vice versa. If you want to be spiritual, you have to live completely in this world of the senses and your ego. You can't be an earthy, sensual, fun-loving person if you don't make peace with the deeper, spiritual questions of humankind. Not only do you have a spiritual practice; that spirit has a direct impact on all aspects of your life. It's implicated, woven throughout, an important part of who you are.

As you go deeper into everyday life, learning the importance of nature and images, you will find your way to many kinds of mystical experiences in ordinary life, such as my walk at night under the stars. Only then will you be prepared to reflect mean-ingfully on the whole of your life and your understanding of what happens after it. Most traditionally religious people start at the wrong end. They begin by addressing the afterlife and miss out on the sacred and the eternal right in front of them. They fail to understand that to have a meaningful idea about the afterlife, you must first appreciate the eternal aspects of this life.

Art is a good place to taste the eternal, especially if it's present with suitable mystery and sanctity. One year our family visited

Siena and walked the enchanted hallways of Santa Maria della Scala museum, some passages having the feel of catacombs and all filled with wondrous art and numinous objects. At home, we get a similar sensation in the Isabella Stewart Gardner Museum in Boston, where art is not alphabetized and historicized into neat categories, but surprises you in lush settings and in nooks and corners. In these two "museums," "museyrooms," as James Joyce said, you are always in a liminal place, between normal life and absolute enchantment.

In the realm of art in general, the sacred and the secular inhabit a passageway where the two overlap, sometimes giving you the dizzy feeling of being in two worlds. This two-worlds-in-one sensation helps heal the gap between religion and secularism.

You might try this lesson in your home and at the workplace: Put the sacred and the profane together in unexpected ways. Place a Ganesha in a place of prominence where people would least expect to find a spiritual figure. Put a beautiful photograph from nature in a chapel or meditation room. Play some spiritual music at work or set up a shrine. Borrow. We have a lovely handmade wood spirit house from Thailand on our summer porch and several Buddhas, a large happy Ganesha, and a Saint Francis. I'd like to see an image of Jesus in a zendo. He belongs.

I never complain about a Christmas crèche in a secular setting. To complain about this is to support a split between the holy and the profane and to worry unnecessarily about the cultural weight of a religious tradition. Of course, those who want to restore Christendom and who fight against secularity have a lot to learn about religion, and they are a threat. But the proper response to them is not to advocate secularism but to express appreciation for the traditions, plural.

Confuse the sacred and the secular in your environment. Create a liminal, neither here nor there, milieu. It is always in the liminal places that significant things happen, so work at creating liminality. Shock yourself and others by refusing to separate the holy and the profane. See the danger in such a separation and avoid it in every instance. This could be a rule in your own religion.

Once you grasp the sacred in the secular, you can, if you wish, go back to traditional religion with an entirely different point of view. Then you will see how the traditional teachings and rituals lead you into the mystical and sacred dimensions of your life. They will have more meaning, not less, although their meaning will have changed because of your maturing spirituality.

The Alchemy of Spirit

Because Jung blended ancient and modern ideas and spoke to both the spirit and the soul, his work is rich and penetrating. It's also complicated and esoteric. When he discovered alchemy, he thought he had found a language for the psyche and the spirit combined. His work became even more a mixture of psychology and spirituality. For him, not only is there the work of making a soulful personality and culture, there is also a work of spiritual development, and the two often overlap. We become more interesting people as we mature spiritually, and we find much of our spiritual resources in what usually appears to be the secular world.

We've already seen that becoming a soulful person entails a process of self-discovery. It may take a long while, and it may involve experiences that are both happy and sad, light and dark, positive and negative. The same is true for the spirit. People often think of spirituality as fixed and settled once and for all. But the spiritual life, too, is light and dark, happy and sad. It requires a special kind of work that bridges external and internal life. It consists of stages in maturing. It's a labor of the heart and mind that at its best gives ordinary life a spiritual glow and spirituality the grounding in mundane experience that makes it real. It may take a lifetime to get the spiritual and eternal thoroughly mixed in with the earthly and temporal. It's not always easy to see the gods in the everyday, or the spiritual in the mundane. You have to train yourself to look with a special kind of imagination, the kind developed in spiritual and religious practice. In a remarkable poem, Rilke says:

> *Gods! Gods! You used to come all the time*
> *and now you sleep in the things around us.*[50]

Like so many good poets, Rilke inspires a sense of divinity that is real but not limited to belief. In our modern world, where both science and religion tend to be too literal, these gods, this appreciation for the divine, have gone to sleep. We don't feel their presence, and so we live in an inanimate world, a world without gods and therefore without a soul.

Some think of the gods and goddesses as metaphors or images in place of psychological categories. That is like thinking of your mother as a metaphor. Certainly mothers have an imagistic and emotional place in the psyche, but they are more than metaphor.

Look around your house. Are the gods sleeping there? Or are they stirring? Imagine if they were alive and awake in the kitchen, the living room, and the bathroom. There would be no essential difference between church and home. And, where the gods are awake, the soul, too, is fully present and offering its gift of deep human connection and creativity.

Don't hesitate to place a good Buddha in the bathroom, or better, a beautiful Venus—the bathroom is her realm. Build a little shrine and light some incense in your office or store. How many office buildings in our secular cities would benefit from some incense and Virgin Marys and Buddhas. Restore deep secularity by getting rid of the anxious, antireligious secularist aesthetic.

---

50 Thomas Moore's translation: "It's time for the gods to come out."

Thoreau lives in the concrete world, but at the same time is always in a time warp of myth, and this crossover, this liminality dependent on his imagination, accounts for the sacredness of his life, his intense religiousness. If living in such a dual realm—the phrase is Rilke's—seems somewhat insane, then this is the religious mania Plato wrote about. It's all right. In fact, it's good and necessary. Without it we are condemned to a flat, one-dimensional, secular-only existence.

In a now-famous statement, Joseph Campbell observed, "The latest incarnation of Oedipus, the continued romance of Beauty and the Beast, stand this afternoon on the corner of Forty-Second Street and Fifth Avenue, waiting for the traffic light to change."[51]

If you are saturated with myth and religion, you will notice Oedipus in a group of people, perhaps a young man admiring a woman who could be his mother. You might see a young woman lovingly arm in arm with a brutish man and wonder what story is being played out—*Beauty and the Beast*? Greek tragedies sometimes ask the important question, when someone is driven mad with some mania like jealousy or unrequited desire: Which god or goddess has been offended here? Which one is responsible for this unfortunate ruining of a life? Hillman says, "A complex must be laid at the proper altar, because it makes a difference both to our suffering and perhaps to the God who is there manifesting. . . ."[52]

Thoreau, Campbell, and Euripides ask the same question for the same reason: What myth is playing out now in life? What sacred, spiritual drama is in play in what appears to be secular life?

---

51 Campbell, *The Hero with a Thousand Faces*, p. 4.

52 James Hillman, *Re-Visioning Psychology* (New York: HarperCollins, 1975), p. 104.

One more example: D. H. Lawrence wrote poem after poem in the tradition of searching ordinary life scenes for their deeper myth. Here's one that draws on the ancient Egyptian mystery of Isis:

> *When I was waiting and not thinking, sitting at a table on*
> *the hotel terrace*
> *I saw suddenly coming towards me, lit up and uplifted with*
> *pleasure*
> *advancing with the slow-swiftness of a ship backing her white*
> *sails into port*
> *the woman who looks for me in the world*
> *and for the moment she was Isis, gleaming, having found her*
> *Osiris.*

In Egyptian myth Isis went looking for the pieces of her beloved and dismembered Osiris. Most of us would like to have an Isis track us down and help put our lives together. She might also be the spirit of kindness and nurturance that might also find us one day and help us be less scattered and more self-possessed. Think about this myth in your life. Has anyone helped you put yourself together after some wrenching misfortune?

Some would read these passages and think of myth as a mere literary allusion: How nice to find mythology in an everyday setting. But when you read more extensively in Lawrence, Jung, Rilke, and Thoreau, you see that they have a special eye that catches a glimpse of the sacred and the spiritual within daily life. They are serious about their theological eyesight by which the eternal appears through the language of myth. Knowing an appropriate myth, they can see through the ordinary to the sacred. They are not playing with literary images; they are discovering the depths of their souls.

The Sacred in the Most Ordinary

Two businessmen in our small town want to convert a classic old and neglected building into a small hotel. They see it as a business opportunity, but they are also committed to keeping the town free of large chain companies and making the place attractive to visitors. As a former monk I see it as practicing the vow of hospitality. It could be a spiritual activity and part of the town's own religion. Following the rule that human beings can do several things at once, you can look to make a profit and make a religious contribution at the same time.

If these two men only consider the possibility of financial profit, they will be neglecting the spiritual aspect of their enterprise and, if they succeed, they won't have the deep rewards religion offers. If they see their project only as a secular endeavor, it won't have the depth it could have. If they keep their focus on the town, on guests, and on important values, they will be enacting their personal religion. I suspect that they will be able to do both: make a profit and act like monks.

To avoid the secularism of the enterprise the businessmen will have to keep a clear focus on the value of hospitality and the vitality of the town. These are spiritual values and have a place within their own religion and the broader religious life of the town. In their design and building they can remember that one of their chief goals is to create the spirit of congeniality and hospitality. If they do this, I suspect that the town will prosper, because human endeavors that split off from sacred values don't have the depth of vision and values needed for long-term sustainability.

Here we arrive at yet another principle in the new religion: It's the spiritual and the sacred that give us health. The secular-only tends to make us sick emotionally and therefore physically. This is true of a community as well as an individual person. Secularism doesn't take the soul or the sacred into consideration, and this fact alone can affect our well-being negatively.

The health of our town needs a striking act of hospitality. If this hotel ever appears, it will be due to the natural religion of the two men and the love of the town. People often toss off the sentiment that God is love, but if that bit of theology were taken seriously, we'd understand that our religion operates on the principle of love. Hospitality is a form of love and is therefore a theological virtue.

By the way, I won't go up to these visionary men and tell them they're being good monks. They're just doing what their heart-inspired spirituality is telling them to do. I'm the theologian. I go around looking for the sacred in the secular in order to teach it and sustain it. It's my job and the work of poets to have the eyesight that grasps the sacred when it appears in the secular.

The Sacred Is Sometimes Deep

The sacred often lies hidden within the fabric of the secular, and it may take an alert and educated eye to see it. Often it helps to make a comparison between a familiar secular experience and a corresponding one that is traditionally within the realm of formal religion. The religion scholar Mircea Eliade, who headed the religious studies program at the University of Chicago for many years, was particularly good at making these comparisons.

In a journal entry of 1973 Eliade reflects on the Japanese tea ceremony and quotes an ancient instruction:

> *The essence of the Tea Ceremony*
> *Simply consists of boiling the water*
> *Preparing the Tea*
> *And drinking it.*
> *Nothing else!*
> *This must be understood well.*

What must be understood well? Eliade says that the most natural and insignificant gestures become soterial, saving—I would say, full of soul and spirit. Then Eliade summarizes: "In this way, humans belong to several universes—the cosmic, the aesthetic, the religious—without rupture and without contradiction."[53] This is my point exactly: We live in several universes simultaneously, including one that is secular and another sacred. If your imagination could reach the point where those words of Eliade make perfect sense, you are ready to become a theologian for our time. His phrase "without rupture" is the key.

For me, though, the significant words in the tea instructions are "Nothing else." For a thing or an act to be spiritual, it doesn't need a cover of spiritually bloated words. You don't call it the sacred tea ceremony. You don't say a group of prescribed prayers before and after it. Let its sacredness speak for itself.

It's the same when you take a bath. Have the intention. Make it sensual, pleasurable, and relaxing. Nothing else! When you go for a walk, walk. Don't practice a form of meditation you're learning. When you drink coffee, drink coffee. Nothing else! Your imagination and preparation will make the experience spiritual and soulful.

Another passionate observer with a firm religion of his own, psychiatrist R. D. Laing, urged us to see the holy in moments of insanity. "True sanity entails in one way or another the dissolution of the normal ego, that false self competently adjusted to our alienated social reality: the emergence of the 'inner' archetypal mediators of divine power, and through this death a rebirth, and the eventual re-establishment of a new kind of ego-functioning, the ego now being the servant of the divine, no longer its betrayer."[54]

Laing is saying that in our normal lives, when our ego is

---

53 Mircea Eliade, *Journal III: 1970–1978*, trans. Teresa Lavender Fagan (Chicago: Chicago University Press, 1981), p. 134.

54 R. D. Laing, *The Politics of Experience* (New York: Pantheon Books, 1967), pp. 144–45.

strong, we may be betraying the divine. We become too secular, too much in control. We don't appreciate another will, destiny, and fate. We fabricate a secular mentality that refuses to acknowledge anything like divinity in ordinary events, and so, as Laing was famous for saying, breakdown becomes breakthrough. The ego structures fall part and divinity once more comes into view.

A whole book could be written about the ego as "servant of the divine" and about dissolving the normal ego, and it would be consonant with this one. For there is a psychological aspect to a religion of one's own. It has to do, as Laing says, with breaking out of a narrow sense of self or the self as a closed room. You don't need to know what is outside the room of your world, but you do need an open door.

Imagine that you felt, as so many spiritual writers have described, that at the core of your heart there is a source or force that is somehow divine and that your ego or sense of "I" is an instrument for this divinity. You would sense your worth and work hard to obey rather than control your destiny. Within yourself, psychologically and personally, you would have a complex and rich religion.

When Plato described religion as a positive form of mania, he, too, was suggesting the value of breaking out of the normal ego. That means finding some distance from normality. You have to be in a state described by Emerson and some Sufi poetry as "inebriated." This is an unusual state of mind, but a creative one. The Greeks would define it as being possessed by the intoxicating god of wine Dionysus.

Norman O. Brown, like Laing influenced by Freud and yet sensitive to religion in a deep way, explores this idea in a book I wish I had written, *Love's Body*. It has been my companion for many decades. I never tire of reading it, especially the chapter entitled "Resurrection," which sees symbol and metaphor as the means of detecting the sacred in the secular. "The symbolical interpretation of the old makes it new; this is the flowering of the rod, Aaron's rod that budded; the bitter waters of Marah made sweet. . . . Life is Phoenix-like, always being born again out of its own death. The true nature of life is resurrection; all life is life after death, a second life, reincarnation."[55]

The core teachings of Jesus focus on this kind of resurrection, the revelation of a hidden, rich possibility in human life. They are mainly about taking life to a new level, making the crucial shift from plain, unconscious living to an awareness of the depth and vast reach of things, especially living from love rather than unresolved bitterness. Brown refers to this shift as resurrection, Aaron's staff growing flowers, the Phoenix rising, water becoming sweet (in the Gospels water becomes wine, yet another natural image for resurrection). Zen masters describe the awakening known as satori in similar terms.

Purely secular life is dead because it has an eye only for the physical and for physical interactions. Life becomes stuck in literalism. Reflection, especially in the form of meditation, art, and writing, wakes us up. To be attuned to the mysteries at work in our lives is to behold the spirit or the sacred in our otherwise secular experiences. And that perception of the sacred transforms life, raises it to a new level. It makes us alive rather than dead and causes the world itself to resurrect.

The theology of resurrection that we find in several religious traditions is about your resurrection, now, in this life. Will you remain soul dead? Or will you wake up with a spiritual imagination, an appreciation for the sublime? The resurrected person has an open heart and a perceptive mind. When he was soul dead, he was not capable of compassion. Now that he has resurrected, his heart is awake and at work. When he was soul dead,

---

55 Norman O. Brown, *Love's Body* (Berkeley: University of California Press, 1966), pp. 205–206.

he took everything at face value. Now he sees through the literal, enjoying the precious power of insight that reveals the many levels of meaning in every event, person, and object in his world.

How do you resurrect in your everyday life? You learn to see through the literal all around you to the greater mysteries at work. Say you feel anger at your child for not obeying you. Instead of literally blasting the child for not being "good," you step back and see the bigger drama, the myth, the gods in play. You offer a small sacrifice to the eternal child in the little encounter. You feel the child in yourself: your childhood, your child psyche. You realize that you don't need to be obeyed, you need to love. You sense the egotism in your anger and release it all for the benefit of the child.

Light a candle. Burn some incense. Invoke the god. Give what is due to the great mystery. Don't act like the offended god. You are not a god. You are a parent, whose job is to help the child learn the rules of engagement and find some middle ground between the desire for vitality and the need to conform to family and society. If you are angry, then you have probably identified with the god, a typical but serious blunder. Ego where religion should be.

Many familiar secular activities are more sacred than is apparent. Let me once again use the example of classical music, though you could tell your own story of your favorite musical genre.

The Goldberg Variations of J. S. Bach have always fascinated me. To me they are sublime in the full sense of the word, as spiritually exalted as the Vatican and as penetrating to the soul as a Zen teaching. Glenn Gould is famous for having recorded them twice, with all his amazing dexterity and courageous, inspired interpretation. For my seventieth birthday, my friend the accomplished musician and pianist George Lopez played the Goldbergs at my house for a small group of friends. George's inspired playing made that evening a special moment in my life that I will always remember, not as entertainment but as a sacred event.

Then I came across the remarkable story of Simone Dinnerstein, who, after having some daimon in her wakened upon hearing Glenn Gould's version of the Goldbergs, shifted her piano studies in a different direction and found her own vision for the piece. I thought that Gould would be perfection for me, but Simone's playing had a vitality and lightness that forced me to rethink what I had enshrined.

I read an interview with her in which she said that people listening to her performances were having mystical experiences. As usual, I took the word "mystical" seriously. I thought that her playing and her reflections fit snugly into my plan to write about natural and personal religion, so I asked her if she'd like to meet and talk.

One winter morning she and her husband and young son happened to be passing through my town and came to my house, and while father and son played pool on our full-size table (some would be reminded of the connection in Mozart's life between billiards and musical creativity), Simone and I had a conversation about music and art.

In her quiet and thoughtful way Simone talked about her experience as a performer. She said that she has to listen to the music as she's playing it because it tells her how it should be performed. She likes the audience to share in her experience of listening and conveying what she hears in the music. She finds that people in a concert audience have a spiritual need for the music and no longer want just a relationship with the performer. She herself prefers to attend a concert in which the performer is exploring the music inwardly as well as outwardly, and she has the opportunity to participate.

"When I was recording the Goldberg Variations, it was the first time I disregarded everything but what I heard." "Everything" would be ideas of how the music has always been played or should be played, concern about perfect technique, and no wrong notes. "I don't meditate," she said, "but I imagine that this is what meditation is like: a loss of self."

I told Simone that my experience of her playing was that she discovered something in the music that hasn't been heard before. Using her refined technical abilities, she is able to bring out that hidden, unknown quality that is in the music, and not just her idea. We listeners are eager for the revelation of this fresh world in art and become absorbed in it. My guess is that Simone has a special following of people ready for fresh revelations. When I hear her play, I'm again reminded of Jesus's words: "Split a piece of wood; I am there." *Touch the keys; I am there.* We are fortunate to hear the secret inner world of Bach, which is a sublime spiritual vision, when she plays the Goldbergs in her own way.

"I grew up without any religion," Simone told me at the beginning of our conversation. Yet she and her audiences are aware that there is something about her playing that takes you to a spiritual place. For having been brought up without formal religion, Simone Dinnerstein is able to give people a mystical experience. In my estimation, she is a theologian in the world of music and a teacher of a certain spiritual discipline in which her method requires a piano.

Just as I have no trouble saying that Edgar Mitchell's remarkable view of his home planet and the cosmos as a genuine mystical experience and in a real sense religion, I can easily see that Simone's audiences have a true mystical experience listening to her play. She plays religiously, not in any sentimental or overblown sense. Like a monk, she devotes her life to practicing and then gives herself to the liturgy of performance. "This is hard work," she said to me about her efforts to maintain the technical skills needed to coax the spirituality out of Bach and Schubert. Yes, the opus is truly hard work.

PART FOUR

A Poetic Life

Thoreau got up each morning and walked to the woods as though he had never been where he was going to, so that whatever was there came to him like liquid into an empty glass.

—JOHN CAGE

Chapter 7

❧

ART AS A SPIRITUAL PATH

There can be poets who know life, who know its
problems, and who survive by crossing through the
currents. And who pass through sadness to plenitude.

—PABLO NERUDA

W aking up is the first act. One day something in you stirs
and you wake up from ignorance and sheer unconsciousness. You wake up from neglect of things that matter. You
wake up to a new vision of your world and your place in it. It is
no accident that the Buddha is called the awakened one, and
Jesus frequently charges his students to go out among the people
and wake them up.[56] Some moments of waking are minuscule.
You hardly know they exist when they're happening, and only
later do you realize that your world has changed. You wake up
many times during your lifetime, if you're lucky, and never stop
waking as you make new significant discoveries.

---

56 This is my translation of a phrase that is often translated "raise the dead"
and taken literally. The Greek word used can mean either "raise" or "wake,"
and "dead" can mean "mentally asleep."

If you really want to be religious in a culture that has lost deep religion either in its secular ways or in hollow religious practices, you have to discover the power of the arts. You need more windows onto eternity and can't dispense with the special portals of music, drama, poetry, dance, and all the other modes of image making. In a sacred milieu, art is not an option but is essential.

I've had countless waking experiences through art. One took place in a New York theater when I saw Richard Burton play the role of the psychiatrist in the play *Equus*. The play itself was a shock to me, to see how modern theater could probe so deeply and imaginatively into religious material, but the startle of it happened the moment Burton stepped out on the stage. He didn't have to say a word. His presence there was enough to move anyone with the least appreciation for acting and stage presence.

That single moment of Burton's appearance stays with me and is like a spring of the Muses. I draw on it when it's my turn to be creative in public. It's part of the lore that sustains my personal religion. I make my contribution to the world through words, my art, which is also my ethics. My memory of Richard Burton onstage helps me stay in touch with my sacred powers and intentions.

My awakening to art took many years and many experiences, like many small lights turning on one at a time. Certain paintings, buildings, music, and books have lighted a candle in my imagination and have allowed me to face my destiny. Your awakening to the possibilities of a personal religion might also happen in small increments. Your task is to be alert and responsive.

What Is the Deep Purpose of Art?

Art allows you to play, express, represent, honor, heal, teach, sanctify, encode, and explore ideas. In Western culture art is often conceptual, presenting ideas and values, but it also depicts the mythic or archetypal themes of two thousand years of challenging life. In traditional cultures, art may have a close tie to ritual and the home environment. It gives a sacred glow to utensils and furniture and, in dance, music, and mask making, helps guide a person through life's passages. You can learn from many different traditions how to bring art closer into the circle of your spirituality.

Some traditions surround the making of art with holy rituals. In Japan, age-old traditional rites are part of the actual building of a temple, from the selection of wood to the final decoration. In India, images of the gods and goddesses come into being through a long process of traditional rites and honorifics. In Africa, images are bathed and then laden with food and flowers. In some societies people honor a new work of art with pageantry and celebration.

We launch new art with an "opening" at a gallery, but we put the spotlight on the artist. Our celebration is usually a vestigial ceremony and not an honest-to-goodness ritual honoring the image and welcoming it into our world. We tend to be personalistic—a direction that represents cultural narcissism rather than religion. But genuine religion lies just beneath the surface of our openings and launches. All we would have to do to make them sacred would be to penetrate beneath and beyond the secular and be more explicit about the spiritual elements.

A small example: When my neighbor Katrina Kenison asked me to help her launch her new book in our small town, I was happy to participate. She had written a thoughtful book about home life. In her books she creates a secular environment where she seeks the sacred.

Our local bookseller was present and involved, since he plays an important role in the spirituality of our community—making a place and events for gathering the community, making good books available in a time when bookstores are disappearing, and caring for local authors. In another context, he would be a spiritual minister of some kind.

Katrina had the imagination to make a simple but real ritual by choosing a special wood-paneled room with, for me at least, monastic overtones and creating a felt community for the occasion in her style and attention to details. A book launch can be part of a community's natural religion if it is done with reverence and a sensitivity to ritual. What is ordinarily secular becomes sacred without losing its comfortable secularity.

Art as a House of Spirit

We tend to think of art as the self-expression of the artist or as coded meanings, but Renaissance philosophers and some traditional cultures use art as a form of power. They believe that when images are made well and accurately depict a certain powerful figure, like the goddesss Venus or a tree spirit, the spirit of that figure is captured, housed, and made available. As you contemplate the statue or painting, you receive the spirit associated with the art piece, and that spirit may be healing and nourishing. According to one widely accepted myth, first described by the Arab polymath Al-Kindi, a piece of art can absorb particular rays of the planets and stars and make that spirit, too, available to the beholder.

In India images are often treated as presences, the statue of the god clothed and anointed and carried in procession, even protected from the sun by a parasol. In the making of the image, many rituals mark each stage until, at last, the statue receives its eyes with which it can see its devotees for *darshan*, the ritual and all-important encounter with the divine, where it's important for the worshiper to be "seen" by the deity. In his beautiful book on images in India, religion scholar Richard Davis points out that statues and paintings are translucent: "While [the artwork] had a substantial presence in itself, it also allowed a viewer *in the proper spirit of devotion and knowledge* to glimpse *with a devotional eye* through it . . . to the transcendent reality of the deity."[57]

Let me underscore a few phrases here: "a viewer in the proper spirit of devotion and knowledge" and "with a devotional eye." To include art in your personal religion, you have to abandon the modern way of seeing images as lifeless representations. This is the most superficial approach to art, even if it is still found in our great museums. In India the devotee comes into the presence of a Shiva or Krishna and beholds the deity, in a certain way of speaking. He is prepared to look at a religious image and get more out of it than a purely secular person might. He has a "devotional eye" rather than the eye of an image tourist. He has been taught, in his spiritual upbringing, how to see. Unfortunately, I have never come across a class in a modern religious institution, and certainly not in an art education class, on how to see in a sacred manner.

Look at a painting of the birth of Jesus. You might well feel the spirit of Christmas or the optimism that the birth represents. Look at the Buddha or Quan Yin in repose and feel your body and mind calm down. Art has the power to affect us and for that reason has served the spiritual traditions of the world in all of human memory. But that power is a two-way affair: The observer has to know how to be in the presence of the artwork for it to have its impact.

One year I felt unsettled because I realized that we didn't have an image of Quan Yin in our home. She is the revered bodhisattva, a sort of saint, in China. She is a graceful, healing figure, often pictured with flowing garments and known as "the one who is attentive to the weeping of the world."

Once you establish a serious connection with the world's

---

57 Richard H. Davis, *Lives of Indian Images* (Princeton: Princeton University Press, 1997), p. 23.

spiritual traditions, you may feel a need for certain objects and rituals. I felt her absence and so we found a Quan Yin, delicately handmade from a lightly grained piece of warm wood, original and evocative. Now she is present in our home, with all the healing, calming, graceful, and humanizing powers of this world-revered bodhisattva. I feel more at peace about it now, though I keep looking at much larger images of her because I know how much spiritual power her image can have. Sometimes size is a factor.

As part of informal religious practice, you could bring art pieces into your home and work environment and introduce the sacred where only the secular has had a place. But, like everything else in this natural, homemade religion, the art doesn't have to represent a traditional religious theme, like a Quan Yin or Saint Francis. It might be a photograph of nature or a city or a human face. It could be a painting of deep peace, like the great dark-hued paintings by Mark Rothko in his Houston chapel. It could be an impermanent ice sculpture by Andy Goldsworthy, known for his reverent work with the materials of wild nature. It could even be a disturbing Lucian Freud depiction of human emotional complexity and physical freakishness. Religion shouldn't always be calm and lovely.

The "Dream Thing"

One artist who has attracted a large following and whose work has a sacred quality without explicit religious themes is Georgia O'Keeffe, whom I discussed a bit earlier. When this book was gestating we visited her museum in Santa Fe and her life search crept into my thoughts about a religion of one's own.

In a letter of 1930 she wrote: "Color is one of the great things in the world that makes life worth living to me and as I have come to think of painting it is my effort to create an equivalent with paint color for the world, life as I see it." This sentence is difficult to parse, but clearly O'Keeffe saw color as making life worth living and she made use of its spiritual potential.

O'Keeffe didn't consider herself a religious person. No matter. She was not unconscious. Unusually sensitive to her environment, she had deep values and extreme sensitivity. Her letters indicate that she was extraordinarily ethical: painting openly and honestly, probing to the deep inwardness of things. Her flowers and her skulls take us to immense depths, to the mystery of who we are and to the interplay of life and death.

She said that she took an ordinary point of view and made it something special. In one show of her paintings she felt that the landscapes lacked something important: "I hadn't worked on the landscapes at all after I brought them in from outdoors—so that my memory or dream thing I do that for me comes nearer reality than my objective kind of work—was quite lacking."[58] The "dream thing" she does with her paintings is to make them art and provide them with her vision.

All effective art does the "dream thing" to our objective world, making the artwork live and giving it spiritual power. It's as though she were placing the eyes on her paintings as a final step in the process. There is a difference between a simply informative photograph of a skull and an O'Keeffe painting of one.

Everyone has a "dream thing" to bring to life and work: an active imagination, an openness to inspiration, and the ability to unveil the invisible, spiritual realm to be revealed. Just as Georgia O'Keeffe relied on her worldly spirituality to bring out the eternal in the ordinary, you, too can render the whole of your life and everything in it sacred. In everything you do, you can evoke the holiness of material, sensual life. Many people have the potential but not the awareness to waken their "dream thing," their own sacred imagination, to resurrect themselves and their world.

Mark Rothko spoke positively about "distortion" in art, a

---

58 Cowart, Hamilton, and Greenough, *Georgia O'Keeffe*, p. 206.

word that at its root means "twisting." The artist takes a commonplace theme, a flower in the garden, and gives it a twist, revealing it as meaningful and layered. You look at the painting of a flower. You don't see a flower only. You see beauty, sexuality, and a hint of the sacred. They are the flower's essence and aura. O'Keeffe also "distorts," showing us what we normally see but don't know that we see—a level of vitality and meaning that raises the most simple things to the level of sacrament, simple outward things signifying sacred mysteries.

Instead of distortion, I usually speak of "deliteralization." I mean that the art piece pulls away the curtain of practicality and one-dimensional thinking that is so common in modern life. The distortion forces us to look deeper and not remain in the practical realm. It gives us a hardly perceptible shock, a hardly noticeable pain, but enough to inspire a shift in vision.

A good photographer, like O'Keeffe's husband Stieglitz, shows us an ordinary world teeming with layers. He photographs an ordinary tree, for example, and unveils the mythic tree that hides there. Roots and branches mirror each other. The image keeps flipping upside down, keeping our vision active. We see a beautiful monster of a tree, and then a satisfying composition of lines and proportions appears. You could hang such a photograph in a church or in your own gallery in a side chapel of your religion.

O'Keeffe's art is sacred because of the distance it takes us from our literal world. Isn't that what religion is about: spiriting us out to the transcendent? Twisting our minds out of our habitual pragmatism? But though she presents the sensation of depth, she doesn't obliterate the surfaces. Instead, she enhances them to the point of slight distortion, all that's necessary to get our imagination to work. Ultimately it's the imagination that reveals the sacred within the ordinary.

As you look at an O'Keeffe painting, you may wonder: "Is that a bird or an abstract form? Is that a real flower? Why is that skull so frightening?" Good religious art distorts, too, and in doing so deepens our thought. The famous Isenheim Altarpiece, now at the Unterlinden Museum in the Alsace region of France, may at first appear disturbingly realistic, but then, in the central crucifixion scene, you see the oddly stretched fingers, the extreme slant of Jesus's head, the striking geometric angle of the figures at the base of the cross. The painting is much less realistic, much more "distorted" than we first thought. That distortion accounts, at least in part, for the spiritual power of the painting, giving us a realistic scene and then turning it inside out to show us something much more penetrating.

We need paintings and other art around us that will shatter our comfort with reality as we understand it. Good art moves us along and keeps us from being complacent. At the same time it takes the whole of our lives deeper. Bad art, especially bad spiritual art, takes us nowhere. It holds us to what we already know and presents a perspective that comforts us without offering a challenge—one way of understanding the sentimental in art.

Bad spiritual art is sometimes sweetly realistic or idealized in a way that stirs only the surfaces of emotion and thought. Unlike O'Keeffe's desert objects and the Isenheim crucifixion scene, it doesn't distort the image in ways that reveal deep and challenging truths. You can look at sentimental and superficial art and then walk away. But encounter a piece of art that has depth and suitable complexity, and you walk away changed and are challenged to live differently.

Formal religion is full of twists and distortions that open up higher and deeper realms. The "thees" and "thous" and exalted statements and lists of commandments and noble truths and pillars. These are a special formulation of the world we live in every day, like the positive distortions of art, and yet they suggest an otherworld, something different from what we take as normal and ordinary. The King James version of the Bible doesn't wake us up to fresh nuances in the stories, as a modern translation might, but its strong, archaic style distorts language enough to make it suitable for sacred utterance, for rituals and special occasions. A Koan doesn't give us a satisfying story easy to grasp. Painfully it twists our minds into knots that need to be unraveled to end their torture.

At a deep level, art and religion move along in tandem, supporting each other's purposes. On my regular trips to Ireland, I sometimes visit the *Book of Kells* on display at Trinity College in Dublin. Other illuminated Bible manuscripts are there as well, and you can see in the intricate beauty of the calligraphy and bookmaking how religion honors the word, a text, and even letters as playing a major role in establishing a religious sensibility. You can contemplate the *Book of Kells* and then go home and find a new appreciation for books and reading and incorporate this discovery into your own religion.

The *Book of Kells* came from an organized religion interpreted in a particular culture. The place of books, words, and letters in your life may be part of your own personal religion. Like the Irish, who put their own mark on Christianity, you may adopt certain religious forms in your own way. You may have your own *Book of Kells*, your own special presentation of inspired ideas presented carefully and beautifully as art. In this way art can serve your personal religion.

In the hall outside my writing studio hang two spiritual texts important in my religion, printed on special paper by a hand-operated press: the Heart Sutra and the Emerald Tablet. Hanging nearby is a framed page from a fifteenth-century illuminated manuscript and a large painting of a squared circle by a contemporary Korean artist. All are in the spirit of the *Book of Kells*, giving life to traditional religious language. That they come from diverse spiritualities makes them part of our new religious sensibility.

For your own religious insights you may want to use words as striking as the image of a lion caught in a mass of knots, as on an illuminated page of the Irish Gospels. I use words and phrases that seem right to me, even if they make the reader uncomforable, because I'm trying to somehow put the *Book of Kells* into my writing. But now you should find your own method and style. Oscar Wilde spoke of the importance of style. I want my words to be forceful, beautiful, and individual, and you, too, can find your own method and style for your insights.

For instance, I find special meaning in the Eastern idea of emptiness, and so I sometimes take photographs of empty rooms or open doors and windows. The *Tao Te Ching* compares spiritual emptiness with windows and doors, pointing out their usefulness. My friend Pat sometimes sends me images of headless Buddhas that for him signify the necessity to forget your intellectual understanding of spiritual realities and know from a deeper place. I have a special appreciation for the Christian story of Annunciation, when an angel appears to the Virgin Mary to inform her that she is pregnant. This to me is a mystery that takes place in our lives regularly and deserves meditation. Whenever I'm in an art museum and come across a painting of the Annunciation, I pause and reflect on this specific representation of a profound truth. As a writer, I'm careful with my choice of words. I try to keep the mystery and emptiness in everything I say.

I often use Samuel Beckett as an example of secular writing that has a spiritual message. Yet another Irish source, he uses language in a special way and employs a peculiar cast of characters to reveal what I would call his own natural religion. He challenges secularism, but he doesn't resort to formal religion, except in passing, to do the job. Some critics say that the two characters "waiting for Godot" are not waiting for God. But who else could it be? We don't recognize God in Godot because we expect God to be wearing a bushy beard. But we're all waiting for the mysterious someone, and ultimately our wait is an essential part of our religion.

Through its distortions, exaggerations, and emphasis on form, art often shows us the world behind our ordinary reality. A portrait may reveal more about a person than seeing him in real life. A photograph distorts by isolating a figure from its moving context and in that way reveals what otherwise may be hidden.[59] Some works of art display the archetypal roots of human experience, like Hamlet trying to make sense of his family situation.

Art presents primary insights into emotions and ideas that run so deep as to have a numinous and spiritual quality. Georgia O'Keefe? At one level, her paintings depict objects commonly found on the land around her home. But most people find her paintings relevant to their emotions and values, revealing more than the physical. She looked closely at the land around her and found divinity.

When it is said that art serves spirituality or religion, the usefulness of art is not just to offer an illustration of spiritual ideas but to take the observer to a place of special vision and realization. It can bring you to a point of awareness where the spiritual is in play, and in many cases this is just the starting point for further exploration of the mysteries.

Art and Soul Work

A piece of art is not something to look at as much as to see through, a portal or window rather than an object. It unveils a world already within you and in hidden layers of your environment. In art you see reality, but not ordinary reality. You see the sacred understood

---

59 Mark Rothko, *The Artist's Reality*, ed. Christopher Rothko (New Haven: Yale University Press, 2004), p. 69. Mark Rothko discusses this aspect of distortion in art, saying that with his own kind of distortion the painter Cézanne "paints the apple-ness of an apple and not a particular apple." In this regard, Rene Magritte's famous painting of a pipe accompanied by the words, "This is not a pipe," is relevant. The image is not a pipe but the image of a pipe, something entirely different.

as the lifeblood and heart of the world. You see myth hidden within an ordinary image, and you behold the eternal, the timeless, and the archetypal only a thin layer away from the everyday.

Every few weeks Sean, a former priest and monk, comes to see me for a consultation. We have much in common and I appreciate his particular way of doing soul work. Just a few years ago he was relieved of his monastic vows and left the priesthood, but he now continues to live an intense spiritual life.

A gifted and educated artist, Sean is especially skilled at making icons according to strict traditional rules, but he does his own free painting, as well. He also teaches young people world religions at a local college.

I'm always happy to see Sean pull up in his car and take out his recent paintings. We discuss what is going on in his life and then look at his dreams and finally spend time with his paintings. Together, we "read" it all, looking for familiar themes and hoping to deepen his search for a meaningful life in his new circumstances. He has to sort out work, relationships, his past, and the job of trying to make a living.

Sean's art is a major part of his opus, his continuing work of creating a soulful life and maturing his spirituality. He has a sophisticated background in meditation and mysticism and now wants to continue in this direction in a new setting. Once, he was eager to live in a hermitage, so strong was his mystical bent. I know of few people for whom art is so much at the center of their spirituality and so important, as he now creates a religion of his own.

Sean's shift from precisely formed Christian Orthodox icons to somewhat freer icons and other types of painting parallels his change from being a monk to living alone in a secular world. He's never made a complete break with his past. In fact, one day I told him about my experience. It has been almost forty years since I left a monastic-style life, and yet it stays with me. There is much about it that I love, and I try to translate its aesthetics and spirituality into my life even today.

I can appreciate Sean's slow shift from mystic to worldly artist and his desire to keep the spirit of the monk in his work and lifestyle. We look at his art and see glimpses of his progress. I consider it fortunate that he has such profound art to serve as a charting of his opus. The art is his alchemical laboratory, the place where he can make images directly from the experiences of his heart.

I don't interpret Sean's art or make obvious parallels to his experience. I don't try to highlight or italicize any meanings in the art or point out any special relevancies. We just talk about the art and about life. I don't worry if I mix in some of my own experiences. I'm a trained therapist. I know better than to confuse my experience with another's or to manipulate the situation for my own needs.

Work with Sean confirms for me that art can be an essential part of soul work and, whether or not it's explicitly and formally religious, it contributes much to the spiritual life. Sean demonstrates that anyone could bring art into life and in that way intensify his own religious experience.

As many spiritual teachers have said, we need effective images to express the ineffable mysteries that we try to evoke in our thoughts and rituals. Often, we get too caught up in the institutional doctrine behind an image and overlook its universal spiritual meaning. We look at paintings of the crucifixion of Jesus and think too much about the person Jesus and the membership-only religion of Christianity. Instead, we might contemplate the greater mystery of a young visionary persecuted for his values and his challenge to authority and tradition. This is a fate we all might face.[60]

---

60 In my book *Writing in the Sand*, I say that I see no evidence that Jesus ever intended to create a formal religion and that he wasn't talking about the afterlife or another life. He was teaching how to live at a higher level in this life. (Carlsbad: Hay House, 2009).

We look at an image of the Buddha sitting under the Bodhi tree in anticipation of awakening and think too much of the Buddha. We all sit under the great tree that is life and wonder about its deep roots and soaring crown of branches and leaves, and we hope to wake up.

Too easily we divide the secular from the sacred and look at a painting by a living artist and fail to see the sacredness of the image. A play by Edward Albee may have as much theology in it as a book by Paul Tillich. And not just Albee, who stands out for the distant reach of his imagination and the ritual quality of his theater. Go into any art gallery where you can find some thoughtful and penetrating paintings, and you will find the usual archetypal and mythic themes that are the explicit concern of religious art. You may have to look closely to see those themes, but they are always present. The famous Turner landscapes, for instance, are not formally religious art and yet they teach you how to see the divine brilliance that shines from within any natural setting. They offer an important theological lesson. The "dream thing" is fully present in them.

Many people don't realize how central the imagination is to religious and spiritual experiences. The object of faith and wonder is impossible to express in our usual logical and factual language. We need images that approximate our spiritual intuitions.

Religion as Devotion

Devotion is one of those aspects of religion that seem to be both spiritual and psychological. Many religious people devote themselves to certain ideas and practices. I learned about devotion as a child seeing how fervently my mother prayed and how devoted she was to certain holy figures, like the Virgin Mary, and to the holy Mass. Every night, after the family had gone to bed, my mother would pray her rosary. As far as I know, she performed this "devotion" faithfully for decades. My wife and daughter are truly devoted to their practice of yoga and to the tradition it comes from.

But people often devote themselves to things not so obviously or formally religious. They devote themselves to their gardens and their homes. Parents are certainly devoted to their children, teachers to their students, and doctors and nurses to their patients. As we think of a personal, more extended sense of religion, we might consider how devotion in the "secular" realm is part of it.

These last three examples—parents, teachers, and medical professionals—seem to be secular roles, but when you look closely at the depth of engagement and dedication in each case, you begin to glimpse the spiritual nature of the work. Devotion is only one part of the experience that looks like religion. Then you might reflect on the fact that in many cultures these roles are treated as sacred. We might do well to desecularize them in some ways, restoring their status as part of a natural religion.

I've thought about devotion in this way for a long time, and when I first considered writing this book, the pianist Glenn Gould came to mind immediately. I wondered about including him, because as far as I know he had no formal religious practice. But I knew, having been a fan of his since my teens, that he was profoundly devoted to music and to the piano. It was his absolute devotion to his vision of playing, performing, interpreting, and recording that assured me of his place here.

Gould's devotion made him eccentric in his performance decisions and in his lifestyle. He played in his own quirky way and made the music come alive as few have done. He wore heavy coats and gloves on warm days, stayed up most of the night, and lived on a diet of eggs. He was notorious for his eccentricities, such as conducting a chorus of elephants, but instead of being mere personal oddities, I have always thought of them as natural extensions of his otherworldliness, his spirituality.

In an essay for *Musical America* in 1962, Gould wrote: "The purpose of art is not the release of a momentary ejection of adrenaline but is, rather, the gradual, lifelong construction of a state of wonder and serenity. . . . Art on its loftiest mission is scarcely human at all." It was in this essay that he made his strongest spiritual statement, one that is very much at home in this book: We need to wake up to the challenge, he wrote, that each person "contemplatively create his own divinity."[61] As I said before, you could borrow his two potent words, "wonder" and "serenity," and add them to the values that will be the basis of your religion.

For Gould the piano was his portal to transcendence and a spiritual practice in his own religion. I take seriously his statement about contemplatively creating his own divinity. He is not making up his own God but rather finding his own means, the piano and his lifestyle, of being in touch with his eternal nature. Listen to his music, and you will feel a strong aura of eternity in his art.

Gould was a good example of Platonic madness or mania. Listen to a recording and you'll hear him humming along as he plays. This was not nonchalance; it was a loss of self and absorption in the music. He also conducts himself. When I saw him perform when I was a teenager, in one of the rare public appearances before he gave up concerts, he seemed distracted, in the sense that he was so in the music that he wasn't completely present in the world. His eccentricity poured out of him. I liked it, but some of his critics couldn't abide it.

At his funeral they played a recording of Gould playing from the Bach Goldberg Variations. This was appropriate on that occasion not just because of the artistic value but because of its spiritual power.

---

61 Tim Page, ed., *The Glenn Gould Reader* (Alfred A. Knopf, 1984), p. 247.

The Religion of Art

Just because you love art and know a lot about it doesn't mean you are a spiritual person and have your own religiousness. Still, art can lead you so deep into your world and yourself that you get in touch with the sacred and the mysterious. It all depends on how you approach art.

I play my piano, as I said earlier, without professional skill but passably, and do it with the intention of entering sacred spaces. It works. The piano is my incense, my lighted candle, and my empty space. It takes me into deep meditation, where I find the sacred just as I might uncover it in a monastery choir stall. The piano has none of the trappings of formal religion, and yet it is effective in sustaining my spiritual life.

Art shows us the invisible in the visible, the sacred in the profane, even when the sacred isn't expressed in explicit religious imagery. A still-life painting or a portrait can reveal the hidden, and sometimes, when it shows how things glow with their essence, you can even glimpse the divine. The history of art has many examples but perhaps none better than the paintings of simple, everyday things, especially ordinary vases and bottles, by Giorgio Morandi. One critic describes his work as "a meditation on time, art, isolation, self-preservation and the ordinary mystery of all of that."[62] "The ordinary mystery of all that" could be the subtitle of this book.

Van Gogh's famous paintings of shoes teach us to see past the surface of ordinary things and behold the poetry in something so commonplace, pointing to our foundations in every sense of the word. The photography historian Tony Bannon, speaking of the monk Thomas Merton as a photographer, says that a photograph

---

62 Holland Cotter, "All That Life Contains, Contained," *New York Times*, September 18, 2008. http://www.nytimes.com/2008/09/19/arts/design/19 mora.html?pagewanted=all&_r=0.

of something as simple as a vine on a window can be a call to awareness. It "expands the horizon of the witness."[63] There is a phrase you can adopt now for your spiritual vocabulary: "Expand the horizon of your witness."

Technology is developing to the point where ordinary people, nonartists, can now take photographs, make movies, and create computer images and graphics. The plus side of this advance is that we can now all draw out the artist in us, and as we experiment with our newfound art, we may begin to see how much more the sacred may shine through. When our photography becomes really good, the gods appear in the distortion of the real that can reveal more than it disguises.

My suggestion: If you have any interest in a camera, or even if you don't, take one out into the wilderness closest to you and take pictures. Do your own dream thing: use unusual angles and various distances, attach filters, look for forms rather than things, find images that evoke emotion. You are using the camera lens to help you see through the facade of fact to an inner realm of imagination. You don't have to go to nature for his. One year I went out at night and photographed mannequins in store windows. In the night setting and isolated from a busy daytime store, these figures had an otherworldly quality. You can use a camera to bring out the interiority, depth, and abiding spirit in anything.

If flower arranging is a contemplative craft, then painting and drawing and photography can be even more so. If you do just a little study of the spiritual traditions, you will learn how to use your artistic skills to transform the ordinary and reveal its

---

63 Chautauqua lecture, "Contemplative Photography and Thomas Merton," http://fora.tv/2010/07/30/Tony_Bannon_Contemplative_Photography_and _Thomas_Merton.

inherent sacredness. In so doing you will be adding an important dimension to your personal religion.

A Pilgrimage to the Museum

I also recommend that you go to an art museum at every opportunity, but don't go only as an art tourist or student. For the purposes of developing your own religion, you can envision your visit to the art museum or gallery as your own kind of *darshan*. You go there to be in the presence of sacred figures, to see them and, in a way, to be seen by them. You go to have your spiritual life nurtured. You go with some reverence and with a contemplative attitude.

Of course it's fine to study art history and technique and the biographies of artists. This kind of study can help you see the art and can be a preparation for art as a spiritual work. But when you go to a museum with your own religion in mind, go first for an encounter with images. Sense their presence. Show them some kind of honor, if possible: a flower, bring an essential oil, not to put on the painting or sculpture but to wear as you meet the image. Do a little chant. Say a prayer. Sit like a Zen master. Meditate on the painting. Write something about your encounter. Compose a poem for the image. Sketch it.

The idea is not to analyze or be educated. With your reverential attitude you turn the museum into a temple. No one else in the vicinity need see what you're doing or understand it. You're doing your "weird" thing. Your own religion has made you eccentric.

Chapter 8

꧁

MUSES AND ANGELS

I would especially like to recourt the Muse of poetry,
who ran off with the mailman four years ago, and
drops me only a scribbled postcard from time to time.

—JOHN UPDIKE

O ne of the foundational stories of my life began to unfold
when I was nineteen and on my way to Northern Ireland
to study philosophy, one stage in the intellectual preparation for
priesthood, between practical training in spirituality and an extensive four-year program in theology. With six of my fellow
monks I took the Queen Mary across the Atlantic to South-
ampton and then took a smaller ship to Belfast. On the Atlantic
crossing, while sitting in a closet-size, unadorned stateroom, a
simple thought came to me: While in Ireland I should find some
way to obtain a piece of Irish art.

This thought came from nowhere. I know just where I was
when it arrived. It was as though I heard it in the air, because it
was not the result of rational thought. I knew I would be in Ireland
for only two years and wanted to bring a piece of it back with me.

After settling in at the priory in the tiny hamlet of Benburb, I wrote to the National Gallery in Dublin asking for some help from the staff. I soon received a warm letter from Thomas Mc-Greevy, the director of the gallery, inviting me to visit him on my next trip to Dublin. So began a friendship that was the beginning of my true waking up to my nature and my destiny. Personal and intimate stories about famous writers and painters made the arts vivid and important in a way I had never been exposed to before. When I met McGreevy I was in a fog. Jung said something similar: Until the day he woke up to his individuality, when he was eleven, he was in a mist. Toward the end of my years in Ireland I felt that I was just beginning to wake up to a more meaningful world and to a bigger context for my own future.

McGreevy was a highly sophisticated man, a published poet who had lived a portion of his life in Paris acting as counselor and guide to James Joyce and later to the Dublin writer Samuel Beckett. He had known many of the great literary and art figures of his time: Eliot, Lawrence, Pound, W. B. Yeats, Jack Yeats. He was counselor to James Joyce and his wife and daughter, and to all of them he was a natural Hermes figure, someone who could walk comfortably in the different artistic circles and serve as an intimate guide. Hermes was known as the psychopompos, the guide of souls, and McGreevy had that inborn gift.

McGreevy became my guide, too, telling me countless stories about his accomplished friends and teaching me how to live with art. After two years in Ireland and several hushed conversations in the intimate room behind the director's main office, I went back home to study theology. I didn't return with a physical piece of art, but I came back with something infinitely more important: the birth of the artist in myself and the hint of a life work for which McGreevy was the midwife. I saw myself not just as a musician but as someone serious about an artistic outlook. It would be years before I discovered that I had a life work as a writer.

Thomas McGreevy apparently saw potential in me. How, I don't know. He gave me lessons so personal and so firsthand that

I could never learn them from a book. This friendship between an older man and a young student had an eternal quality, the air of an archetypal event. It moved me into my future by inspiring me. McGreevy told me that I was an important figure in his old age, but to me the weight of significance was all on his side. I was the primary beneficiary.

Recently, on one of my frequent trips to Dublin I was walking the same streets on which, fifty years ago, I had had a few of my important walking conversations with Thomas McGreevy, I noticed an ad for an exhibition of W. B. Yeats memorabilia at the National Library on Kildare Street, and so I went in. I remembered how McGreevy had talked so fondly about "W. B.," though he had been dead for twenty years, that tears came to his eyes, and he remarked how difficult it was to be in Dublin without him. With my memories heavy on my heart, I couldn't pass by this exhibit of Yeats.

Inside the National Library I walked slowly through the dimly lit and intimate presentation of Yeats's books and letters and stopped cold in front of a display of Yeats's wife's automatic writing, the practice of putting a pen to paper and letting your hand make letters and shapes that you then interpret and use for guidance in life. Yeats had married a woman who, though not the object of his dreams, was a genuine companion in his life and work. Soon after they were married, he discovered that she could provide him with raw material for his most well-known poems and other writings and generally serve as his muse and, with her intelligence and insight, his companion.

Years later, when I was in graduate school in the field of religious studies, many of my classmates and I were reading Yeats's *A Vision*, a remarkable journey in ritual poetry centered on the moon, electrified by images of spinning gyres, and inspired by Yeats's wife, Georgie. As students of religion, we were interested in any kind of connection between the human and the mysterious, whether it was a revelation on a mountaintop or scribbles on paper made by a spouse.

At the exhibit, by the way, I was surprised to see how automatic Georgie Yeats's automatic writing was. It consisted of drawings and unusual figures, as well as words that seemed more nonsense than sense. Some of the images reminded me of the quaint magical figures I had seen in old Renaissance texts, like the Picatrix, I had studied while writing my dissertation on Renaissance natural magic.

To appreciate more fully what Yeats and Georgie were up to, you could take a pen now, close your eyes or look away, and let your hand scribble some figures on a piece of paper. They don't have to make sense, though you will probably recognize some of the forms that appear. Now think about the images that have shown up.

I just did this little exercise and came up with the following: 4 3 g y. The "g" and "y" are recognizable but not formed in the usual way. I happen to like the way they've appeared. The stem of the "y" has a nice wiggle in it. When I reflect on the figures, I think of $4 + 3 = 7$. As everyone knows, "7" is a number of good fortune. Saint Augustine said that if you add the four Gospels to the Trinity you get "7." The "G" is fluid and open. In the introduction to this book I mentioned using "G" for "God." "Y" is a character in a novel I wrote twenty years ago: Mrs. Y. As I was writing the novel I thought of "why," why am I here, why do I do what I do, why has life turned out this way? Her name was Yolanda, but I called her Mrs. Y. She was a seeker, asking the important questions, a facet of my own psyche, no doubt, a bit insane because of her curiosity.

Now, use your imagination with your automatic writing, and don't worry about being good at it or doing it correctly. Trust your imagination and then trust yourself to find hints of meaning.

Is a Muse Real?

A muse is the experience of inspiration felt as subjective and having a human face. Many people speak of inspiration as coming from a "voice," not necessarily an actual voice but something like a voice.

Sometimes people think they hear an actual voice of inspiration—in a room or outdoors. They hear words that give them ideas, though on reflection there were no words to be heard. At other times, the voice is one of a real person who speaks as or for the muse, like Yeats's wife, or, for me, Thomas McGreevy. In Ireland, in particular, it was a common belief that a "little person" might appear in the guise of an actual person. Yeats himself presents such stories in *The Celtic Twilight*.

We usually think of a muse as being so subjective, a inner part of a person or a mere metaphor, that we don't discuss the role of the muse in the spiritual life. But I think the muse belongs in our discussion. After all, Christians have listened to angels and saints and the Virgin when they have appeared with messages. Mormonism is based on such revelations, and in Islam Gabriel reveals the Qur'ān to Mohammed over twenty-three years. Gabriel interprets the dreams of Daniel in the Old Testament and has a role in the sephira of the Kabbalah, Yesod.

The point is to be a good listener and keep your ears open for the subtle sounds, the utterances that are not spoken with vocal cords but are there to be heard anyway, or are actually spoken but mean more than intended. As I travel, people often tell me things that slip past the surface and touch me. I remember them afterward, and sometimes they lead to new work and interesting decisions. Recently a man in a crowd said to me, "You should write about growing old." Something in his voice, like a muse, allowed his words to penetrate. I thought about them and now feel them churning in me. I'll be surprised if I don't write about aging now.

The muse doesn't just inspire; it churns things up. It can be disturbing as well as comforting. It may give you an idea you'd rather put off indefinitely. When it offers a challenge like this, that may be the best time to give it your attention.

How Do You Listen to a Muse?

To have your own religion you need inspirations. You need to be like Virgin Mary heeding the angel or Mohammed writing down what he hears. But we are a generation of skeptics with a compensatory tendency toward fundamentalism. We tend to be materialists in life, even if some among us are strong believers in traditional religion. We believe in our research methods and our machines and seem to fear the autonomy of the imagination.

We're interested in seeing the world that is invisible to the naked eye and therefore base our medicine on what appears in a microscope and our sense of the cosmos on what we can see in a telescope. Yet there are other invisible factors that can't be seen through a physical lens. We need a particular kind of imagination for these factors, and our contemporary worldview stands in the way.

So the first and more general answer to the question about how to listen to a muse is to ease up on your anxious modernism. Take seriously what many of your neighbors and friends would dismiss as imaginary and fantastical. Listen for the voice of inspiration and heed it.

A Calm, Alert Mind

As with many different kinds of intuition and inspiration, you have to be alert. These messages often come and go quickly and are usually subtle. You could easily ignore them or fail to give them attention. You can't be busy thinking about things or planning. That's why some people look for inspiration while taking a shower or walking in the woods. You need an inner calm and an alert but not a busy mind. Maybe you need to be doing something habitual and not important so that your mind will be open for revelations.

When a creative thought first appears, it may not show itself in all its glory. It may be only a seed that will blossom later. It helps, then, if you can see the potential in a fresh idea or image.

"Care of the soul" was a phrase I had read many times and over many years. One day it suddenly stood out—clearly the effect of a muse. Only then did it serve me creatively and give me not just a book, but a life work.

We know that a muse can inspire an artist, but we don't talk much about it waking up the spiritual self. But if you scan the religious movements in history, you find that founders often started out with a dramatic message from somewhere mysterious.

A good example: the Shakers. In 1774 their founder, Mother Ann Lee, was living in England when God told her to create a community free of sex. She had been coerced into marriage and had eight children, none of whom survived into adulthood. She didn't feel good about sex.

Mother Ann's community did well in the United States, and in the 1850s went through a phase called the Era of Manifestations, when several members had visions or went into trances and were given ideas, songs, and poems. Ann Mariah Goff, for instance, said that Mother Ann appeared to her and told her not to be wasteful, but to be neat, industrious, and humble.[64]

Certain members of the American community were called instruments, because they had the capacity to be inspired. Eventually, the period of intense "manifestation" ended, but the Shakers built their religion on the messages some of their members had received. Their famous song "Simple Gifts" is an example of a gift received in this special way. As part of your spiritual practice, you might learn how to be an "instrument," a feather on the breath of God, as Hildegard of Bingen puts it.

The Shakers believed that to be open to inspiration they should keep their living space in order and they should fast, rest, kneel, pray, and look into themselves. These are good suggestions: You need a clear space to see and hear something as

---

64 Stephen J. Stein, *The Shaker Experience in America* (New Haven: Yale University Press, 1992), p. 170.

delicate as the voice of a muse. You can train yourself to be an instrument.

The Shakers said the veil is thin in certain circumstances. For myself, I would prefer to write in the early morning, but I have learned that ideas come to me more readily late at night. So I often write from ten to midnight. For me, music also interferes with my writing. I can't help focusing on chord progressions and other technical aspects of the music and can't be open to inspiration. Some days I know that nothing will work. The door to what Emily Dickinson called "the Heaven" is closed. I wait for another day, but I always trust that the muse will appear. Waiting is a spiritual skill especially useful when you're looking for inspiration.

For me the steadiest and most reliable muse has been my memories from life in the religious community. Those memories are like a well of inspiration, constantly giving me ideas on how to shape my own religion. Sometimes I'm quite concrete and try to give my life a monastic feel, but at other times I freely adapt certain practices and styles. I still listen to music, but not always Gregorian Chant. I still meditate, but not the way I did in the priory.

In Greek myth the nine Muses are Daughters of Memory. My neighbor Gary Pinette writes songs, and he says that remembering certain stirring events of his life, both positive and negative, inspires him. According to Plato, an artist "remembers" in a much deeper way, as well, keeping important lessons about life that as a society we've forgotten. I think of the great films of Ingmar Bergman, which help us remember deep and forgotten truths about being human.

The voice of a parent can have the quality of a muse. I remember certain sayings of my father: "When you're trying to fix something, never force it." Words from a father can be the inspiration for a way of life. A parent's words detach from the actual saying of them and have an eternal, guiding presence in the mind of the child. Abraham Lincoln confessed, "I remember my mother's prayers and they have always followed me. They have clung to me all my life." Clinging is a good way to express the constancy that a parent's words can have as they sound, muse-like, in a child's memory.

A muse may be inside or outside. Marsilio Ficino, an Italian Renaissance independent scholar, wrote to his friend Giuliano de' Medici, "My great love for you has long impressed your image in my soul. And just as sometimes I see myself out there in a mirror, I often see you within me in my heart." What an inspiring image: a reverse mirror. This is Ficino's definition of a soul mate. It is also a good description of what happens when a real person transforms into a muse. He takes up residence in your heart and speaks to you, guides you, and inspires you.

Often a muse is more an impulse than a person. The words "daimon," "spirit," or "angel" may indicate that the muse seems to be from another dimension or is out there and in here. The important thing is not to explain this puzzle but to learn to live with it effectively.

Angels and Muses

The word "angel" means both "message" and "messenger." In the religious imagination of many traditions the main job of an angel is to serve as a go-between, linking the divine with the human, often by delivering messages. In the Gospel, an angel in a dream warns Joseph, the husband of Mary, to leave town because of danger to their child. Here we get two good pieces of information about angels: They can warn about threats and they can do their work through dreams.

Of course, as we develop a personal and natural religion, we're not going to be naïve about angels. They don't exist the same way people and animals do. But to dismiss them is to be blind to the possibility of a spiritual presence. Have you ever felt the approach of a threat and took caution? Without losing any of your modern sophistication you could describe that warning as the work of an angel.

Angels also inspire, as when Gabriel visits Mary to tell her that she is pregnant in a spiritual way. The father of her child is a holy spirit, Gabriel says, and he assures Mary and tells her not to be afraid.

Angels are cousins of the Muses, the messenger aspect. In art and literature they both speak for divinity and protect the mystery. I'm not recommending that we suddenly restore talk of angels or even that they have a necessary place in your developing religion. But I do suggest looking closely at angels in painting and sculpture. You'll find them in several written traditions and in the art of temples and churches. Notice how they are presented and think of them in the most sophisticated ways, as representations of inspirational experiences you may have.

Let me offer more specific advice on this theme. I recommend going to a museum that has paintings from the Middle Ages and early Renaissance in Europe, and from other cultures as well. I have no doubt that you will come across some extraordinary images of angels. Now, sit down in front of one of these angels, and without being at all naïve about it, learn from the image what qualities an angel has. Notice especially the wings, and see them as a kind of poetry, as images and not representations. Imagine that this image portrays a mysterious experience that you may have in your daily life. You don't see angels, but you sense an angel-like factor in certain special events: protection, inspiration, epiphany, or invitation.

Once, James Hillman and I together gave a weekend seminar on inspiration, taking it seriously and exploring Hillman's theory of "personifying," restoring an appreciation for imaginal figures. In this context Hillman says, "We need to recall the angel aspect of the word, recognizing words as independent carriers of soul between people."[65] The muse resides in our language as well as in our heads. Looking for the right word requires a small muse, one that can inspire momentarily and in a precise way.

Hillman was always interested in the way our ancestors inspire us today with their written words. Their "voices" speak to us and give us direction and hints for our own creative work. Renaissance artists and writers had a practice of honoring a particular list of ancestors whose ideas were behind their own. This ancestral line, unique to each person, is a powerful muse. I sometimes worry about always referring to the same historical figures in my books, but they are on my list, which is long but limited.

In *Walden*, Thoreau makes a slight reference to angels, but when I first read it I felt that a whole theology or angelology was suggested in a few words. Reflecting on solitude and the various neighbors and animal companions he has, he mentions the importance of the lake. "It has blue angels in it, in the azure tint of its waters." To the casual reader, this reference to angels may be just a metaphor and a figure of speech. But Thoreau was a secular theologian, someone prepared to see an angel when it appeared. To see the angelic in the blue waters, perhaps in the flickering light on the small chop of the waves, is to turn a spiritual eye on ordinary nature. Seeing the angels there, Thoreau knows that he is living in a sacred place.

Later, he hints at how nature can transform a person. One goes into the forest "as a hunter and fisher, until at last, if he has the seeds of a better life in him, he distinguishes his proper objects, as a poet or naturalist it may be, and leaves the gun and fish-pole behind." Emerson had written that only a poet can really know astronomy and the other sciences because he goes beyond facts and reads the things of the world as signs.

Emerson opens his celebrated essay "Self-Reliance" with a

---

65 Hillman, *Re-Visioning Psychology*, p. 9.

quotation in Latin that translates: "Don't look for yourself outside yourself." Then, in a short poem, he write these two lines:

> *Our acts our angels are, or good or ill,*
> *Our fatal shadows that walk by us still.*

From Socrates's love daimon to the first-grader's "guardian angel," people have always felt accompanied by an invisible spirit—Emerson's "fatal shadows," an interesting way to think of an angel. "Daimon" is an ancient Greek word for an inner presence. Socrates felt that his daimon was focused on the place of love in his life and more often warned him against making a wrong decision than giving him positive inspiration. When I was a child, nuns taught me that I had a special angel with me to protect and guide me. Emerson's "fatal shadow" is less sentimental and hints that a guiding inner presence may at times be something to contend with. We have a shadow self, not dark in the sense of evil or dangerous, but the shadow that follows us wherever we go, a companion figure that inspires, warns, and guides.

Thoreau often gives himself a pep talk, encouraging himself to make his life meaningful. In a journal entry of October 26, 1853, he writes: "I must attend to my diet; I must get up earlier and take a morning walk; I must have done with luxuries and devote myself to my muse."[66] He knows what every inspired person understands: You have to prepare yourself for your muse, and sometimes you have to clear a space in a busy and cluttered life.

Thoreau didn't want to be caught up in the concerns of the average person. He was like the monks, of whom we'll speak later, who resisted the affairs of the world. In September 1851 he wrote in his journal: "Though I have been associating even with the *select* men of this and the surrounding towns, I feel inexpressibly

---

66 Thoreau, *I to Myself*, p. 206.

begrimed. My Pegasus [winged horse associated with the Muses] has lost his wings; he has turned a reptile and gone on his belly."[67]

Another hint about the muse: Try not to be "begrimed" by the normal concerns of the world. Keep a distance. Don't get unconsciously caught up in its values and way of seeing.

My own rules for living with a muse, my shadow self, are similar:

1. Find some solitude without becoming a loner.

2. Practice the art of waiting.

3. Trust the information provided, even if it isn't yet complete or clear.

I often tell the story of the time my friend and fellow writer Chris Bamford and I were having lunch at a diner on the Taconic Parkway, talking about the idea of care of the soul. There it was, staring me in the face, the idea for a book that would change my life, and I didn't see it. I was passionate about the ideas for the book, but my thought was that Chris and I should write it together. I didn't see myself as an accomplished writer. I felt I was a yeoman, an eternal amateur. I suspect that this image was part of my *puer* nature, the part that doesn't grow up. This psychology of mine almost ruined the greatest promise of my life. It was getting in the way of the muse and remained a block until I began to take my work more seriously. Then the muse began to speak, or I began to listen.

Lover Muse

There is another kind of muse, far different from the one we learn about in Thoreau's journals, who wakes up our soul through

---

67 Thoreau, *I to Myself*, p. 101.

attraction and love. The heart goes into motion and feelings swell and, as Plato said, you become at least slightly mad with infatuation. Plenty of literature discusses how a lover can be a muse.

Consider the following fictional account from a hard-boiled story told in delicate language by the stylish writer Craig Holden. The passage tells of the main character, a whiskey runner during prohibition times, falling in love with the woman he would marry: "It had come to him, in his contemplations, that a woman with her intelligence and beauty and spirit and self-assurance could become, in and of herself, a man's impetus. His catalyst. His reason. . . . [S]he could inspire anything. And justify it. And sweeten it. And, by so sweetening, jeopardize it as well. . . . [T]here was nothing else he wanted so much as her."[68]

Every phrase in that description tells us something about this kind of muse. She is an impetus, inspirer, and sweetener. And she has a shadow side. By making him crazy, giving life a romantic glaze, and causing him so much longing, she can interfere with the man's projects, as well. Still, because of her, he wants to stretch beyond his limits and accomplish more than he imagines himself capable of. Now he wants to takes risks that before he would have avoided. He is extravagantly inspired.

A religious figure is often the object of an infatuation. Jesus, the Buddha, Mohammed, the Virgin Mary, Mother Ann—people fall in love with them and are inspired to live special lives and to be creative in their spirituality. Obviously, it can be dangerous to become so besotted with a spiritual figure, but it can also motivate.

In your own religion you may also come across figures who nudge you in a certain direction. In this book it's clear that Thoreau, Gould, and Simone Dinnerstein have inspired me to press further in my work. They provide ideas, an impetus, and a

---

68 Craig Holden, *The Jazz Bird* (New York: Simon & Schuster, 2002), p. 85.

desire to be creative and effective like them. I can't imagine working creatively without this kind of muse.

By the way, a nonromantic friend or partner, too, can be a muse. I've already told the story of how James Hillman entered my imagination, taking up room and board there for decades, giving rise to much creative work. He has done the same for many other people because of the seminal quality of his thoughts and writings. You read him and the seeds get planted in the soil of your mind and sprout in good time. Then you don't know for sure if the ideas are yours or his. He wrote about people starting out in childhood like an acorn destined to be an oak, but he himself is an acorn. You have to read him with care, lest you lose yourself in his brilliance.

Hillman's anima, his soul, his aesthetic sense mixed with his sharp ideas, the spark of imagination within him, revealed the nature of his muse.[69] He inspired with his imagination and with the world he loved. On the other hand, to me Hillman was a muse taking on the disguise of a friend.

You could take this idea seriously in your own religion: noticing how friendship can inspire your creative work, whether that work is artistic or in some other area such as business, medicine, or academics. You can be open to the influence of friends to offer ideas and to inspire your creativity.

Friendship is a form of love. It is not usually the hot, flaming, romantic kind of love but rather a cooler, more extended, and yet maybe even more meaningful connection. I can't separate my feelings of friendship from all that I owe to James as a muse. When I think of key ideas I learned from him, I remember the

---

69 On the male muse, see: "The Female Poet and the Male Muse" in *Magma Poetry*, 37. http://magmapoetry.com/archive/magma-37-2/articles/the-female-poet-and-the-male-muse/.

setting, what we were doing, how he expressed himself. I always remember the deep feeling of connection I had with him, his laughter and the expressive movements of his eyebrows.

For example, once we were walking on his street, and I was telling him about a client who had an extraordinary passion for French napoleons, the rich pastry with layers of cream and cake and light and dark frosting. This was no ordinary culinary passion. My client couldn't stop eating these things, and there was a French bakery in my neighborhood. He'd buy several every time he left my home office, and he had a serious weight problem.

James stopped there on the sidewalk and put his face close to mine. "This is an important symptom," he said. "Tell me how it all unfolds." Then he pointed a finger. "You have to notice these small things. How the psyche works. What you eat!" Whenever Hillman spoke about the psyche, he was fierce. No wonder people were so affected by him.

Daimon

A similar shadow self, spoken of since ancient times and mentioned by modern writers such as Jung, Yeats, Rollo May, and Hillman, the daimon may be a voice, an urge, or a sense of warning that can guide and inspire. But unlike an angel and a muse, the daimon is a figure you may have to wrestle with.

"Daimon" is an ancient Greek word for an inner presence or force that guides by urging one direction or another, or by warning of dangers in a certain activity. In Greek mythology the daimon may appear beside the hero, admonishing him and urging him on. Poets speak of the daimon as a force to reckon with, the source of creative power and necessity. The daimon adds strength and firm, explosive power to the more familiar notion of a muse.

Jung warns that you can't use this daimon for your own willful purposes. "The autonomy of this ambivalent figure should be religiously borne in mind, for it is the source of that fearful power which drives us towards individuation."[70] The daimon pushes us toward our own fulfillment, but it does so in its own way, often trying to steer us away from our best plans and strategies. It's fearsome because it often demands so much from us.

Yeats called the daimon "the other self." It can give you creative inspirations, but it is a challenge, precisely because it speaks for fate and destiny rather than personal will and desire. Yeats thought that out of the struggle of daimon and self you can be your most creative.

Because the daimonic conveys a strong air of otherness, it serves the spiritual life, which is in large part the interplay between self and the invisible other. The spiritual life is also not a static process, but a dynamic one that invites you to further and deeper engagement with life. But it is not the fully external engagement as expressed in modern terms. It's a mixture of inner, outer, and beyond. It is deep, engaged, and transcendent, all at the same time. The depth element often goes unnoticed, especially when the accent is on transcendence. The depth process includes various personal developments and our past experiences, as well as deep-seated emotions and relationships. Working out an important friendship or romantic involvement engages the spirit—you may have to wrestle with both your desires and your inhibitions—and may be a significant element in your own religion.

The daimonic may appear in the form of a person or place—traditions speak of a spirit of a place, and that spirit can be felt even in our modern times. I have a daimonic relation to Ireland. Maybe it's in my blood and my heritage, or maybe Ireland is not a real place only but part of the geography of my imagination. It's a place of power for me, even though my appreciation for Ireland is mixed. I see the social problems and some habits of the people

---

70 C. G. Jung, *Alchemical Studies* (Princeton: Princeton University Press, 1967), p. 437.

that disillusion me. For the most part, though, the place still retains a significant amount of fantasy. It enchants me, an indication that the daimon still resides there.

In Hillman's case I felt that the daimon was his genius and the power that often burst through his personality. He saw it as anger, an emotion that got him into trouble frequently but also accounted for his creativity. I saw his daimon as a power to reimagine anything that came to his attention. It was akin to the near-inhuman abilities that some musicians and athletes have. In Hillman it was close to what the Spanish poet García Lorca described as "duende," the creative power that seizes a person and drives them toward an almost insane creative state. "The arrival of the duende. . . brings totally unknown and fresh sensations, with the qualities of a newly created rose, miraculous, generating an almost religious enthusiasm."

Creative people often seem tormented, but it isn't clear what causes them so much struggle. If we were to take the daimon or duende seriously, we might understand that you can't be inspired regularly by a shadow self without being buffeted by it. Read Lorca's essay "Play and Theory of the Duende" and you'll get an idea of how shattering the creative life can be, how shattering the spiritual life is when it is really lived as a response to an invitation, rather than as an ego project.

Most of the people I have mentioned as having created a religion of their own were both creative and troubled in some way. Thoreau had the reputation of being a difficult person. Gould was eccentric to a fault. Scholars today can't agree whether Emily Dickinson had a mental illness or was just unusual. Socrates was executed in part because of his professed relationship with his daimon. I could go on with similar examples.

Married people easily confuse the daimon for the self. They struggle with the daimon raging in their partner, thinking of it as a personality quirk, easily tamed and controlled. It would be better to understand that everyone has a daimonic force in them, perhaps some more than others, and the person affected is as much at its mercy as people in the vicinity.

The ancient Romans used the word "genius"—the genius that resides in the head or the genius *loci*, the daimon of a place. They referred to a woman's genius as a *juno*, a daimon special to a woman. The spirit she was born with, a woman's *juno* accounted for the creative unfolding of her life over the years; she would celebrate this *juno* on her birthday and give special attention to her eyebrows as sacred to the *juno*. (Remember my reference to Hillman's eyebrows.)

Eyebrows can say a lot about a person, sometimes betraying someone's passions and fears. You may look to the eyebrows and see the *juno*, the non-ego personality at work in a life.

To the Romans, the genius and *juno* also accounted for a spirit of optimism and well-being. To some extent it was the Roman equivalent of the Greek "soul" and was both in a person and outside, an aspect of individual life and a quality of the family and community.[71] In Roman thinking, not only are the genders different in surface areas but they are inspired and moved by inner presences special to each, a genius and a *juno*.

If two thousand years ago the Romans sensed the active presence of a *juno* in a woman, then that presence is still there today, even if we don't normally appreciate it because of the limitations of our ideas and language. A woman has a *juno* that is her creative force. Any man who has stood in the presence of a woman should understand this: There is a force there that is not due to the personality but to the womanness, a presence that is

---

71 For information and debates on these fascinating ideas, see Richard Broxton Onians, *The Origins of European Thought* (Cambridge: Cambridge University Press, 1988), pp. 127–130.

more feminine and more potent that a person herself could ever be.

Here's an interesting religious practice you could borrow from the Romans. You could make or somehow obtain a statue that would represent the genius of your home and place it in your garden, as Jung did with his Bollingen stone, a large hewn stone on which he carved mysterious words in several languages and the image of a small human figure. The Romans preferred the image of a snake. You could also use a snake or an animal that more effectively evokes the spirit of your place. Find the perfect image of your *juno* and place her in your home to keep that relationship alive and concrete. I wonder if our wood-carved Quan Yin is the *juno* figure in our home. If you're a woman, by all means find an image for your *juno*, and keep it close. You need your *juno* to have sufficient passion to get through life creatively.

Jung says that a word like "daimon" has more numinosity or spiritual charge than "unconscious," and in his private life he addressed the daimon in the language of "thou," and advocated taking such spirits seriously, painting and carving images of them. In a religion of our own we might follow Jung's practice rather than his theory and address the spirits that inspire and direct us as "you" rather than "it."[72] You might also study closely the way Jung gave body to the daimon in his painting, calligraphy, stone cutting, building, and unusual spiritual writing. Consult his "autobiography" *Memories, Dreams, Reflections* and *The Red Book*.

---

72 I first heard the word "daimon" used in a psychological context in the mid-1960s, when friends played audiotapes of the existential psychiatrist Rollo May. May generally spoke positively about the daimon, as in his book *Love and Will,* where he wrote, "The daimonic is the urge to reach out toward others, to increase life by way of sex, to create, to civilize; it is the joy and rapture, or the simple security of knowing that we matter." He also warned that the daimon can get out of hand and become destructive.

The paradox in all of this is that a daimonic urge, outside of will and decision, is actually more human and more personal. As we respond to daimonic impulses we are being more ourselves than when we try to live from will and intention. We are what inspires us, not what we intend and make ourselves to be.

I once knew a man who was a successful banker and had a hobby of taking art photographs. He told me once that photography was his real passion, but he wanted to make a decent living. His words "real passion" were, perhaps, his way of talking about his daimon. Eventually he quit his job at the bank and devoted himself full-time to photography. He said that he was letting his true self out, and he felt so much better for it. His bank job was a practical identity, while his photography allowed him to be an individual.

The conscious mind is small and weak compared to the emotional and spiritual power that we call daimonic. It may be the urge to create, take risks, and love. Life may be simple when you avoid the daimon of love, but it is also less passionate and meaningful.

In our contemporary situation it would be difficult to use angel language for the daimonic inspirations that come our way. We concretize angels too quickly. But it would still be instructive to study angels and get to know the real experience that they represent. We might become more aware of the subtle ways in which the spiritual works in everyday experience. We could also incorporate in our natural, personal theology notions of angels in the writings of Rainer Maria Rilke and Wallace Stevens, two poets who have employed a highly sophisticated, contemporary, and subtle kind of angel in their thought.

One day in the winter of 1911 Rilke was alone in the castle at Duino at the northeastern limits of Italy, a castle on a point that juts out into the Adriatic Sea. A storm was blowing up in that dramatic setting and a potent line came to him: "When I cry out, who among the choirs of angels would hear me?" It became the first line of his *Duino Elegies*, poems about his experience of a world whose interiority unfolds "like an angel, blind, looking into itself." The first elegy goes on:

> *If one of them held me against its heart,*
> *I would disappear in its tremendous being.*
> *Beauty is only the beginning of a fear*
> *that we can hardly stand.*
> *We are in awe of it because it calmly sinks to our level*
> *to do us in.*
> *Every angel is terrifying.*

Rilke has a way of evoking the power and awesomeness of the daimon and angel. In his writing, these are not abstractions. Similarly, a religion of one's own is not a reasonable, placid, or convenient way to be spiritual. It's an opening to the full thrust of what it means to be part of vast, mysterious, and powerful existence. Like all real religion, it is basically a willingness to stand at the edge of our existence, like Rilke at land's end, open to the full potency of what it means to be alive.

Living a religion of one's own is not for the weak or pusillanimous, a melodious word that means "small soul." Notice "anima" in the word. Remember the depth and force of some of your fears. Recall the strength of certain desires and longings. The soul is filled with potential urges that overcome the will and can cause distress. As you amass the ingredients of your own religion, prepare yourself for a life requiring courage and focus. This is where the spiritual warrior and the spiritual jihad come into play. To maintain your religious convictions, you will need every bit of courage you can summon up and every ally and resource you can reach for. Religion is not just a nice thing to do. It's always a matter of life and death.

PART FIVE

Beyond the Self: Inner Guidance

Sometimes if I stopped writing and drew one hand over another my hand smelt of violets or roses, sometimes the truth I sought would come to me in a dream, or I would feel myself stopped when forming some sentence.

—W. B. YEATS, *A Vision*

Chapter 9

✿

SKILLS FOR
AN INTUITIVE LIFE

> Words and paper did not seem real enough to me;
> something more was needed. I had to achieve a kind
> of representation in stone of my innermost thoughts
> and of the knowledge I had acquired.
>
> —C. G. JUNG[73]

O n my first trip to Italy I asked some friends to take me to
the Villa Medici in Careggi, just outside Florence. The
villa was then part of a medical center and had been preserved
and maintained, especially the beautiful gardens that, though
modified in the nineteenth century, showed off the spirit of the
Renaissance. Walking through the exotic plants and trees, I came
upon an extraordinary sculpture. I don't know if it comes from
the times of Marsilio Ficino, who met at the villa in the 1480s to
discuss the soul with his friends, and I haven't been able to get
historical information on it. It is an image of an old man with a
child's body and bird claws for feet, sitting on an owl.

---

73 Jung, *Memories, Dreams, Reflections*, p. 223.

It was common in Renaissance times to portray in fantastic and grotesque images the paradoxes that are often rampant in life. Grotesque doesn't have to mean ugly; it may refer to a beast that is a mixture of many species, a chimera. I took a photograph of this statue during that visit many years ago and have contemplated it many times since. The old man with the young body is familiar as the senex-*puer*, a tight blend of youth and age. An example is my father, who at one hundred years old still had a youthful spirit. Or it could be someone who is able to imagine new possibilities freely and yet is also skilled at making his ideas workable and even financially successful. Sitting on an owl, the old man is even more enabled. The owl itself is a senex-*puer*, a spirited bird, but one associated with wisdom and underworld, both brilliant knowledge and night vision.

The lesson I take from the mysterious image in the garden is to realize how important it is to deal with life's mysteriousness, using your imagination and intuition, prepared for paradoxes and surprises, able to appreciate how intricate the path toward fulfillment can be. It isn't enough to be reasonable, to follow the crowd, to do what is expected, and to be normal and adjusted. We have to be like that figure in the garden: old and young, feeble and birdlike, infantile and wise.

Finding your own way toward a unique religious life isn't like preparing for a profession. You don't go to school for it, and you won't find a ready-made plan. You have to follow inspirations, revelations, surprises, turnabouts, and intuitions. I don't use the word "intuition" lightly. I don't mean a simple hunch. I'm referring to a deep kind of knowing that doesn't follow the rules of logic and can't be found through research and reasoning.

A Dreamcatcher

"Intuition" comes from a Latin word that means "to keep watch over." To be intuitive is to be prepared to see some new kind of information or insight that is faint and passing. Intuitions come and go quickly. You have to watch for them. You need something like a dreamcatcher, a feathery net, to grasp them when they appear. They are like subtle messages coming at you, but so delicate and thin that you might easily let them go by. Because they are not the product of reasoning and factual research; you have to learn to sort them out and eventually trust them.

I present these "rules" from experience. As I get older, I become more intuitive and live more from intuition than facts. I have to watch for intuitions, grab them before they disappear, evaluate them rather quickly, and then trust the ones I decide to keep. Each of these steps requires practice and experience. I get better at them the longer I deal with them. I realize that intuition is a valuable way of getting along in life, but I'm also aware that it is a skill.

Strong powers of intuition are useful and maybe necessary to establish a religion of one's own. It's a subtle business to grasp the hidden truths in nature and in oneself, to know how and when to act, and to appreciate mysteries when they are in play. In our personal religion, intuition is akin to prayer in formal religion. It's a special form of dialogue and communication.

Intuition is more like contemplation and meditation than research and experiment. It is more interior, more subtle, less provable, and more elusive. It isn't easy to trust what you sense intuitively, mainly because there are no external facts to bolster your conclusions or give you confidence as you act on them.

Religion isn't essentially about facts but about matters of faith, hope, and ethics. It requires inner vision as well as outer. Especially when it comes to making decisions and determining how to live, formal religions often offer tools for intuition, such as scripture passages that can be interpreted in various ways, or retreats that help you still your mind to be open to inspiration.

Intuition and Timing

In the Gospels, at the moment when Jesus is gathering students and followers and sending them out to teach and heal, he says, "The moment has come in the fullness of time. God's kingdom is close. Allow yourself a change of heart and trust this good teaching" (Mark 1:15). The word for time here is the much celebrated word "*kairos.*" It doesn't refer to a quantity of time but to quality—the perfect time to act. It suggests opportunity and good fortune. Things have reached a point where now it's good to make a move.

Such a moment came to me one day when I was still living in a religious community. Over those thirteen years I would sometimes wonder if I would remain in the community. Many of my classmates left, but I persevered to a point only six months away from ordination. I remember in my last year there my father saying with some relief, "I guess you're over the hump now."

"I hope so," I said, and I thought I was.

But one morning I woke up and knew that the calling had vanished. I could no longer live like a monk and aim for the priesthood. That very morning I had a meeting scheduled with the prior to discuss the upcoming ordination. He asked me if I had doubts about going on.

"Yes," I said, "I have serious doubts, and more than doubts."

"Then you can't be ordained," he said. "You can wait for next year's ordinations."

No, I couldn't. I felt the pressure of the fullness of time. The word used with "*kairos*" in Mark's Gospel is a verb form of pleroma, fullness. I knew that I couldn't delay my life. My experience as a monk had apparently reached its pleroma. This was the exact time for me to make a change.

From the outside it may have looked as though I was deciding against religion, Christianity, and the Gospel. But as I see it now, it was just the opposite. I was making a religious decision, in the fullness of time, following a profound change in my heart, that was in complete accord with the Gospel. I was choosing against a formal religious life and leaving open the possibility for a religion of my own. Years later I would read about Emerson coming to a similar point of decision, rejecting the formal tradition, and for him, too, it was a matter of becoming more religious, not less.

Parenthetically, let me say clearly that the gist of this book, the discovery or creation of a religion of your own, is not an option. It's a necessary step in your spiritual unfolding. Resist it and hide either in a religious institution or in a fully secular world, and your soul will be stuck. You will have symptoms and will not be happy. You may spend years wondering what is wrong with you: why you're sad or sick, why your marriage isn't working out, why you can't find work that you can love. You may wonder what it's all about.

I now believe that it would have been irreligious of me to stay in the Church instead of following through on my intuition—that's what it was—that fate had a different life in store for me. I didn't know what the future would bring. Like stepping off a cliff, I was going into free fall. I had no assurance that I would find a more meaningful existence and I didn't have any clues as to what the future could be. I was at the mercy of pure intuition asking me to surrender.

Intuitions can be challenging: They are difficult to grasp, keep, trust, and understand. Yet they are essential, especially in spiritual matters.

An essential phase in the spiritual life is to discover your destiny, your calling, or God's will for you—whatever way you want to put it. This important issue requires a constant and deep intuitive reading of events. The ultimate question is, Who am I and what am I called to do in this short life? It's a question that can only be answered in mysterious ways. You may have to follow the advice Rilke gave to his young poet friend: Keep deepening your question until an answer evolves. The best way of deepening is to pursue a string of intuitions, discovering to some extent through trial and error where your destiny lies.

When I look back on my life, I realize that the truly significant, positive changes took place in the midst of considerable discomfort: leaving home to embrace my destiny, leaving the monastery when I knew it was time, being denied tenure at a university and knowing that a new chapter was beginning, having a child when I didn't think fatherhood was in the cards for me.

Nicole Kidman, a real artist whose acting I admire, says something similar about her work, which requires an intuitive instinct at every step. Her intuitions were tangled up with a tendency toward the unusual and the dark. "As a kid, I was always a bit, I suppose, darker. I was drawn to things that were unusual. And that's partly to do with my parents. My mom's always questioned things, wanted us not to conform. So, with roles, I like to be in a place of discomfort. I do my best work in the most complicated roles. I don't have the capacity to be lighter, and I so wish I did. I'm working on it."[74]

"I like to be in a place of discomfort" may be the secret to her successful career. It is certainly an aspect of living instinctively, reading the signs and following an inner compass. It's similar to John Keats's celebrated "negative capability"—when a person is capable of being in "uncertainties, Mysteries, doubts"—essential not only in art but in religion. People sometimes turn to formal religion for comfort, but a deep, personal religious sense may require the opposite—the capacity to be with uncertainty, to take risks, to ask the most difficult questions, and to avoid the easy answers. Maybe this is the difference between formal religion and the spiritual path you find on your own: With the latter you allow yourself the pressure of doubt and wonder.

---

74 "Nicole Kidman interview with Jennifer Aniston," *Harper's Bazaar*, January 5, 2011.

The first prerequisite for a religion of one's own is the ability to be connected to the mysteries without having to explain them. Recently a woman in therapy with me, Patricia, said, "What is going on with me now? Why am I in so much pain? And what are you and I doing, sitting here talking about it? What is it all about?"

This was a woman whose life had been clear and ordered for many years, but it had also been shallow. Her work was meaningless to her, her marriage superficial, and her parenting only half-engaged. From the outside it looked to everyone like a perfect life, but to her it was a failure. Then it began to fall apart. She felt the pain of its disintegration, but I could see the necessity. I didn't see how she could change without a real experience of chaos. I kept in mind Jung's words about Hermes or Mercury, a development that takes shape or a mood that comes over us when we need to change and find our depth: "This spirit corresponds to that part of the psyche whose transformation and integration are the outcome of a long and wearisome opus. It leads those it overcomes neither upwards nor beyond, but back into chaos."[75]

Most people understand a spiritual path to be one that leads "upwards and beyond," but Jung was aware that it may bring us back into a deeper and creative chaos, a state of origins and beginnings that allows new life to form, a process of transformation that is "a long and wearisome opus," not a brief and exciting rebirth. Some people don't have the stomach for it and give it up. Even some spiritual movements embrace a positive philosophy exclusively, neglecting the role of disintegration in the making of a soul.

A religion of one's own is a process, not a static state, with forward and backward movements. It is rarely a steady evolution.

---

75 C. G. Jung, *Mysterium Coniunctionis*, p. 252.

It is both painful and wearisome and full of uncertainty. It is spiritual and psychological, theological and emotional, social and intensely individual. Like the work of an alchemist, it involves frequent changes and various temperatures, colors, and smells as one adventure follows another.

You need your intuition in high gear to stay close to developments and to know where to go next. Your guide, if you have one, needs equal amounts of fortitude and instinct. It would be good to have some tools available to support your intuitive processes.

Guides and Markers

When you read the stories of men and women who have struggled to find their way toward a deep understanding of themselves and their world, an important aspect of their own religion, you may notice how certain people and events serve as guides and markers for them.

One example that always inspires me, probably because I have been a Catholic monk and come from a certain generation, is the Cistercian monk Thomas Merton. He was an ardent searcher all his life, but especially in his youth, when he sought answers and had a strong intuitive pull toward religion. He didn't know for a long time if that pull would lead to formal or informal religion.

He had many serious questions, and one big step in his march toward monasticism was a book. Merton read a heavy tome by the philosopher Etienne Gilson, *The Spirit of Mediaeval Philosophy*. "What a relief it was for me," he writes in his early autobiography, "to discover not only that no idea of ours, let alone any image, could adequately represent God, but also that we should not allow ourselves to be satisfied with any such knowledge of Him."[76]

---

76 Thomas Merton, *The Seven Storey Mountain* (New York: Harcourt Brace & Co., 1998), p. 191.

Merton was an intellectual looking for religion with his mind. Today more people seem to be on the hunt with their hearts. But Merton's search for satisfying religious ideas is still relevant, especially the idea that God is beyond any particular expression. Many people could find sure guidance avoiding ideas about religion that are too certain and fixed.

The other, more general point is that a book can be a life-changing guide to intuition. A book can help you formulate your vague intimations and sharpen them. It can spell out more clearly what you have found in the fuzzy regions of your tracking. It can take your thoughts and wonderment further, not necessarily providing clear answers, but furthering your process.

Next, Merton had the impulse to actually go into a church. "First, there was this sweet, strong, gentle, clean urge in me which said: 'Go to Mass! Go to Mass!' It was something quite new and strange, this voice that seemed to prompt me. . . . When I gave in to it, it did not exult over me, and trample me down in its raging haste to land on its prey, but it carried me forward serenely and with purposeful direction."[77]

Merton's story is full of intuitions, an openness to an inner voice that would at first reject and then finally accept. Gradually, step by step, he found his way to the Abbey of Gethsemani in Kentucky, where he lived the rest of his life in relative isolation and yet in dialogue with the world, fulfilling his hungry search for a spiritual home.

I'm reminded of another Catholic, a friend who has gone out of his way to help me, the actor Martin Sheen, who also tells a tale of chaos, search, and discovery. He was at a low point in his life, dealing with disorientation and alcohol and in the wake of a heart attack, when he made perhaps his most powerful film, the aptly titled *Apocalypse Now*. His life really changed, he says, when

---

77 Merton, *The Seven Storey Mountain*, p. 226.

he bumped into the director and screenwriter Terrence Malick in Paris in 1981. Malick helped him personally and gave him a book, Dostoevsky's *The Brothers Karamazov.* "It transformed my spirit. When I finished reading it I put it down and literally got up and walked to Saint Joseph Church. I banged on the door and this Irish Passionist priest opened the door and said, 'What's going on?' I told him, 'I have been away from the church for a long time and I'd like to go to confession.'"[78]

Then, through the channels of his Catholicism, Martin became an activist. As he says, "For the spiritual life to be active you have to put your body where your spirit is. We must find a way to unite the way of the spirit with the work of the flesh." One day in the late 1990s, Martin and I went for a walk in Santa Monica and then attended Mass. After Mass he invited a number of young men to join us for dinner at a nearby restaurant. I noticed how he offered himself in a caring way to each one of these men, who were on their own paths toward meaning. He sat at the head of the long table and engaged the men in a penetrating conversation. The scene echoed the Last Supper, and I could see that Martin had not just found Catholicism, but his own religious identity, his own way of being Catholic. That evening at dinner he wasn't a sheep hiding in the flock. He was taking the role of his inspiration, Jesus, sitting at the head of the table, offering himself to a group of men, disciples for the moment, looking up to him.

For both Merton and Sheen, their deep intuitive quest for a religion they could reconcile with their needs and values found focus through friendship, another useful tool for intuition. A good friend can offer a book, an insight, an opportunity to reflect, and emotional support. The best friend might be one like Malick, who gave Sheen something to think about and was the

---

78 Sr. Rose Picatte, interviewer, "On 'The Way' with Martin Sheen," *National Catholic Reporter* (October 7, 2011).

impetus for a crucial spiritual development. Friendship, of course, works two ways. In your own religion, you could be the kind of friend ready to suggest books to read, lectures to attend, and travels to make on behalf of the other's spiritual life.

Synchronicity

Over many years I have found other tools useful, though they may seem unusual in our science-based culture.

The first, synchronicity, associated with Jung, is simply noticing when two or more things happen at the same time in a meaningful way, though there is no causal connection between them. The novelist Herman Hesse tells the story of how he was searching for some answers to his life questions when he happened to find a life-changing book on an empty seat in a train. A passenger had left it inadvertently, and Hesse found a trail to his answers.

Readers have told me many stories about my book *Care of the Soul*. I'm sure other authors have similar accounts. A person is traveling and finds an old, worn copy of the book in a used bookshop in a foreign country. It becomes a lifesaver. Or, a person has had the book for years sitting on a shelf in his bedroom. One evening he picks it up and starts reading. It speaks to him and leads him along—at just the right time. One woman told me that she was moving to a new house and thought she had thrown away most of her books. As she was unpacking, *Care of the Soul* fell onto the floor. She picked it up and found a new direction for her life. Books seem particularly prone to synchronicity.

You can cultivate synchronicities by paying close attention to the times and places of certain meaningful events. You don't need causal connections, just coincidence and timing. You can make decisions based on synchronicity. You can also extend the idea to any matters involving time, timing, season, and decisions. Farmers used to plant in a waxing moon and harvest in a waning moon. You could so something similar in any area of life.

The religious aspect in this is cooperating with nature or connecting your life with that of another—another person, being, time, or place. My friend Pat reads lightbulbs. When a streetlamp flashes out, he sees it as a punctuation of meaning, something to take note of, like a red flag in e-mail.

I take synchronicities as signs and guideposts. Reading them regularly and giving them some attention makes your world come alive. You live with imagination rather than with facts. You notice levels of meaning that would otherwise pass you by. In this realm of imagination and startle, you are less encased in your head and more in touch with the life of the world, especially its signals and invitations.

I have tried different kinds of intuitive devices, starting with the *I Ching*, which is a profound instrument for bringing imagination to life. I usually use the coin method and watch closely as one hexagram turn into another—it's called The Book of Changes. Then I tried reading Tarot cards. I'm quite familiar with traditional spiritual imagery, so the cards were rich and suggestive. But for me, the way I used them, they didn't fire up my imagination and intuition. Then I discovered tea leaves.

Tea leaves appear to me as an alphabet or automatic script, pictograms that suggest an unfolding imagery that has meaning as your imagination goes into action. I can't explain them, but I find reading tea leaves an effective way to stimulate intuition. The process is not just one of reading images, like interpreting dreams. There is something about the tea, the cup, and the tradition that has some potency. There may be echoes of the Japanese tea ceremony inherent in the notion of tea, as well as my grandmother, whose experiments with tea leaves were so striking that she eventually gave up on them.

Whatever the explanation, my intuition comes alive when I look into a teacup that has been drained and has leaves stuck to its sides. Recently I was having a cream tea with my wife in a beautiful tea shop in England. She asked if I'd look into her cup.

As sometimes happens with these things, immediately images began to appear and without thinking about their meaning, I began to get ideas about her work and her future. I told her what I saw. She has a habit of listening closely to my intuitions, as I do hers.

I realize, of course, that I could be ridiculed for these practices, especially the tea leaves. But I have also found that people enjoy them and many even take their "messages" seriously. I used to be reluctant to present this side of my interests to professionals like medical doctors and psychiatrists, but I have found that many of them want to escape the heavy rationalism that pervades their worlds and are eager to explore alternatives.

Mirrors

This issue of tools for intuition brings us to a discussion of natural magic. The two areas overlap to some extent. In that respect, a number of years ago I visited the British Museum on a day off in London. I asked the officer at the door if there might be an exhibit on alchemy. He said I should go to Oxford for alchemy, but they had a small collection of items belonging to John Dee. I was even more excited by that news.

For years I have studied the history of natural magic that includes John Dee, astrologer, mathematician, and seer of Elizabethan England. He was a learned and well-read man who employed assistants who were skilled at using a scrying mirror for insight. That day at the British Museum I saw Dee's mirror, made of black obsidian, a volcanic stone, and highly polished. When I returned home to New England I told my family what I had seen, and later my son gave me an obsidian mirror as a gift. I put the mirror on my desk, where it sat for several months. I'd look into it and see nothing. Then unexpectedly and quite dramatically the mirror suddenly "turned on."

Later, I realized that working with tea leaves taught me something about tools for intuition. I learned how to see past the images that formed from the leaves and listen for thoughts that arose in the process. Suddenly, the mirror came to life in ways even stronger than the leaves. Now I can look in the mirror and, on most days, get insight into any issue I bring to it or that someone else raises. Intuition has suddenly risen a step or two in my estimation and among my priorities.

The magnetic power of the mirror is so strong that one day, when I was sitting with a friend in a London coffee shop, I happened to glance at his oversize cup of coffee and felt my eyes become fixed on the reflections in it. In the early days scrying mirrors were sometimes simply dark-colored bowls filled with water. The scryer read the reflections in the water. It wasn't my intention at all to "read" my friend's coffee. But I couldn't help myself. I kept my thoughts to myself and tried not to let on what was happening. He didn't know about my interest in the mirror. But ideas shot out from his cup. We discussed these small revelations that took us quickly to issues that had been much on his mind. He was grateful and wondered how I knew about his worries.

Nowadays, just before I'm scheduled for an hour's consultation, I may take a quick look in the mirror. I gaze for only a few seconds, but in that time I usually see two things: a pattern of some sort that serves as a symbol for what is happening in my client's world, and then I get a more particular idea of how to proceed. I don't use this information in a heavy way but only think about it now and then during the conversation, especially if the mirror material suddenly comes to mind, as it often does. In work like therapy it's important to be intuitive, and the mirror jump-starts that power that is usually napping in me.

The mirror has taught me to perceive intuitions immediately. I no longer need any intermediary of thought and reasoning. I can also sense when the timing is right for such a method—it isn't always the case. I have become more of a receiver than a doer and a thinker. I've learned to trust more and insist on less.

I've discovered how much significant information passes us by every day, when we aren't alert and receptive. Often we don't have time to wait for the full and perfect message but should take the nuances that are available. I know now that important ideas often come in tiny packages that zoom past our senses.

A mundane example: I was checking in at a hotel. The person at the desk gave me a plastic card for a key, and I noticed just as I turned to head toward my room that I hesitated. A thought shot though my mind that this key wouldn't work. But I dismissed the thought, probably because I had no reason to consider it, no information that would make it a rational idea. When I got to the room, I discovered that the floor I was on had locks that required ordinary metal keys. If I had paid attention to my passing intuition, I would have been spared the trouble of sorting out the keys. Nowadays I try harder to give credence to the small sparks of intuition that streak through my awareness.

Prophecy

The traditions teach that a person who has made real progress in religion of some sort may develop a gift for prophecy, the ability to glimpse the future. Many people turn to religion to become more ethically sensitive, to prepare for death, or to make sense of life. Another motive, especially for a religion of one's own, is to cultivate out-of-the-ordinary personal powers, not to astonish friends but to live more fully in a spiritual sphere, to be relieved of the limits of a purely materialistic existence.

As a therapist I have found it helpful to cultivate my intuition. It isn't enough to listen to a person's problems or life story, analyze it rationally, and look for ways of improvement or a route to health. A human life is profoundly mysterious and calls for deeper and less rational ways of responding. I use dreams in all my work, as I have already described, and they take me to a deep, reflective place that is far more intuitive than cognitive in the usual sense. They float me away from pure rationality toward insights about the future. Where is this person headed? What will be the likely outcome if he continues on his present road or if he changes? I could arrive at answers to these questions by trusting my education and technical training, but I will come closer to a livable answer through intuition.

Therefore, let's add one more intuitive power: prophecy. Without being too strange about it, taking ideas about the future as a normal part of life we could cultivate intuition in this direction. We could pay more attention to our hunches about what will happen and test them as events unfold. We could also use any of our tools for intuition to help ignite and intensify our thoughts about the future as it develops.

I'm not talking about some prestidigitational magic in predicting the future to the astonishment of all. I'm imagining the ordinary, everyday use of intuition concerning the future that would give you hints about what could happen. Prophecy has always been part of religion because it represents a power out of the ordinary, appropriate in a spiritual way of life and suitable to a religion of one's own.

The year 2001 was an important one for me. I moved to Ireland with my family and lived in a small village, more a suburb, on the south side of Dublin, a walk away from the sea. I have always had a deep love of Ireland, from the stories my family told me when I was a child and from studying there for two years when I was just turning twenty. I hoped to write about Ireland during our sabbatical, but things didn't turn out as we imagined.

My daughter's school didn't work out as we had hoped, either, and, feeling cut off from the exciting life I had been living in the United States as a busy author, I got depressed. I was happy to come home, though not really so happy to leave Ireland.

In this context something extraordinary happened. In August, back in the United States, I was teaching psychiatrists, as usual, on Cape Cod for a week. One morning I woke up with a disturbing dream: Planes were attacking buildings in an American city, billowing dark smoke and branching flames all around. I woke up thinking that the country might well be attacked soon and told my family about my anxieties. This was three weeks before September 11.

I don't know why this dream would come three weeks before the event it depicted, but the timing is interesting. I can't think of any practical reason for it. I've spoken to others who had similar dreams, and for the most part their dreams also appeared two to three weeks before the fateful day. The sense of prophecy, in dreams or waking, may give you a jolt and it may have the sheen of the mysterious about it. This is a sign of breaking through beyond literalism and secularism to your mysterious powers. I take them as being natural but out of the ordinary. Ficino said that this kind of daily magic is like grafting the limb of one kind of tree to the trunk of another. The power is natural, but we have to "graft" ourselves solidly into nature in order to enjoy the special powers that are so unusual as to be magical.

One of the underlying themes of this book is the opportunity we have in a new century and millennium to stretch beyond the myth of fact and the scientific worldview that has both given us a treasury of gifts and at the same time has limited us. Now we can explore worlds beyond the factual and the measurable, with full use of our intelligence, and recover new kinds of knowing and a basically fresh approach to mystery and religion.

Chapter 10

❧

NATURAL MAGIC

If you want to obtain solar gifts, notice when the sun
is ascending in Leo or Aries on the day and hour of
the Sun. Then, wearing a solar robe of a golden color
and having laurel on your head and, burning the solar
aromatics myrhh and incense on an altar, spread
flowers like heliotrope on the ground.

—FRANCESCO DIACETTO, STUDENT OF MARSILIO FICINO[79]

In 1971 Phil Knight, the founder of Blue Ribbon Sports, at the
time a company struggling to succeed, was developing a
brand of athletic shoes and needed a logo. Fortunately, a graphic
design student, Carolyn Davidson, was in an accounting class he
was teaching and took on the task of coming up with several
possible logos. Knight wasn't thrilled with Davidson's "swoosh,"
but he liked it best of the bunch and decided to use it. Davidson
billed Knight at two dollars an hour and presented a bill for
under thirty-five dollars. The famous "swoosh," still the logo of

---

79 D. P. Walker, *Spiritual and Demonic Magic* (London: Warburg Institute,
1958), p. 32. TM translation.

Knight's new company, *Nike*, had a powerful impact on customers. In 1983, at a gathering honoring her, to show his gratitude Knight gave Davidson a diamond swoosh ring and an envelope with Nike stock.

The Nike swoosh has been celebrated, envied, manipulated, and copied, but it hasn't been seen for what it is: magic. Magic is a way of acting that is effective and powerful but doesn't use the usual cause-and-effect, rational methods of science and common sense. A shoe company wants to convince people to buy its product, but it isn't enough to explain how good and economical the product is. The company will look for language or a symbol that will speak to people in a nonrational way, perhaps emotionally or symbolically, and set the fires of desire in them.

The Nike swoosh suggests speed, grace, and success. For the Greeks, Nike was the goddess of victory and was pictured with wings and she was holding a feather. In the war of the Titans, Nike stood by the side of Zeus, father of the gods, offering him confidence and counsel. Like most magic, there is a hidden element that adds to the power of the symbol or language. A person buying a pair of shoes doesn't need to be told the mythological story of Nike. He only has to see the swoosh, and the history of the logo has its effect.

Sometimes magic is due to the power inherent in a word or image. Many ancient books of magic picture strange symbols that according to tradition have special powers. The athletic company's swoosh isn't in these books, but it could be. It has kept the company successful for many decades by attracting millions of loyal followers. Any company would be happy to have such magic.

Most people don't realize that there is a long history of sophisticated magic in the West. Ramon Lull, Tommaso Campanella, Marsilio Ficino, Abbot Johannes Trithemius, Heinrich Cornelius Agrippa of Nettesheim, John Dee, and Robert Fludd were all magicians—not sleight-of-hand tricksters but serious, altruistic people who drew on powers hidden deep in ordinary life. Some, like Lull and Trithemius, were especially interested in the power of alphabets and words; others, like Fludd and Ficino, also saw special powers in music and the visual arts.

These early figures referred to their work as "natural magic," to distinguish it from supernatural magic. Often they understood magic to be quite ordinary, like Trithemius creating alphabetical codes that would seem simple today and yet were astonishing in his time. Think of writing a letter to someone in code where every other letter of every other word spells out the message. Although Trithemius spoke of words having daimons in them, he meant that his coded words had special hidden powers.

For Americans, the words "We, the people" have the power to inspire and move. "I do" at weddings is far more than an affirmative answer to a question. In the Catholic Church, "This is my body" has the momentous effect of making the Christ present in ritual. In the Heart Sutra, chanted, written, and memorized around the world, the word "empty," "*sunyata*" in Sanskrit, has a mesmerizing effect as it is repeated many times.

Some religions judge magic as devilish and dark, unacceptable. They won't confess that some of their activities are magical. The Catholic Church distinguishes between magic and sacrament, but in some cases it would be difficult for most people to pinpoint the difference. If you have a positive evaluation of magic, as I do, you have no problem admitting that your religion contains magic. The same is true for a religion of your own: Appreciating the magic in life helps you live life outside the perimeters of reason. In that way magic serves religion.

I want the space in which I live and work to have a spiritual dimension. I put statues and paintings and quotations all around and notice how they magically influence the way I work. They support my intention to give a spiritual quality to my writing and my way of life. I learned this in part from the Renaissance author on "natural magic," Marsilio Ficino, who would put quotations on the walls where he taught, understanding this practice as a form of magic. The magic is in the impact carefully chosen visual words can have on the awareness of people exposed to them.

The Archetype of the Sky

You may know the word "magus" from the Gospel story of Jesus's birth, when magicians or astrologers—the Magi (plural form of "magus")—arrived with gifts. In the Western world, there was a long line of magi, each following a particular approach to magic. Natural magic entails recognizing and employing the hidden power in words, alphabets, and images. Many a magus in history has developed certain abilities and skills to have a strong effect with unusual and often mysterious means. But the magus was also usually interested in applying magic to ordinary situations. Ficino helped painters find powerful themes and images. John Dee advised navigators so they wouldn't get lost. Today advertisers are always looking for words and images that will have the power to influence people You and I can use magic in our everyday worlds to navigate issues at work and home.

My friend Ruth lives just outside Zürich and one day several years ago went looking for a place in the Alps where she could go for a personal retreat. She found an old cabin in an enchanting clearing. At the door was a large coiled snake, at the window a busy hummingbird, and off above the trees an eagle. She felt that the three animals represented the earth, the soul, and the spirit, and she made her home in the mountains there. She followed the magic of the place rather than any rational reasons and has enjoyed many happy years in her retreat. Now she has incorporated the persona of the magus into her way of life.

As I was writing this chapter, I was sitting outdoors having lunch with my wife and daughter next to a rushing river when we spotted a tall, thin blue heron standing still on a rock in the water. We watched him closely for several minutes, and then a man came along anxious to see the heron he had just heard about. He got his glimpse and then said he could go back to work. This magnetism of nature is a kind of natural magic, as well, not unrelated to Ruth's sight of the animals at her cottage. A lucky glimpse of what is usually undetected has a magical impact, difficult to explain but obviously powerful.

Most people realize that you can't accomplish much in life through mental effort alone. You need luck, as we call it, or perhaps less rational tools of imagination. You can rely on intuition, imagination, and, as we've seen, prediction. Normally we don't pay much attention to these nonrational modes of perception and judgment, but we use them anyway. The magus makes a profession out of them.

In the past, the magus kept an eye on the sky. He lived in an astrological world and included the movements of the planets in his calculations about how to interpret events and what to do. Today we have seen the dusty rocks on the moon and on Mars and find it more difficult to imagine the planets as meaningful factors. But, as usual, we think too literally and concretely. Even knowing what we do about the planets from science, we could still benefit from a religious attitude toward the sky.

You can begin thinking astrologically by noticing the sky in ordinary ways: look at the clouds, be aware of the weather, stop to watch a special sunrise or sunset, know where the moon is on its monthly course. These simple, everyday practices can be the basis of your astrological awareness. They can enrich your life and increase your sense of participation in a greater universe that has its schedules and changes. You can even fit your behavior and decisions into this grand movement in the sky and realize that you are not small but are part of a grand, dynamic cosmos.

In 2001, as we began a year of life in Dublin, Ireland, my wife, Hari Kirin, a serious painter, developed an imaginative art project that had a strong ritual aspect. When we arrived with our two young children, we had to register at the immigration office as "aliens." We felt odd and uncomfortable being put into such a category. Then, as we tried to convince the officers that we had financial resources, we saw how people from many countries in the same room were finding it more difficult to prove themselves worthy to enter. That's when my wife conceived her idea.

She decided to paint the Irish sky every day at four a.m. and four p.m. The timing of her work echoed a monastic rule, and, in addition, she felt that these were the most liminal or "thin" moments of the day. The clouds in her paintings suggested that the borders we enforce so strictly between nations are irrelevant when seen from the sky. Quiet and undisturbed, they pass over these artificial boundaries constantly, paying them no heed.

She made her paintings on small pieces of canvas the size of an Irish pound note, the currency at the time. When she had completed three months' worth of paintings, she arranged to exhibit them at the very immigration office that had originally inspired them. Some of the officers there tried to prevent her from showing her paintings, but, an Irish-American, strong-willed herself, she stood up to them and got her one-day exhibit.

Because this project, made up of several hundred beautiful small paintings, portrayed the sky on its daily schedule, it qualified, in my mind, as an astrological project and had its own kind of magic. She painted on her strict natural schedule and portrayed the mystery of the clouds. She helped people reflect on the limitations of national borders and offered a concrete view of our common global humanity. The project was both aesthetic and ethical. And it was magic.

It's no coincidence that religions around the world pray to a sky father—"Our Father, who art in heaven [sky]," or that church spires point to the sky and church ceilings are painted in sky-blue colors and dotted with stars. It's interesting that in Christianity, Easter falls on the first Sunday after the first full moon after the spring equinox and that Christmas coincides roughly with the winter solstice. These dates are determined by what is going on in the sky.

Mircea Eliade's *Encyclopedia of Religion* describes sky aspects of the *Ka'bah* at Mecca, which is "the highest point on earth because it lies directly beneath the polestar, the 'center' or 'gate' of heaven and the opening in the celestial vault through which the 'sky stone' must have fallen. The Ka'bah thus marks a visible point on the axis mundi along which communication between the divine and human worlds takes place in an especially powerful and significant way."[80]

We could practice some simple natural magic by climbing a mountain to experience that imagined contact point between earth and sky, the finite and the infinite. We could have a photograph of the night sky accessible for reminding and reflecting. We could paint a ceiling light blue to bring the sky into our living space. These are simple magical ways of participating in the ancient ritual of honoring the sky as an image of spirit.

The sky is the literal space above us, but it is also a natural symbol. No one invented the symbolism of the sky. It's simply a fact that when you gaze at it you may think about spiritual matters. A domed church makes that experience more symbolic and yet still rather effective. From a certain point of view, the dome is a tool of magic. The Pantheon in Rome, with its open circular "eye" at its top, is another example. The sky may be the most comprehensive and most affecting images for spirit in general, and so we often see it represented in religious art. We might take a lesson from sacred art and give the sky special attention in our own practice.

In the summer of 2012 I spent a week at Oxford University teaching a group of highly qualified astrologers. I was impressed by the sophistication of their astrological knowledge and techniques

---

80 Mircea Eliade, ed., *Encyclopedia of Religion* (New York: Macmillan, 1987), vol. 13, p. 347.

and appreciated their openness to my more general ideas about relating to the sky and living in an animate, ensouled world. They taught me new ways of using astrology as practical spiritual poetry, a tool for imagining life's rhythms and one's natural raw materials.

At dinner one evening, the master astrologer Lynn Bell sat across from me at the headmaster's table, identical to the one used for dining hall scenes in the Harry Potter movies, and talked to me about my Jupiter returns. Jupiter returns every twelve years into each person's sign, and so those times—at ages twelve, twenty-four, thirty-six, forty-eight, etc.—are times of good fortune and significance, a time for opportunity and self-reflection. She asked about events in my life that coincided with Jupiter's arrival at twelve-year intervals. It was like sitting with a good therapist, and the conversation helped me restore my sense of life rhythms and my connection to the natural world. Think about your own Jupiter returns. Did anything remarkable happen at the twelve-year intervals in your life?

This is an effective way to make connections between your own life and the movements of the sky, to align yourself with nature in its specific aspect of the heavens. It is simple natural magic that expands your idea of who you are and how you are connected to the cosmos.

Some Principles of Magic

We are entering a new era. On the one hand, we are aware, as never before, how our world changes with developments in information, communication, science and technology. But there is a backlash. Many are also interested in the more esoteric ideas of Jung, new spiritual communities, and magical elements of traditional religions such as Tarot Cards and the Kabbalah. We are headed for a new style of thinking and living, and some old and rejected perspectives may well return with a new dignity. It simply makes sense to offset our material gain with an expansion and deepening of our spiritual place in the world. I expect astrology and magic to be part of that cycle of return.

The magus of old teaches us, first, to time our lives and activities well. Stay in tune with the rhythms of nature and the pulse of our lives. Be open to the *kairos*, the right timing, and the good signs. Be ready to slow down and halt when the winds are not favorable. Abstain from eager desires when the climate isn't right and then move ahead when indications are strong.

The alchemist, another kind of magus, stares at his oven and glass vessels and adjusts the heat. Know when to keep things hot and when to cool down. Know how to boil and simmer and remove from the heat. Understand the purposes of cool and hot, as the ancient Greek philosophers advised. Know, too, what to keep moist and what to dry out, what to add to your life and what to take out. An alchemical imagination of ordinary life is part of natural magic.

The magus also sometimes uses music as a way of healing, calming, and persuading people. The music may be actual sound, as in Marsilio Ficino's use of what he called his "Orphic lyre." The music could also be metaphor, as in Robert Fludd's fascinating charts showing the many octaves of experience that resound in our actions. We all know how different kinds of music can affect our emotions, but how? Try to explain it. One way is to see the special power of music as a form of magic. Fludd's idea of the music of everyday life is also common.

A man tells me that his grown son won't talk to him openly about any matters of importance, even though he, the father, is very open-minded. But as the father talks, I hear in his words a strong need to control, to have the son do what the father wants and expects. The father sings a tune of openness, but another voice in him hums quietly about control. The problem causing conflict between this father and son, from a certain angle, is a matter of music.

The magus of former times wanted to break through to

higher and hidden worlds. Some tried to conjure angels. They used mirrors, bowls of water, crystal balls, alphabet wheels. They read the flight of birds, spirals of smoke, animal tracks, clouds. They meditated, prayed, traveled, collected books, experimented, and studied with each other. Many had thin boundaries between their astrology and their humanities, their practice of magic and their scientific and mathematical studies. All searched for ways to be effective in the world that were mysterious and largely nonrational.

The Tools of Magic

Deep intuition and foresight need some kind of instrumental catalyst, a concrete method. Today some read Tarot cards or ancient runes to stimulate their imaginations and draw their perceptions closer to prediction and insight. The reading of tree leaves rustling in the wind, once a practice carried on by a few, appears outlandish, while studying rats in a laboratory seems quite rational today. The modern researcher doesn't realize the limits of the knowledge available in his highly controlled studies. Maybe the person reading runes discovered other interesting truths about human experience.

The magus thinks that like cures like: When two things are similar, often in relatively insignificant ways, they can share power. Marsilio Ficino said that when you are in need of vitality and spirit you should wear a piece of amber on a yellow string around your neck. The amber and the ribbon are the color of the sun, and you are evoking solar spirit when you wear a sunlike color.

This may not seem to make any sense. But go into a room where the ceiling is painted sky-blue and see if you feel any quality of the open sky. Notice how you feel when you wear a particular color or fabric or style of clothing. Isn't there magic for many in jeans? Jeans may evoke the spirit of relaxation and simplicity that you crave on a weekend away from the rigors of work. The makers of jeans know all this and use magic in their advertising. My daughter, a singer, thought carefully about the photo to be used on her first album. She was singing yoga music and decided to wear her spiritual white veils and a denim jacket. Many people told her later that they were entranced and uplifted by the veils but comforted by the ordinariness of the denim. Again, it is all a matter of ordinary, natural magic.

I consult with hospitals and recommend, à la Ficino's magic, that they pay attention to the colors and materials they use for decor and make choices that promote the health of their patients—using magic for health. They probably wouldn't paint a hospital hallway black—they know that much about the power of color—but what colors would be healing?

I have visited many hospitals where one strategy in particular is effective in creating a healing environement. For example I walked the quiet hallways of Greenwich Hospital in Connecticut, where attractive and calming floor carpeting has a remarkable healing effect. Magical carpeting is like William Morris's brilliant wallpaper, which also works magic in a room. Morris passionately resisted the trend in his time toward industrialization and the breakdown of humane values. He responded by making beautiful books and by creating such vivid wallpaper, usually with stunning images from nature, that his patterns and colors are still in use today. Using his rational mind, he wrote essays expressing his passionate thoughts, to which he added the magic of craft to make concrete the kind of changes he was advocating.

Fountains, atria, megalithic sculptures, hanging fabrics, dramatic lighting, flowers, and plants—they can all transform a space magically. Ficino, the father of natural magic in the West, said that architecture is the most important magical art, but in practice he also included music, painting, color, jewelry, clothing, aromas, and herbs. He was a complete magus, deeply concerned about both soul and spirit, and willing to experiment with a wide range of methods drawn from many traditional sources.

Food is another example of an ordinary substance that has magical properties. Why use fluted glassware at a party? Because it magically creates a festive atmosphere and helps people enjoy themselves. Why have a bountiful table on Thanksgiving? Because it suggests comfort and nourishment in a family and embodies an important aspect of the holiday. Why use cloth napkins instead of paper? Because a more refined material raises the experience to a more meaningful level.

From manna in the desert to Jesus saying over dinner, "This is my body," to the Jewish Seder and the Sikh Lungar, religion has observed the power of food to signify holiness. If you accept the idea that one purpose of formal religion is to show how to treat life as sacred in ordinary circumstances, then the widespread ritual of eating carried on in the religions of the world teaches that any gathering over food can have a religious quality and purpose. Eating is not just for the body but also for the soul and spirit.

Preparing and presenting food is full of magic, from the use of spices to making attractive shapes and color arrangements and assortments of flavor. We all know that a good chef is a magician: he or she can do things in a kitchen that you and I might like to do but, even when we follow directions perfectly, turn out badly.

Intuitively we know that food has magical properties. When we are going through an emotional struggle, it is quite natural to ask a friend to lunch to discuss the situation. Why lunch? Because food has a magical power to help people feel their closeness and to speak with special potency. Over food, you enjoy intimacy and community and thus pave the way for deep, friendly conversation. Accordingly, I've advised people who are lonely and cut off from people to take cooking lessons or at least to give more attention to food. Rather than try to solve their problem abstractly, they could make use of the magic of food.

Magic and Religion

Religion is all about establishing and maintaining a connection with the eternal, the mysterious, and the transcendent. Magic is a powerful kind of action that has its effect outside the usual cause-and-effect operations of normal life. The magus usually claims that he is only using neglected powers of nature, and in this magic shares something essential with religion. For a religion of your own, magic can be a way of stepping outside materialistic ways of thinking. It can place you in a liminal space that is shared by religion, where things can happen without the force of will and literal manipulation.

Magic stands next to mystery, and mystery is the heart of religion. Magic is an obvious tool for formal religion, but it can also play a part in the religion you devise for yourself. You can become a master of the invisible and the mysterious, not just to show off but to be effective in making life rich and meaningful.

Some religions use a method like bibliomancy—opening a book at random, selecting a passage with your finger, eyes closed, and reading the text indicated by your finger. You can try this method anytime. Many Christians make the sign of the cross before doing something special. That's magic. Muslims spit the words of the Qur'ān on a person who is sick, hoping for a cure. That's religious magic, as well.

Thoreau built a small, ordinary-looking cabin on a small lake, and today, almost two hundred years later, the spot is honored and a replica stands in the place of the original cabin, where people make their pilgrimage. They're not coming to learn how to build a cabin; they are drawn by the magic of Thoreau's conception, his view of the world, captured in the physical presence of a small building. Making the cabin was his form of magic.

You may have found your current home through magic of some kind. People, like my friend Ruth, often tell stories of how they found their house through a series of improbable events and coincidences. This kind of magic adds a significant dimension to something as important as a home, a dimension not entirely unlike the magic of Thoreau's cabin. Ruth found her cabin in the mountains by magic: She paid attention to the animals that appeared when she first visited. This is easy magic requiring just a little imagination: observing the behavior of animals and using your imagination to read the signs.

To establish a religion of one's own, you might consider not doing everything logically and in a fully controlled manner. You might look for signs and coincidences. You could follow up on sychronicities. You could do some simple magic by placing your finger blindly on a map, opening a book to a page and a line, swinging a pendulum pendant, picking a card from a deck. These are all very simple forms of everyday magic that lead you nonrationally toward your objectives.

Many years ago my wife and I were trying to decide whether to leave our modest but beautiful home outside Amherst, Massachusetts. We were part of a good community and liked the region. Our children were just about to reach school age, and we didn't know if we should remain in an area of five colleges, filled with university students, many of them drinking too much and getting involved with drugs. So we consulted the *I Ching*. I don't remember now just which hexagram we got, but it clearly indicated that we should follow through on the idea of moving to New Hampshire. And we did.

Today, almost twenty years later, I sometimes long for the simple house in beautiful Western Massachusetts. But then I think of the good life we have had in New Hampshire, how the children got an education here, and the children's wish now that their children grow up here, too, and then I feel good about our *I Ching* magic. The result of your magic may not be pure and perfect, because life is complicated and rarely black and white.

You can learn how to consult the *I Ching* from one of several books that teach you the easy method and give you all the basic readings. Get a beautiful edition of the Tarot cards. They are full of traditional images that relate to your life. Read them as you read a dream. Use a book to help you with all the symbols. I do. But try to use your intuition more than your rational intellect. Let the cards inspire your own thoughts. Don't just interpret what you find there.

Then graduate to more refined methods. Tea leaves and the mirror require some serious letting go of rational thinking. Still, you may be someone who can be inspired. I taught a course on natural magic in which, out of fifty participants, a dozen people seemed to make progress with the mirror. I thought that was a good ratio. You may be among the dozen.

Depression, aggression, stress, and purposelessness are some of the common symptoms of our time. People wonder why we are plagued with such things and how to get rid of them. As I see it, the problem is that we have lost religion—in the deep meaning of the word. We have formal religions that contain the seeds of genuine religiousness, but they are weakened by many problems: my usual list includes fundamentalism, moralism, empty ritual, misunderstood teachings, and general irrelevancy. In our time of cultural change, they are becoming so weak as to be lost to history.

To feel alive and ready to live, we need to live in a world that is alive and not just a collection of objects for our use. We need to encounter this world and take on life with all its mysteriousness. To the secular mind, life is a problem to be solved, but to the religious imagination it's a realm of mysteries to be engaged. But to engage a mysterious world, we can't be mere exploiters and manipulators. We need magic in order to tap into the hidden powers of life.

PART SIX

✤

Soul and Spirit

To enter the realm of spirit is only a part of the solution to the dilemma proposed by this found process, life. The remaining art resides in living well, in the particulars of our movement through the day and night. And this means attending to the second impulse of inner life—being interested in the feet of God, the parts that are still visible and have not ascended out of the picture. These toes and calloused skin are the neglected element of the divine, the bit that ouches the earth, the bit we have.

—JOHN TERRANT

Chapter 11

✺

THE CLOISTER IN
THE WORLD

[Monks] have not come to the monastery to escape from the realities of life but to find those realities: they have felt the terrible insufficiency of life in a civilization that is entirely dedicated to the pursuit of shadows.

—THOMAS MERTON[81]

For centuries and in many parts of the world, men and women have left their homes to live in a monastery, a spiritual utopia, where they could pursue what they called a life of perfection. Today most of us don't go off to a monastery, but we may seek a utopian life of our own. It makes sense then to look closely at monastic life to see if we can adapt some of its ways to modern secular life. In this way we could create not just a religion but a monastery of our own.

In my early monastic years I found it deeply satisfying to live

---

81 Thomas Merton, *The Waters of Siloe* (San Diego: Harcourt Brace & Co., 1949), p. xviii.

in a community of people dedicated to spiritual values and loving life and looking out for each other. There is something secure about having a minutely determined daily schedule punctuated by the chanting of psalms and songs and eating in silence and going to bed early and rising with the sun. It all had its shadow side, of course—the challenges of celibacy, the dominating authorities, the occasional wacky confrere, the monotony of the schedule, the loss of worldly pleasures, and the lack of freedom. But I miss it and try to evoke the spirit of the monastery in my secular life. I recommend it as a model for anyone creating a religion of one's own.

You can evoke the monastic spirit in small ways that don't interfere with your busy secular life. I'm not suggesting a radical shift in lifestyle, but rather ways to season your usual ways with themes that come from monasticism. Small and brief allusions to the monastery, whether aesthetic or practical, as I present in detail in this chapter, can bring a new atmosphere to your experience and can help change a completely secular existence into a spiritual one.

Vows Shape a Life

Strictly speaking, a monk or nun is someone who lives in a community dedicated to spiritual teachings and remains there. Thomas Merton was this kind of monk in a strict order of Cistercians, where they observed silence at all times and rarely left the grounds. In spite of his seclusion Merton had a significant impact on the issues of his day. Many know of Hildegard of Bingen, too, a twelfth-century abbess who was both a cloistered mystic and a serious player in the politics of her time.

Some, like the Servites, where I spent my time, take vows of obedience, chastity, and poverty, each of them designed to make community life tight and intense. With the vow of obedience, you live where the authorities tell you to live and do the work they think you're needed for. Chastity usually means celibacy, not being married, and generally toning down your sex life severely. Poverty entails owning everything in common, with the suggestion of living sparsely and frugally.

Lived strictly, these vows foster community life and a spiritual focus. Married couples could be dedicated and spiritually active, but coupling takes something away from intense communal life. Besides, spirituality thrives best when the appetites are thinned out. People moved to create a spiritual lifestyle aim for simplicity: less money, simpler eating, plain housing. Overall, the vows do two things: They increase a sense of community and allow a strong focus on spiritual matters.

Imagine using these monastic vows as a general model for crafting your own personal religion. You could think of them not as solemn promises but as dedication to a particular value. A medical resident once told me that she was going to be celibate for two years, just to prepare for her career in family medicine. She wondered what I thought of her idea, since her friends and family were doubtful. As a former monk, I immediately recognized the impulse and thought it was an excellent and rare inspiration. I encouraged her. Preparing emotionally and spiritually for a major life change is something monks and nuns do routinely, a valuable practice the ordinary person might neglect.

Make Your Own Monastery

The physical layout of a monastery can give you some ideas for making your own religion. In the various priories in which I lived, the main rooms were the chapel, the refectory (dining room), the recreation room, the private bedrooms, and the library. In most cases there was also considerable land around the priory for solitude, for walking, and for manual labor.

For example, during my years of philosophy training I lived at Our Lady of Benburb Priory in County Tyrone, Northern Ireland. A river ran through the land that was big enough for several football pitches and acres of pasture and lawn. The ruins of an old castle jutted out over a flowing river, and I felt that this ancient building helped create a sense of timelessness that also fosters the spiritual life.

Look at the physical layout of monasteries, as well as their activities and schedules, and see how you might borrow their approach and adapt it to your own purposes. You might be quite literal or entirely metaphorical with your adaptations: a big, heavy door in your home or a massive bell standing ready to ring in your garden, or an atmosphere of quiet and retreat.

One of the most extraordinary examples of a person making his own monastery in a secular environment is C. G. Jung building his tower in the village of Bollingen in Switzerland. In his memoirs he says, "I had to make a confession of faith in stone. . . . It was settled from the start that I would build near the water. . . . It is situated in the area of St. Meinrad and is old church land, having formerly belonged to the monastery of St. Gall."

Jung's tower accomplished many things for his psyche and his spirit, giving him a sense of expansive time, putting him in touch with his ancestors, helping him live a primitive life in the modern world, offering him the means of contemplation, and serving as a concrete reflection of his own psyche. The fact that his "tower" was on land belonging to a once powerful and famous monastery added the dimension we're talking about.

I enjoy a monastic spirit in my home. I've already described my writing room, my own scriptorium, but let me add a few details. I am surrounded by books from the floor to a high ceiling. Throughout history monks have been associated with study, copying manuscripts and collecting books. I have art around me from many different spiritual traditions: several Buddhas, Saint Thomas More, Daphne, Asklepios, Helios, and unnamed idols. Just outside my door is a beautiful framed print of the Heart Sutra and across from it a lovely painting on handmade paper by Korean artist Kwang Jean Park, depicting a squared circle (one goal of the alchemists), and down the hall is another hand-pressed print of the Tabula Smaragdina, the Emerald

Tablet, an ancient statement about the connection between Heaven and Earth, upper and lower, a central theme in my own religion. The holy word is the primary language of the monastery.

Out my window I see the beginning of many acres of wooded land. We live at the edge of town, on the border between town life and farmland and forest. My wife is a contemplative person who spends much of her time at yoga and art in a chapel and art studio above the garage. So with the general quiet and meditation going on, our home has a monastic feel to it. That may not appeal to many people, but for me it keeps my past and present linked and especially satisfies the longing for a monastic lifestyle that must have gotten me into the monastery in the first place.

A monk's home isn't a noisy place, though monks are known for their deep belly laughter and hearty wit. You may need some physical aids in your home to foster a quiet and contemplative atmosphere: a meditation room, contemplative colors, statues of a Buddha or bodhisattva, a saint, or paintings, indoor plants and trees, or just photos or paintings of nature. A water fountain can be effective, or a contemplative image from a spiritual tradition perhaps placed near a plant or flowers. You can get help with this physical arrangement by studying pictures of actual monasteries.

Monks often have a cloister. The word means either the monastery itself that the monk rarely leaves, or a colonnaded walkway, part of an enclosed garden. Anyone living outside an urban environment can make a cloister in or near their home or else just give the suggestion of a cloister with a partially enclosed garden and maybe a pillar or two. In an urban setting a very small rock garden, a painting or photograph of monks, a shelf of spiritual books, a desk for writing or even practicing calligraphy might evoke the monastic spirit. Look at an old cloister and get some ideas for one that would suit you and your lifestyle. The generic principle here is that the mere suggestion of a traditional form is often enough to evoke the spirit of it.

Monks have a refectory rather than a dining room. The word refers to a place where you're refreshed, almost identical with "restaurant," which means "restore." What could that mean to an ordinary person? Of course, you have to use your imagination and consider your own tastes and lifestyle. For the monk, "refectory" implies eating without conversation—monks often sit on only one side of a long table. You could set up a lunch nook where anyone in the household could eat alone and quietly, when they are so inspired. This doesn't mean that it is not also valuable to dine in convivial company, talking loudly and excitedly. Monks do that, too. In ordinary secular life we are usually good at creating a congenial dining area, but we may overlook the private nook for a snack or lunch.

Monks usually have a garden where they can walk in meditation. You could easily set up a garden that is more monastic than simply floral. You might make a walking path as part of it, or a stone or wood walkway. A Zen garden, of course, is a good way to go. The emptiness evoked by the sand, rocks, and plantings help clear the mind. You could look at photographs of classical Zen gardens to get ideas, and, as usual, you don't have to make it a copy but rather a garden inspired by Zen. This new kind of secular spirituality is not literal in its inspirations.

You might also learn from the Islamic garden, a reminder of Paradise and a place of rest and seclusion. An Islamic garden has its own aesthetic with an emphasis on clean lines, long shapes, a water feature, mosaic, and arches.

Knowing the importance to monks of a library, you could make something of your collection of books, understanding that a library is more than a utilitarian way of storing books. You could make your library, however small, a real and distinctive place, where your books create an atmosphere for study, reflection, or beauty. You might even have objects around you that evoke a monastery: old types of pens and paper, a magnifying glass, special inks, a calligraphy set of tools, an antique lamp or desk, some very old books, or even a manuscript. I have framed medieval manuscript pages on my wall to evoke the monk's love of a beautiful handmade page. I keep picture books of ancient illuminated Gospels on my shelves. My books on Shaker buildings and furniture also suggest a unique kind of communal art that fits in with the more classical monastic arts. I don't want my monastic pieces to be too literal or to reflect only a single spiritual tradition.

Today, as the book is replaced more and more by e-readers and other high-tech devices, a library of books, old and new, will be even more special and require care and attention. At the same time, a home library today will seem more monastic than ever and send the imagination back in time, which is a way of going deeper. As bookstores and libraries change or disappear, we could convert our sadness, if that's what you feel, into determination to collect special books, noticing their bindings and typography and making a particularly beautiful library for them.

I set up my library so that books by Ernest Hemingway, Jamaica Kincaid, and Ralph Ellison are out of place but within reach. They are my inspiration for style. I don't come even close to them in their artful use of language, but still they guide me and serve as models for the perfection I set for myself.

Celibacy

People often ask how a vibrant person could live under the vow of celibacy. I found obedience the more difficult vow. Not having a typical sex life seemed relatively easy because there is so much satisfaction in living in a close community, where friendship is often intense. Sexual relationships tend to cause considerable emotional complexity, too, and so the less convoluted connections in a community are in some ways more enjoyable. For all the compulsive emotions that drive us toward sex, there is also, for some, pleasure in being free of the entanglements and anxieties around it.

If you define "sexuality" and "celibacy" broadly, you can bring the vow of celibacy over into ordinary life, giving it an added spiritual cachet. You can even be celibate in marriage or other intimate partnerships. Sexuality in marriage is, of course, very different from the monk's experience, but marriage entails a dedication to one person, a vow, that puts a check on the desire for others. You may have celibate moments, as when you or your partner are apart or simply not interested in sex at that time. You can use times of separation as opportunities to positively enjoy a temporary celibate life.

Many people, of course, are not involved in sexual relationships. Maybe they don't have a partner, they're too busy with work, they're sick, or they're just not available. These situations can be difficult if there is no spiritual motivation. On the other hand, a loftier viewpoint can change a burden into an opportunity, because celibacy fosters spirituality and can be both liberating and fulfilling.

If you're living a celibate life, it helps to sublimate in careful and imaginative ways. You can consider the rewards of a sex life and try to work them into life in a more generic way. Pleasure, sensuality, beauty, touch, and other erotic delights can be part of life in general. Obviously these qualities may not fully replace sex, but they help turn repression or deprivation into a less focused kind of sexuality. Eroticism and celibacy go well together.

Let's remember that we're talking about making a religion of our own and shaping a spiritual life around our own needs and circumstances. Strict celibacy is a major tool men and women have used to construct a spiritual existence, and so we should consider it in our efforts to create a secular spirituality. We don't have to abstain from sex literally, but we could bring the spirit of celibacy into our ordinary lives.

We're back to Hillman's psychological polytheism. I'm interested in how to be fully sexual and fully celibate without repressing my sexuality or taking celibacy on as a burden. Both repression and the burden go against the polytheistic spirit.

Just as the vow of poverty involves a toning down of the

desire for possessions and money, the celibate spirit tones down fascination for things sexual without moralistically denying an erotic way of life. There are situations where you can enjoy life more by holding back on your sexual interests and cultivating your innocence. Even in an intense sexual relationship you can find activities that are positively pure and innocent. In general, the wholehearted enjoyment of sex helps support a wholehearted celibate spirit, and vice versa. Of course, the actual monk or nun doesn't look at it this way, but the rest of us need a different way of bringing celibacy into our ordinary lives.

Hospitality and Stability

Some monks either take a vow of hospitality or, like the Benedictines, think of it as a major concern. In my visits to Glenstal Abbey in Ireland, the one quality that has struck me most is the dedication of the monks to hospitality.

On more than one visit Father Christopher, the former abbot, with good humor helped me with luggage, made me tea, answered my questions, and generally made me feel like an honored guest. His humility and kindness were genuine—hospitality without servility. I felt that without intending it he was giving me lessons in how to be hospitable and attentive without any loss of dignity or pleasure. The current abbot, Father Mark Patrick Hederman, is always ready to pick me up at the airport, drive me where I need to go, or travel to meet with me. Whenever I contact him and ask him if I can stay at the monastery for a few days, there isn't a beat before he welcomes me with stunning openness and grace.

Hospitality may seem less important than, say, celibacy, but the effect of this spiritual practice is to create an atmosphere of warmth and friendliness rare in our busy, self-absorbed world. We may know this degree of service only in good hotels, where we pay dearly for the experience and sometimes question the motives. Many people work in the "hospitality" industry. They might take some important lessons from the monastic form of

hospitality. In the monastery, hospitality is one of the funda-
mentals of a daily spiritual practice. It shows how we might all
make our spirituality concrete by treating each other with special
attention and service.

Selfless, out-of-the-ordinary hospitality also creates an atmosphere of a utopian community, an ideal of monks and nuns. They
often see their purpose as showing how the new life of their
beliefs—Christian, Buddhist, humanitarian—looks when put
into practice. The monastic community serves as a model for how
life could be if it were lived according to highly refined values.

Ordinary people can adopt this ideal of the perfect example,
as well. Monks and nuns want to be different from the run-
of-the-mill secularistic society. They aim for a level of lived
perfection. We could do this in our secular lives by refusing to
sink to the level of inhospitable, aggressive, and competing ways,
practicing what monasticism calls *"contemptus mundi,"* a rejection
of the usual worldly values for loftier, utopian ideals.[82]

A Monk's Religion

It's difficult for a former Catholic monk to write about monasticism without always going back to Thomas Merton. In his
early years he was a brilliant young man living in New York, attending Columbia University, loving jazz and pursuing ideas,
cultivating lasting friendships, and discovering radical social
work. Although he was raised in France and England as a humanist and then an Episcopalian, in New York he became interested in Catholicism and monasticism and finally became a
Cistercian monk at the Abbey of Gethsemani in Kentucky. This
was a strict religious order under the close authority of an abbot.

Even in such seclusion Merton flourished as a writer, com-

---

82 *Contemptus mundi* does not mean contempt for the world. It's more a decision not to be satisfied with the narcissism and shallow values of a secularistic society. It's more the refusal to participate than contempt.

menting on all the issues of the day, as well as writing many books on monasticism and contemplation. For a while he was responsible for training new monks in their year of novitiate. But even though he had found his calling in a strict monastery and had taken ordination to the priesthood, he was never fully settled. He became seriously interested in monasticism and contemplation of the East and hungered for more solitude, finally being rewarded with his own hermitage away from the monastery buildings.

Late in his life, while being treated for an illness, he fell in love with a nurse and managed to carry on something of a relationship. His feelings for the woman, whom in his notes he called "M," were strong and serious, but eventually he decided to stay with his vows.

My point in telling this complex story in a few words is to suggest that even someone like Thomas Merton, living in a monastery where his entire life was set out for him and most decisions made by an abbot, was forever hard at work making a religion of his own. In that regard it seems somehow fitting that it was on a rare trip away from the monastery, in Thailand at a conference of Eastern monks, that he was accidentally electrocuted and died. His books, especially his diaries and notebooks, show a complicated man who never felt finished developing his religion.

I've been reading Merton most of my life and in some ways have modeled my religion after his. When I lived in the priory, I stretched the rules as often and as much as I could, while remaining quite faithful to the spirit of the place. As a writer now I try to speak for the deeper issues at work in society, as Merton often did. I even try to learn from his writing style. I particularly like having a monk as my model. It pleases me when occasionally a listener calling in on a radio show confuses me with Merton.

Merton was often in trouble for his efforts to make sense of his life, and this is one aspect of sustaining a religion of one's own that we might overlook. You might think that once a person enters a monastery, everything is settled. You just follow the rules and avoid difficult choices. But religion is a dynamic thing, always in process, forever bouncing back and forth between some given standards on one hand and experiments on the other.

I once had a brief conversation about Merton with the poet Wendell Berry, who knew him, since they were neighbors. Berry told me not to romanticize Merton because he was a complicated man. I already knew he was difficult for his superiors and some of the people around him, and I could understand that his restlessness might make him a challenge to the authorities and even his friends.

To put that much intellectual and moral energy in a strict monastery is to ask for trouble. Yet Merton's unwillingness to surrender completely to a highly regulated life gave him vitality that I have always found attractive. Forever dealing with his passions and desires, feeling frustrated and trying to stretch the rules, made him very human. It teaches us that working out our religion is a strenuous job that won't necessarily win friends or commendation. You have to remain loyal to your inner calling, no matter how conventional or unconventional it may be.

A Dedicated Life

Besides adapting the traditional monastic vows, you could also find your own. I have a vow of beauty and try to arrange my life around the beautiful, getting support from my favorite classical authors—Plato, Plotinus, Ficino, James Joyce, and James Hillman—for whom beauty was essential to the soul. I learned it during my monastic days, when I wasn't explicitly taught the importance of beauty but learned it from the grace of my surroundings, including the Gregorian chant that I studied seriously and sang daily.

I know people who have a vow of humility, not in a formal sense but in the way they live and relate to people. When you meet these men and women, you sense their dedication to keeping their will out of the way. Maybe they never made an outward solemn promise to do this, but obviously they made a serious decision in this direction that they observe and honor in everything they do.

The possibilities for taking "vows" are infinite. I've considered vows of pleasure, parenthood, walking my talk, friendship, and gracefulness. Some of these are relatively easy for me to observe, but others are a challenge. They flow directly from a place deep inside me, but I live them in my daily life in a very concrete world. Each of us could select vows proper to us, promises to oneself that help structure and maintain a spiritual way of life.

The Model of the Monk

One of the problems with religion and secular life as we've known them is that they are usually separate and too distinct. The monk and the nun bring them together and use many concrete methods to maintain a spiritual life that is well integrated into activities like work and community. This linking of spirit and world could be our ideal as well, as we try to craft a religious practice that is an expression of who we are.

One striking aspect of monastic life is the way an ordinary day has many moments of meditation, chanting, and praying. We could learn from monks to intensify the spiritual side of life by incorporating a number of relatively brief times for meditation and reflection during the day. Peppering a day with spiritual practices helps make the whole day both meaningfully secular and thoroughly spiritual.

Scheduling your day is a simple way to follow the monk's style. Instead of just letting your days unfold spontaneously or being at the mercy of an inflexible, busy schedule with family and work, you might set up a few regular activities, like meditation before breakfast, listening to music before lunch, being quiet after ten p.m., eating simply in the morning and taking a quiet walk afterward, if only for five or ten minutes. This would be a monk's walk for contemplation, perhaps not the same as a brisk walk for cardio exercise. Thoreau said that just getting up early can be a sacrament, a spiritual act.

Another method is the monk's way of dressing. It sets the contemplative apart from the people around him. The cowl or hoodie symbolizes and invites a contemplative attitude, covering the head as a metaphor for thought and identity. A long tunic covers the body, suggesting that this life is dedicated to spiritual ideals and has little to do with the ego. Sandals may symbolize simplicity and poverty. By the way, these associations are quite ancient.

The artist and craftsman Eric Gill and the arts and crafts pioneer William Morris both dressed like monks. But you may prefer a more subtle approach: a hat or hood and sandals or a long and ample shirt. You may find your own way of dress, not directly related to the monastic garb, to symbolize your particular spiritual values. I met a taxi driver in New York once who wore black pants and shirt and a white knitted skull cap. I asked him if he was part of a community that shared this way of dressing, but he said it was his own uniform that expressed his own outlook on the world. A monk taxi driver.

Monks in Spirit

Monks and nuns live their lives as though they were on a lifelong retreat away from their homes, and they have done this for millennia all over the world in a variety of spiritual traditions. Monastic life is still going on, but anyone may learn from the monks how to adapt many practices to ordinary life in the world. You can be monklike as you foster a contemplative lifestyle, see your work as a spiritual practice, or give your home qualities of quiet, beauty, and conviviality.

The strong sense of community that monks try to achieve in their monasteries is meant to be a model for others, a spiritual hothouse for experimentation and living out ideals. Monks often call it the perfection of life. You might attempt utopia in your own home and in that way conjure up the monastic spirit. You create a model community in a troubled world. You aim for perfection, not in a neurotic, perfectionistic manner, but in a spirit of conviviality.

Instead of going off to a monastery you can bring the monastery to the secular society. In common areas in our towns and cities we could install more and better places for contemplation, indications that we are a community, and images that evoke spiritual values. We could be more like monks and less like secularists, more like thoughtful men and women who make all of life sacred and less like unconscious citizens who have nothing more at their disposal than ego and instinct. The monk is pursuing a much higher and deeper calling.

In public spaces we could place hints of a cloister, places for meditation, places and times of quiet, simplicity, and modesty, and a deeply felt sense of community. A workplace could have its cloister, a place where workers could refresh themselves with a taste of nature and quiet. It could have a schedule that included moments for meditation, a place for a quiet snack, resources from many traditions for spiritual reading.

In a quiet neighborhood in Houston, Texas, the Rothko Chapel sits on a small open space with a quiet pond and piece of sculpture. On an ordinary day when there is no event to make it seem busy, the chapel is a place of reflection in an active city. The architecture, furnishings, and, of course, the large black paintings of Marc Rothko create a special atmosphere for reflection. If you look at the schedule of events and the books that are available, you'll see that every spiritual tradition imaginable is represented.

This is a rare resource for those of us trying to maintain a religion of our own. It's current with where religion is in life today. It's based on art, it offers a suitable place for reflection, it draws on all the traditions equally and positively, and it's located in the midst of city life. Beyond that, it's welcoming, friendly, and intelligent. It's effective in creating local community experiences and in sustaining a feeling for world community. All of our cities—I mean the cities of the world—would benefit from many of these "chapels" to sustain the personal religion of their citizens.

I've called this new approach a religion of one's own, but as you can see, as you pursue your own religion you'll immediately begin to see connections with the whole of life and with community defined both in the most local of ways and with all beings in the cosmos, including those we have yet to meet up with. This religion need not be narcissistic and limited.

What I am envisioning is a return to a sacred environment and a sacred sense of self. A divided world has rendered secularity a source of insanity and aggression, and it has made religion vapid and unhelpful or fanatic and dangerous. So this new kind of religion reinstates both secularity and sacredness, one deepening the other in a fruitful tandem. We need to enjoy secular life, and we need a sense of the sacred for depth of sensitivity and meaning.

Oddly, in monasticism I discovered the joys of secular living, and with that memory I recommend the adoption of a monastic spirit in the very thick of fully secular living. None of the pleasure or joy of worldly existence will be lost, but a new pleasure in its depth will arise. At some time in life we could all be monks. Every day we could all bring the monastic spirit into the world, making it alive, profoundly communal, and joyous.

Chapter 12

A SACRED WAY OF LIFE

> Let the rain beat upon your head with
> silver liquid drops . . .
> I love the rain.
>
> —LANGSTON HUGHES

To foster your spiritual life, you need an effective method especially suited to you. Buddhists call it *upaya*, "skillful means." When I first heard about *upaya* many years ago, I felt excited because it helped me make sense of the many odd things we do in the name of religion. It's important to have good ideas, but you also need to be skillful in your method. The practice of religion requires precise and thoughtful action.

In the Lotus Sutra, a long lesson in *upaya*, you'll find a story about a father trying to save his children from their burning home. In a moving parable he tells them that wonderful carriages are outside waiting for them filled with toys and things they will love. When they follow the enticement and are out of the burning building, they don't find a carriage but they have their lives. For me, the spiritual traditions, my memories of monastic life, my books and friends, and my music are the skillful means I need. And just as the carriages of the Lotus Sutra father represent the teachings of the Buddha, so my piano represents the arts and the idea of sensual, home-based meditation.

What is your *upaya*? What means do you use to be a real person, open to the world around you and to the mysteries of your birth, death, and the events of your life, the direction it has gone? You may pray, meditate, go to a place of worship, and try to live a good life. As an adult you have to ask yourself: Are these methods effective? They may not work because they are not you, not you of this moment in time. It may be appropriate now to tweak those methods or look for different ones.

When I think of one of my lifelong models in the spiritual life, Thomas More of England, I see methods he used that are similar to the kind I advocate here: prayer, spiritual reading, ritual, a life in law (culture), educating his children carefully, caring for animals, making a good home, and being a leader in his community. He was a passionate man with some significant faults and blindness, but, more than most, he knew how to make a religion for himself.

Some schools of Buddhism teach that *upaya* goes along with two other aspects of the spiritual life: compassion (*karuna*) and wisdom (*prajna*). I'd like to borrow this Buddhist trio of virtues for my own religion. What could be more perfect than basing your life on wisdom, compassion, and skillful means? What better way to describe religion than as a deep way of life that takes into account your mind, your heart, and your hands?

In my own private book of spiritual practices, along with these three central ingredients I would add wonder and serenity, two items I borrow from Glenn Gould. That gives me a five-legged table on which to build my religion: wisdom, compassion, skillful methods, wonder, and serenity. I've borrowed them all, but now, in this new configuration, they become mine.

Anyone can do this, especially now when we need a return to theological thinking: seriously considering the essentials of a life and finding ways to respond to the mysteries we face every day. It's foolish to take the modern approach of trying to explain and control everything. Religion teaches us how to relate to the mysteries in such a way that they give us our humanity and make our lives worth living.

I appreciate my five virtues as being basic for my own religion. In the past people criticized me for being too intellectual, but study and reading and the exchange of ideas has not only made my life interesting, they have also been the source of my values and actions. I am what I am because of my ideas, and I don't apologize for enjoying the life of the mind and imagination. Intellectual people have also criticized me for being too much in the heart, being too involved in people's lives and not maintaining a distance proper to a writer and thinker. They also accuse me of being lightweight in the realm of ideas, but I think they may be reacting to the interests of my heart and my attempts to make rich ideas attractive to all kinds of people. Some want me to be more of an activist, some want me less easygoing, and some want me to be part of a movement or an organization. Meanwhile, in the din, I play my piano and write. It isn't always easy to practice the virtues of wisdom, compassion, skillful means, wonder, and serenity. Especially serenity. The world might like you to do something else.

Do Something

In formal religion the emphasis is on belief, morals, and church attendance. In a religion of your own, the first thing is your own special vision, and then ways to embody your vision concretely. Emerson lectured, Thoreau built a cabin and wrote a diary, Dickinson wrote poems, Kevin Kelly arranges flowers, Simone Dinnerstein plays Bach, you may make gardens, I study and write books. Just as we each may have a religion of our own, we may also have our own rituals and narratives and express our intuitions in ways that are most comfortable to us. We not only see the world in a sacred manner; we make our lives according to that vision.

The great stories of Christianity, Buddhism, and the other formal religions echo in the stories we tell about our lives. Whenever you want to expand your own religion, you can always go back to the traditions and get good ideas. You can also trust your inspirations and intuitions. Here, then, are two energetic or dynamic elements for your religion: borrowing from tradition and listening today for inspiration.

Just as I was about to write the last chapters of this book, my wife's cousin Eva, a writer and teacher who lives in Dublin, Ireland, was on her way to the Boston airport to go home. I was driving her and remembered that we would be passing close to Walden Pond on our way from New Hampshire, a place she had never been. She asked me to stop, and we walked to the edge of the lake. It was a brilliant September day and there were just a few people at the pond. We were in a hurry, but she said she just had to step into the lake to honor the man.

Later, I asked Eva why she wanted to stop at Walden and put her feet in the water. She responded, "I honestly did not realize that I had taken off my shoes to go into the water while we were at Walden Pond. It must have been instinctive and in the moment. So these explanations of mine are speculations in retrospect. I can only think that I might have been trying to do something simple that Thoreau might have done in his time there, or to absorb more deeply the spirit of the place by putting my feet in the water, or by this ritual to secure my own intention to move towards simplicity and stillness, with help from the strength of his example."

Eva performed a religious act by walking in the Walden waters, and then she tried to make sense of it. Medieval Christian theologians said, "*Fides quaerens intellectum.*" There's another good saying to keep in mind: "Faith looks for understanding." You start with your intuition, like Eva's to enter the sacred Ganges of

Walden, and I ask her for understanding. Her beautiful statement is a perfect example of the kind of religion I am espousing in this book.

Notice how strong Thoreau's power and influence are. I believe they come from his habit of obeying a will deeper than his own. He let himself be inspired and certainly didn't worry much about what other people thought. As a result, his actions and words speak to our world over 150 years later. I would go so far as to say that the moral power in Thoreau's words and actions comes from a *siddhi*, a special gift, that came to him as a result of his "obedience."

Iconic Walden

The cabin Thoreau built at Walden shows how someone can independently follow an inspiration and create something that marks his own religious life and also addresses the needs of the world community. Thoreau had an inspiration, a philosophy, and the chutzpah necessary for building his temporary hermitage on the lake. Interestingly, by following his inspiration he found his way further into life, by doing an action that drew its power from his spiritual being and then caught the imagination of the world.

You can also follow your inspirations and strengthen them with reading, study, and learning. Thoreau had an educated spiritual imagination. He was not just letting his wild inspirations dictate his life. Many religious people have inspirations that we call "unhinged," a good image for an imagination disconnected from an intelligence. You want to be inspired intelligently, preparing yourself through reading and a spiritual practice to make the most of what you receive in those special moments of revelation.

When I was living at the priory, part of the daily routine was focused not on spirituality but rather the spiritual life, the accent on "life." Today spirituality often seems to be separate from life and focused on the self. Maybe we need a new etymology for religion: "real-igion." Make it real. Spirituality is a dimension of living, not a way out of life. Thoreau, the secular monk, said he went to Walden to "front the essentials of his life." The purpose of our own religion is similar: it's a way of facing the life that is given to us and making the most of it.

Toward the beginning of *Walden*, Thoreau warned about having the wrong motives for any action that you do. He didn't like the idea of repentance, for example, that is common among some religious people. They seem to live from guilt rather than a sense of community. Thoreau said he was familiar with his town of Concord and knew that the citizens there were "doing penance in a thousand remarkable ways." He goes on to explain that many people had to work hard in the fields to make a living. In notebooks written a few years later, he explains further: "A wise man will dispense with repentance. . . . God prefers that you approach him thoughtful, not penitent, though you are the chief of sinners. It is only by forgetting yourself that you draw near to him."[83]

It isn't easy to see the big ego in self-effacement, but it's there. If you think it's good to suffer because of bad things you've done, just consider the suffering involved in everyday life: hard work, difficulty in relationships, sickness. The real penance in Thoreau's neighborhood was being done by farmers working hard in the fields, not by people beating themselves for having sinned.

Today we are all doing penance every day. We're working hard, trying to make money to keep a roof over our heads and food on the table, trying to maintain a good relationship or marriage, trying to keep our children safe and happy and educated, trying to keep the world from blowing itself up. We don't need any more penance. We need some joy, an ideal, encouragement,

83 Thoreau, *I to Myself*, p. 47.

a philosophy worthy of us, a real community, neighbors to keep us from having to go it alone. We need our own religion: our sources of inspiration, hope, and healing.

Natural Rituals

In formal religion a ritual is any action that contributes to the spiritual life. It has a transcendent purpose and serves the spirit. It is often full of symbols and usually is more about poetry than practicality. As we discussed earlier, a wedding, a good example of this kind of ritual, may have certain legal implications, but its many symbols, like the rings and the exalted language and the formal dress, take it out of the merely legal to address deep and spiritual levels of meaning. The ceremony helps the couple realize deep in their bones that their marriage is profound and lies within the realm of the eternal.

I grew up in a religion that made the most of ritual. The Catholic Mass uses music, costume, incense smoke, water, wine, bread, gesture, word, and movement to present the mysteries of Catholic belief. Some religious reformers have found such rituals excessive and meaningless, preferring moral persuasion through reading and speaking. The same is true in life: Some people like a plain and practical way of doing things, while others enjoy symbol and ritual. Some people like to celebrate their birthdays in style, while others like to be quiet and reserved.

To me, the boundaries between formal religious rituals and natural ritual easily overlap. Christmas is a good example. Christians sometimes become irate because of the commercialism of the holidays. They want to put Christ back into Christmas. But I see the parties, the gift giving, the carols, and the images of Santa Claus as very much in the spirit of Christmas. After all, Christmas comes at the very bottom of the year, at the solstice, when the nights are long and there is a noticeable and sudden shift toward light. Naturally, it is a time of hope and light, a time to celebrate.

This natural time for ritual fits well into the Gospel teachings of Jesus, and so the formal theological and religious aspect of Christmas is important for those who follow him. But many people adopt Christmas without a particular interest in Jesus and Christianity. A winter solstice celebration is suitable also for the Jewish Hannukah, a festival of light, for Kwanzaa, the Buddhist Bodhi Day, Boxing Day, Saturnalia, Soyal among the Hopi and Zuni, and many other formal and informal spiritual rites. I say we should put Santa—his name means "saint" or "holy," the spirit of conviviality and generosity, without reference to any particular formal religion—back into Christmas. Christmas is everyone's religious holy day, and its "true" meaning is universal. As someone profoundly devoted to Jesus and enthusiastic in my appreciation for the Gospel infancy narratives, I say, "Let's put Santa back into Christmas."

Ethical Acts

I have an old and loyal friend, Mike, who is intensely interested in developing his own theology, though he may not put it that way. He's also a gifted athlete. Twenty-five years ago he happened to notice at a gym that people were throwing away their old athletic shoes before they were worn out. He got the idea to round up all the shoes he could, wash them, and send them to children around the world who needed them. He made a small nonprofit business out of his idea and has helped thousands of children. He's particularly concerned about those who are walking barefoot in regions where they pick up parasites and bacteria.

Mike's "job" has no external religious aspects, but it fulfills his spiritual vision and serves as a concrete ethical practice, making his work a religion of his own. Mike's personal practice evolved out of years of studious interest in several spiritual traditions, but it is also personal and informal, having no connection to a church. According to my definition, it qualifies as a personal religion.

I asked Mike to write down any thoughts he may have about his own religion. His response is rather long, but it's a beautiful statement that puts a face on much I have been writing, so I'll quote it in full:

Forty years ago, I saw a photograph of some children standing in a line, somewhere in Africa, all of them dying from starvation. I'm sure I knew at the time that there were children out there somewhere in the world who were suffering, but it was something that I had never had to face before.

For two years, I fasted, I read, I meditated, and I prayed. At one point, I asked God to take my eyes and give them to someone else if I was never going to be able to see with them any better. Then, one morning, I woke up to a world that I had never seen before. I picked up the phone to call a friend to tell him what I saw, and what I now know. But I couldn't speak. I didn't speak at all for days.

What I know is that the Kingdom of Heaven is at hand. I know that Truth is a way of being in the world, and that it is independent of any religion. The people that I know who have discovered it honor Jesus, and honor the Buddha, but do not consider themselves to be followers, much less worshippers of either of them. And I know life to be a blessing.

In 1989, I started a program called the Shoe Bank that provides shoes for children wherever critical needs exist. Someone with a mission group I sometimes work with recently sent me a photograph of some children standing in a line, somewhere in Africa, all of them waiting to receive a pair of shoes that would protect their feet from parasites. What immediately came to mind was the photograph from forty years ago that set all that has come to be into motion.

⚬━╍━⚬

In 1991, I had a son, Michael, who started helping me with the shoe program when he was in kindergarten. The only videos I have of him are from when one of the local television stations would be doing a feature on the Shoe Bank, and would film us together picking up or delivering shoes to one of the local shelters. My life's work has never allowed for me to set money aside that would have helped Michael to pay for college. But I believe that the time we spent when he was young, caring for others together, will serve him better than anything that money can buy.

Mike's statement contains several of the items I would include in a religion of one's own. He's aware of the traditions and draws from more than one. He has his own theology and translates it in a powerful, individual, ethical work. He also sees how his young son could develop a religion of his own through the experience of his father's good actions.

Communitas

Most people who hear about this idea of a religion of one's own ask: What about community? Isn't that essential?

Let's distinguish between being a member of a group and having a deep, transformative feeling of community. Sometimes a town may be a closely woven community, but when tragedy hits, the deep feeling of community rises. You can almost see it and touch it. The anthropologist Victor Turner uses the word "*communitas*" for this feeling, and recently his wife, Edith, published an enlightening book on the idea.

She describes many different facets of *communitas*, including the power of spirituality, humor, and common effort to bring it into play. You don't manufacture it the way you might organize a meeting, and in fact, control of the individuals involved is almost certain to dispel it. It's a special sense of community that embraces not only every other human but other species and things, as well. Edith Turner says it simply and elegantly: "What indeed is this *communitas*? It keeps appearing as a togetherness that seeks the whole universe as its boundary."[84]

You can experience this feeling of community if you're worried about being somebody, being noticed, being valued, or being seen. You need freedom from the anxieties of narcissism. You need your heart open to the other, to the stranger, and to the unknown. Writing about paranoia, Hillman makes an interesting point: If you are not open to influence from within, you won't be open to others in the world.

Repeated sensations of deep community create the climate in which each person can develop a personal code of ethics. An example from my life takes me back to the late 1960s, when I joined several busloads of fellow students from the University of Michigan on a trip to Washington, DC, to protest the Vietnam War. I took the place of a young man I hardly knew and wore his badge. I knew no one else on the bus or at the rally, and I didn't even have my own identity. Yet, standing there on the National Mall with tens of thousands of men and women sharing a common concern, I felt deep community as I have rarely experienced it in my life.

We were bound by a shared ethical passion, one that gave the occasion a strong feeling of spiritual action. The very place felt like holy ground that day and, interestingly, Edith Turner refers

---

84 E. Turner, *Communitas*, Kindle Edition (New York: Palgrave Macmillan, 2012), locations 792–793.

to that very location as a sacred space. Community, place, and ethics go together to create an event in one's personal religion.

Many people feel a need to be part of an identifiable group. For them, a local community could be a bridge to a larger, less concretely defined community. For myself, friends around the world, fellow writers everywhere, and a widespread number of readers of my books give me the community I require. Of course, I have my precious local neighbors and friends. But I prefer the feeling of community in a larger and expanding sense of connection to a gathering of those who share a common belief. Especially today, the planet is small and we are all in touch with each other. There are few degrees of separation. We might not understand that there is only one community, the beings of earth. And that community may well expand should we encounter others in our universe.

Postlude

✥

LIVING YOUR BLISS

Things fall apart; the centre cannot hold;
Mere anarchy is loosed upon the world.

—W. B. YEATS, "THE SECOND COMING"

I have heard these lines of Yeats countless times in sermons and
lectures and seminars, and yet they never seem to grow old.
Today people feel them in the core of their hearts, as politics,
economics, family life, and city streets seem to have lost the soul
or spirit that has given them a heart. We feel the spirit of our
times as "mere anarchy," a falling apart that lacks any nobility.
The more we look out into deep space and behold the spheres of
planets and suns around us, the flatter our world and our lives
appear to be.

The feeling of apocalypse, so palpable in Yeats's poem and
among the citizens of our world, is not ours alone. Generations
before us have felt it, as their cultures, too, faced seemingly impossible problems. You could say that it's mythic or archetypal, a
mood that comes over humanity when it has reached a point of
entropy.

To add to the weight of our particular feeling of end-time is the absence of widely accepted, authoritative, and comforting established religions. We have nothing to give us vision and to ground our values and hold us together. To create new religions of the old variety or to revivify the old traditions is impossible, given our new sophistication in so many areas. To take the purely secular path is suicide, because science simply doesn't go deep enough in its vision to guide us at our depths, and the ego of psychology is also far too small to navigate the mysteries that overshadow us. The pleasures of technology are empty without a deep guiding philosophy. The only way is to imagine a new religiousness that embraces the secular and steers away from sentimental solutions to our unsentimental problems, a religiosity built on all the traditions but not stuck on them. We need a religion of one's own.

To create a religious life of your own, you have to think things through and be critical of the information you find. You may have to do some digging to find good resources and then experiment until you are satisfied. You have to ask probing questions and when you realize the teacher or community you have landed on isn't worthy, move on. You may have to travel, read, study, go on a retreat, take a workshop, or search the Internet to find answers to your questions, answers that don't insult your intelligence. In the spiritual realm especially, you need a nose for flimflam and unsubstantiated ideas.

All of this amounts to an antidote for unconsciousness. The best part is that living consciously gives more pleasure than the dull stupor of automoton thinking ever could. Yes, sometimes giving up old, cherished ideas can sting, but the pleasure of knowing is far greater than the satisfactions of ignorance. "Pleasure," a word made ignoble by many religious traditions, is the secret to the future: deep pleasure, nothing less than erotic satisfaction and, truth to be told, bliss.

Bliss

I've been using words like "pleasure" and "satisfaction," but the word used more often in traditional religious literature is "bliss."

I have in mind especially two important sources: the Upanishads of ancient India and the beatitudes of Jesus.

Early Indian theology said that there are three essentials in the religious life: *sat-cit-ananda*. Let's translate these important Sanskrit words as "being-awareness-bliss." Long tomes could and have been written about these three little words, but let's consider them simply. Being is accepting your situation as it is and sensing your individuality. I've been stressing this quality throughout the book by speaking of a religion of one's own. Thinking of religion this way, we emphasize being a person over feeling lost in the crowd. Awareness is obvious. We could phrase it "being conscious." This is also a major theme of this book. The third element, "pleasure," is oddly missing in many formal religious presentations.

I would guess that most people equate religion with discomfort: going to church when you don't feel like it, not doing things you'd like to do, depriving yourself, and generally believing that working hard and even suffering makes you a good person. Interestingly, throughout history many thoughtful writers have suggested the opposite: that pleasure is a good thing and is even a sign of soul.

Those who follow this philosophy are sometimes called Epicureans, after the philosopher of moderate and deep pleasure, Epicurus. Many philosophers of soul have been Epicureans—Ficino, Wilde, Dickinson, Morris. In my work on the Gospels, I suggest that Jesus, too, was an Epicurean. Compare his philosophy of life as presented in the Gospels with the teachings of the church leaders who have spoken in his name, and you see an odd difference. Jesus recommends all the usual Epicurean virtues: friendship, eating together, caring for each other, enjoying life, and having a loving attitude. His followers often stress self-denial, judgment, fear, and submission, and they often do it in strict, punitive tones. You may well ask, Where is the love?

So, it may be counterintuitive for me to suggest that a

religion of one's own could be based in pleasure rather than pain. I recommend getting out of the sadomasochistic pattern of rules, punishment, fear, submission, authority, and male dominance altogether. But I want to go deeper than pleasure. I want to suggest that the goal of this new religion is bliss.

I'm using this word precisely and carefully. Bliss is the special pleasure you find when you live from the center of your life, when you are in tune with your fate, and when you have an opening in your mind and heart to the source of life, acting in accord with the deep laws of your nature. This is *ananda*—joy, bliss, or deep pleasure.

I want to distinguish between ordinary happiness and bliss. Bliss is neither a superficial pleasure nor an extravagant wish. Understood against the background of the religious traditions, it's the special joy and relief of being in tune with nature, including your own nature. It's a religious virtue and the result of a long period of search, experiment, and practice.

When Jesus taught the beatitudes, he used a special word that we traditionally translate as "blessed," as in "Blessed are the meek." But his word "*makarioi*" refers to the island of bliss where the gods and goddesses go to find peace and rest. It's a place of divine repose, not just superficial happiness. For humans, bliss is not an option; it's essential if we are to enjoy health of body and soul and remain free of desperate, symptomatic acting out. One wonders if excessive entertainment, certain drugs, alcohol, and consumerism are not neurotic, ineffective ways of reaching for bliss. Like all symptoms, they offer a taste of what is missing but do so in ways that are ultimately ineffective and often harmful.

In the early 1970s I had an intense conversation with Joseph Campbell over breakfast. He had not yet made mythology popular with his books and his videos with Bill Moyers, but he was well known and on his way. We were discussing his idea of being faithful to your "wyrd." Later he would say, "Follow your bliss." He meant watching closely for your inner, unfolding destiny and making decisions based on it. He said that this would lead to bliss, and he alluded to *sat-cit-ananda*.

His word "wyrd" refers to the ancient image of three women who spin out our fate—the wyrd sisters—and, of course, it gives rise to our word "weird." As you follow your inner promptings and remain faithful to your own weird guidance, you do certain things that generate your own existence, including a religion of your own. You may one day understand that to be a joyful person you have to stand out from the pack and live your own life— follow your wyrd. You may become eccentric and do things that society questions and your loved ones worry about.

Bliss is the joy that arrives when you are released from the pressure to be a small self. Bliss descends when you open yourself to life in all its abundance and breathtaking power and let it so suffuse you that you forget your worries about being somebody and justifying your life. You give in. You let life take over. You become a holy person instead of a secular egotist, and then you discover that your holiness is the base of your own religion.

A Final List

People like lists. I like lists. So let me add a list of items you can keep in mind as you make a religion of your own.

1. *Redefine traditional terms and ideas.* Don't unconsciously assume the old meanings and old language. Feel free to reinvent and redefine. Don't accept the usual meanings of "God" and "religion." Don't think of ethics the way you always have. Don't imagine rituals and gatherings in the old archaic ways. Reinvent. Reimagine.

2. *Don't be too literal about community.* Remember that your community includes all beings and objects in the universe. Don't be narrow in your view of who or what is in your community. Include animals, the things of

nature, such as trees and plants, things and objects, and beings we have yet to encounter in the universe. Remember the paradox: Local community works best when you are mindful of the earth and cosmic community, and vice versa.

3. Feel that you have a right to learn from and practice anything from the world's spiritual and religious traditions. They are yours. You can be a member or not, focus on several or just one or two, try one after the other or several at once, remain close to your family tradition or move away from it, embrace the traditions or explore your agnosticism.

4. Understand that many things, if not everything, that are usually considered secular are sacred, if you have the eyes to see it. A religion of your own is different in that you can keep the sacred and secular bound to each other tightly, seeing the sacred in all secular activities.

5. Be a mystic in your own ways. This is not an option. To be fully human you need some sort of mystical experiences regularly. Nature and art become especially important in this regard.

6. Don't think of ethics and morality as a list of things you shouldn't do. Think of them as positive things you should do, often unique to you, that contribute to and help the human community.

7. Wisdom, compassion, and method. You can borrow my three central factors, themselves borrowed from the East. You can add the two from Glenn Gould—*wonder* and *serenity.* Make a religion of your own out of them. Add two more of your own.

8. Use the arts for your spiritual education and welfare. Approach them in a special way, as routes to spiritual insight and experience. Don't go to a museum for education but for *darshan*: make it a pilgrimage, contemplate the images.

9. Be intelligent about everything involved in your spirituality, but also use your intuition, trust it, and develop it with concrete methods. Remember Plato's word for these ways of knowing: "mania." You may feel like a maniac listening for your daimon and caring for your *juno* and following your intuitions.

10. Embrace eros; don't be afraid of it. Make it part of your everyday life. Follow your desires and cultivate deep and solid pleasures. Build your religion on joy and bliss. Understand that enjoyment of the human body, yours or someone else's, is only a step toward living joyously in a sensual, material world. This is the base of a spiritual life and the necessary foundation for a religion of one's own.

"Every church has a membership of one," Emerson said. I don't intend this book as a critique of formal religion. Whether you are an ardent member of a spiritual community and tradition, or not, is not the point. Whether you are a member or a seeker, you can create a religion of your own. The resources available to you are vast and beautiful. All you have to do is get over the bad habit of arguing over who is right and who possesses the truth. In these matters I recommend giving up the word "truth" altogether. It only gets you into trouble.

I'd like to turn the world upside down and develop an educational system in which everyone learns first about art and religion. Once you've made headway with these two essentials, then you're ready to look for a profession or a job. Then, and only then, are you prepared for marriage and parenthood. Only then will you be able to age with grace and wisdom.

Our society does crazy things routinely because it has forgotten religion. It is trying to go it alone. It thumbs its nose at mystery and suffers the consequences. We need to be skilled (*upaya*) at dealing with the mysteries of love, illness, work, intimacy, and death. It's difficult to imagine, but if we could turn things around and become a wisdom culture instead of an information culture, we might have a chance.

If we could discover the importance of play over hard work, image over interpretation, and love over control, we would be inching toward bliss. If we could each have the pleasure of living a religion of our own, we might live in harmony and mutual joy.

Acknowledgments

I have been able to explore my "weird" ideas these many years only because I have the support of friends who accept me for who I am. I can't list them all, but I'll mention a few who had a direct impact on this book: Pat Toomay in New Mexico, Cheryl Holmes, Brian Clark, and Geoff Sweeting in Australia, Heather Bass in Maine, John Van Ness in my neighborhood, Aris Boletsis in New York and the world, George Lopez in Maine, Simone Dinnerstein in Brooklyn, Veronica Goodchild among the crop circles, Mike Berringer in Texas, David Chadwick in Zenland, Kevin Kelly in Kansas City, Carla Marie Greco in Santa Rosa, Katherine Gotshall English in the neighborhood, Gary and Patrice Pinette never too far away, Sean Kramer in Manchester, Eva O'Callahan in Ireland, Chris Robertson in London, and Dr. Clare Willocks in Glasgow. Brendan and Hazel Hester's support from Dublin means more than they know. I'm happy to be working again at Gotham with Bill Shinker and Lauren Marino, grateful that they saw the value in this book, and publicist Lisa Johnson, and my daily coworkers Emily Wunderlich and Beth Parker. Thanks to Father Mark Patrick Hederman at Glenstal Abbey for helping me keep my Catholicism in my own way. To Hugh Van Dusen for always advising me wisely. To Chris Bamford for key ideas and publishing advice. To

ACKNOWLEDGMENTS

Aftab Omer for helping me understand my work and to Mark McKinney and Byram Karasu for their love and loyalty. Thanks to Patricia Berry for constant friendship, and to Rev. Karin Kilpatric for bringing my ideas to life. Thanks to Kim Witherspoon and Alexis Hurley for early guidance. The book really owes its existence to Todd Schuster, who helped me shape the idea and get it into the world. Thanks, too, to Jacob Moore for his role in that process. My family is as much a miracle as Emerson's blowing clover and falling rain: Abe is such a complete person and Ajeet such a gifted and loving daughter. Hari Kirin can advise and support me in just the right ways and all the while teach me about love and soul and spirit. With love and gratitude in my heart I thank all of these highly creative and visionary people for having a part in making this book.

Index